José Esteban Muñoz

Readings

Theory and History of Literature
Edited by Wlad Godzich and Jochen Schulte-Sasse

For other books in the series, see p. 157

Readings

The Poetics of Blanchot,

Joyce, Kafka, Kleist,

Lispector, and Tsvetayeva

Hélène Cixous

Edited, translated, and introduced
by Verena Andermatt Conley

Theory and History of Literature, Volume 77

University of Minnesota Press, Minneapolis

Published by the University of Minnesota Press
2037 University Avenue Southeast, Minneapolis, MN 55414
Printed in the United States of America on acid-free paper

Library of Congress Cataloging-in-Publication Data

Cixous, Hélène, 1937–
    Readings : the poetics of Blanchot, Joyce, Kafka, Kleist, Lispector, and Tsvetayeva / Hélène Cixous ; edited, translated, and introduced by Verena Andermatt Conley.
       p.   cm. — (Theory and history of literature series ; v. 77)
    Includes bibliographical references and index.
    ISBN 0-8166-1940-9 (hc)
    ISBN 0-8166-1941-7 (pb)
    1. Literature, Comparative—History and criticism.   I. Title. II. Series.
PN871.C55   1991
809—dc20   91-12384
                                                            CIP

Contents

Acknowledgments

My indebtedness goes to Hélène Cixous, whose readings are the basis of this project.

As for the first volume, *Reading with Clarice Lispector,* I would like to express my gratitude to Iowa State University and James Dow for making the initial stages of this project possible through a summer grant. My thanks to Miami University of Ohio for providing me with the generous award of a research leave leading to its completion.

Special thanks go to Marguerite Sandré for her patient recordings and her general help, to Claudia Guimarães for helping me with the Portuguese translations, to Susan Bennett for her help with the Russian translation and bibliography, and to Audrone Willeke and Ed Plater for providing bibliographical information on Kleist's translations.

I would like to thank David, Francine, and my parents for their patience, and above all Tom Conley for his continued assistance and especially for his wonderful sense of Irish humor.

Introduction

The present volume can be read side by side with *Reading with Clarice Lispector* (University of Minnesota Press, 1990). The readings included were given in seminar form by Hélène Cixous between 1980 and 1986 at the Université de Paris VIII, at the Centre d'Etudes Féminines. The selections are my own, except for the passages on Kleist that Cixous wished to have included. The organization into chapters, as well as the selection of about 600 pages for the two volumes from among the original 2,500 pages, are also my own. I kept those passages that seemed the most significant — at times the most controversial — of Cixous's thought. Much of the material under discussion — all eminently readable because of the pedagogical tenor of the seminars — is elsewhere transformed poetically in her fictional writings. In these pages she explains what her fiction performs. The seminars can be read as laboratory for Cixous's fictional and critical practices.

Given the oral nature of this material, the problems in translation, as outlined in the first volume, have to do mainly with recurring expressions. To avoid excessive repetition, I have modified some of the prevailing use of the *il y a*. For Cixous, the deictic expression *il y a* constitutes a statement of no origin that brings with it a gift of language. The implied sense of a gratuitous "giving" has had to be somewhat attenuated. A number of other expressions also remain difficult to translate. For example, *du côté de,* "on the side of," is one of Cixous's favorite formulas, used in the context of her simultaneous reading of several texts at once. It was rendered variably as "in the direction of," "toward," or "leaning toward." *Etre dans quelque chose,* "to be into something," which has a colloquial ring in English, has been changed to "to engage in" or other synonyms. The neo-Hegelian expression, *travailler sur quelque chose,* "to work on something," has been transposed as "to study," "to explore," or "to see." For the literary texts discussed by Cixous, at times I have modified the English translations to make them correspond more closely to her own readings, which are based primarily on French translations, especially where the latter seem closer to the tenor of her analyses.

A result of Cixous's reading practices, the juxtaposition of texts in the two volumes across centuries and national boundaries opens possibilities of multiple readings in various directions that acquire many shadings, flickers, and refractions. Cixous's reading of texts side by side, at times dialectical by implication (for example, in the chapter on Blanchot and Lispector), is always in movement and prevents mastery or appropriation of the text by the reader. The primary carrier of Cixous's readings is an ongoing interest in poetry attached to the proper name of Clarice Lispector, whose texts are read alongside those of Joyce, Kafka, Kleist, Blanchot, and Tsvetayeva. Many of these proper names have crisscrossed Cixous's texts since the beginning of her career as a writer. Lispector has been a concern for a number of years, but the shift toward Eastern Europe is recent and now (in 1990) indicates how artists' interests announce political events that follow. If the texts chosen by Cixous reflect in various ways a preoccupation with writing as well as an insistence on pleasure, they are also linked to current issues in literary theory. Cixous's analyses offer at times welcome divergences from more established canonical lines. She takes up now-consecrated literary figures, mainly from the past. Rarely do her analyses extend to contemporary culture in a specific sense. She chooses to stay within the aura of what she calls "poetic writing." Cixous's purpose in these seminars seems twofold: to essay certain kinds of textual readings without advocating a style or a simple interpretation; and to develop further discourse concerning ethics.

Despite a synchronic approach to the texts and a concentration on generations of writers rather than surrounding facts (dates, sources, filiations) or, more broadly, literary history, nevertheless a shift in interest emerges between 1980 and 1986, from work on the origin of writing and the primal scene, or love and the gift, to problems of history. There is an avowed change, in Cixous's terms, "from the scene of the unconscious to that of history." The artist is now viewed caught in historical turmoil. But emphasis is still placed on the scene, on the word and poetry, on topics that do not immediately mobilize an overt activism. Cixous's general, almost clichéd pronouncements on history may startle the reader but her close readings of texts are always compelling.

Next to a growing interest in cultures of the Third World (here in the seminars mainly those of South America), the holocaust, and Eastern European countries, something else now comes forward, in the *après-coup,* that is manifested in her strong affiliation with the Jewish question and with its cultural representatives past and present—Freud, Kafka, Lispector, Celan, Derrida, and others. The question is treated mainly in Cixous's association of Jew and poet. Through the wandering

Jew and the poet given over to wandering, outside society, Cixous asserts her own belief in a poetic absolute. Here too one can sense a shift, moving away from an earlier need to disconcert the reader, toward a search for a technique that would best render, if not an adequation, at least a proximity between life, milieu, and writing. Poetry is not understood as subversive, as a ''revolution'' in and of language, but as that which precludes strategies of capture or containment and that — contrary to philosophy — allows for otherness. Cixous's belief in the virtues of poetry in its largest sense is much opposed to the development of a certain prose common to modern technocracies, in which discourse favors the efficacy of clarity and the pragmatics of meaning and fills all the gaps and fissures for the purpose of appropriation. Poetry, not in its Apollonian form but as a residue of Dionysian culture, insists on a necessary *part sauvage*.

Her emphasis on poetry points to a tradition that can be traced across time but that has become particularly marked since the early nineteenth century; this tradition invokes attention to nature, the literary absolute, and a view that art must take a leading role in social change. These traditions are glimpsed through the names of Schiller, Schelling, and others. This also suggests why Cixous — and a long-standing literary relationship with James Joyce and *fin-de-siècle* aesthetics confirms the point — is more attracted to early and middle romantic writers or to those whose aesthetics reach back to them. She chooses not to question the limits of a poetic art form in a technological age other than through overt rejection of media-generated writings that she calls ''noise machines.'' Identification with the romantic topos of writing poetry with one's eyes closed does not allow for consideration of the pervasive impact of film or the media, or of what Paul Virilio calls a general *''politics of speed.''* Cixous's main concession seems to be a move from a private to a public sphere, or from the autobiographical novel to the collective stage.

The lesson taught in these pages — and a lesson is to be learned, not in the sense of a constituted morality, but in that of an apprenticeship of life, joy, and pleasure — is based on *other* forms of exchange. Cixous does not confine herself to any one critical theory, and blatantly claims that she has no debt to pay to anyone nor any peer to please. Although the gesture may appear supercilious enough to disconcert many of her readers, Cixous does not hesitate to associate a writer's proper name with the text. Hence the ubiquitous formulas such as ''Clarice says,'' or ''Kleist shows,'' seemingly a recovery of the self-identical author that would be heresy for many contemporary critics. The formula must not be read as naïve regression to the plenary self, but rather as a way, like in Proust, to keep the text under study separate from both biography and the real person. Similarly, the proper names in the texts read, be they Ofélia, Penthesilea, or Toni, are part of a network of forces more than references to ''real characters.'' Cixous listens to the writer's text somewhat in the way an analyst listens to speech. Her readings, close to analysis, do not herald a so-called rigor that would be demanded of a disciple of any school but point out the law that establishes the theoretical truths.

Over the years Cixous's writings, like those of others of the French vanguard, have run the gamut of experimentations with writerly techniques. They have never been devoid of a strong sense of the *real,* even if the effect of reality is a psychic one. Her readings are at their best when irreverent in respect to certain master texts, which she does not hesitate to approach, turn inside out, look at closely or hold at a distance. She never relies on a priori, mystifying signature-effects. Central for her is an apprenticeship of and through life, a necessity to experience pleasure no matter what the circumstances; her texts do not center on an affirmation of one's own alienation. The reader's enjoyment and apprenticeship may be derived from Cixous's radarlike perceptions of all the shadings of human relations that can serve as lessons of life. Accent is placed on the necessity of an *accord,* a vibration—that is, on a linking with the world rather than on a break with it. Yet for Cixous, there *is* an "outside" of the text, a world and reality. In that way, reading and writing are both exploration (utopia) and consolation (redemption). She is aware that certain things are made possible through writing, but also that others are possible only in writing. Cixous privileges the absolute—that which is outside a social world, with its laws and median desire. This absolute metaphorized most often by a summit, maintains little relationship with collectivities, especially in their present form of increased massification and not simply of "crowds" (as Cixous would like to have it in her reading of the Soviet space), and may no longer be viable today.

The seminars veer away from some of Cixous's more militant feminism of the seventies. Though still present, the demarcation line between objects good and bad is attenuated. In the wake of Lispector, Cixous looks straight at a person or an object and sees, hears, everything, rather than selectively, and chooses elements needed for given ideological battles. The opposition between men and women fades even in its derivative form of "masculine" and "feminine," or those who retain and those who give. Rather, she decants poetry and its representatives— that is, poets from all over the world and across the ages. Of importance is their communication through communion with each other and with the world. Some residue of an opposition between men and women still exists, with its ensuing rivalries, similar to the conventional strife between philosophy and poetry. It surges, for example, in what Cixous has called her "ongoing dialogue with Jacques Derrida," with whom she obviously also shares much, from her Jewishness to her North African origins. Though Cixous's seminars are infused with philosophy, here especially with a kind of Kantian Hegelianism in her reading of the sublime, she uses Derrida's textual philosophy for the purpose of working against it. Cixous becomes the poet who can do what philosophers cannot, that is, account for the living or for otherness within a realm of intelligible experience. Poets can live with noncomprehension where philosophers are in constant need of co-opting the limit through concepts. A certain verticality pervades all of Cixous's discourse. And while we readily agree that there is invention only through a leap, why then the need to refer back constantly to a theory that serves as *point d'appui* (a basis) for a rivalry? Yet Cixous's comments in this volume on a few pages from *Margins of Philosophy* in relation to alterity, noncomprehension, and the limit count among the most unusually perceptive readings of Derrida.

The valorizing of poetry, language, and the experimental text in Cixous's double fight against personal and institutional repression echoes, at least in its second part, that of other thinkers who have come out of May 1968, including Derrida, but also Jean-François Lyotard, Gilles Deleuze, Félix Guattari, and Michel de Certeau. Such emphasis can perhaps be historicized on the hand by the kind of restrictions imposed by the French academy and by existentialist poetics that focused on subjectivity and intentionality, and that thinly disguised philosophical dogmatism to mobilize their dialectical efficacy. On the other hand, the refusal of institutionalization can be read, perhaps, as a reaction to the strong presence of the left, an outcome of the French Resistance, in its collusion with the Communist party and the problematic adherence to cultural politics reducing arts to dogma. We may recall the controversy documented in the official party-line review, *Les Lettres françaises,* directed by Louis Aragon — the very review in which Cixous will profess in an interview in November 1970 the necessity for both experimental texts *and* universities in France — around Picasso's drawing of a peace dove during the Korean War. The drawing was condemned by the social realist canon for being "too abstract." It is perhaps in such a climate of philosophical and political dogmatism that the necessity of a writing *not* attached to an institution, even that of literary history, emerges.

Possibly for cultural and historical reasons — though there is always in Cixous an affirmation of the necessity of the real and of the art of doing, of the *faire* — Cixous privileges the word over action and activism. For her, contrary to descendants of the Enlightenment, the world is not just acted upon and reality is not just constructed. Other articulations can and must be sought, such as those that favor life in all of its forms and that look much more for an accord with the environment in its widest sense.

To a linear, teleological line, Cixous prefers other, often non-Western modes of thinking. Perceptions radiate, reverse their courses, and diffract in all directions. With oriental echoes, she tries — especially through affinities with Lispector — to act less on a milieu or an object, a particularly Western obsession, but to be in harmony — or in a moment of grace, perhaps — with a person or a milieu. This implies a necessary passivity in activity, something that, a decade ago, might have been called femininity in contrast to a more Western, phallic masculinity that proposes change through violent action. Less idealistic than mystical, Cixous's meditations — evident in not just her readings of Lispector but also of Kleist — center more and more on ethical dilemmas, which might be called ecological and can be read in Cixous as well as in other writers. They will no doubt lead to major changes in the status of art. Over the last hundred years or so, the avant-garde has been thought to be mainly subversive. It will henceforth need to be more corrective, if not prescriptive. Attention to a milieu or an environment cannot be heard either by those who simply prefer activism or by theoreticians questioning the issue of the origins. Yet Cixous's "origin" never refers to a fixed point. This "origin" is not that of the phenomenological subject, but of a subject with as little subjectivity as possible, one in tune with its environment and always in movement. Away from the habitual dismissal of Kleist as naïve and innocent, hence simplistic, her readings of the writer are particularly striking. Other assertions may disconcert the reader, such as the ubiquitousness of the Heideggerian expression of being "without shelter," "at risk" — which, even in the exalted and poignant discourse of Etty Hillesum, marks an elevated contrast with most critical accounts of the holocaust and is, it can be said, a worn-out metaphor, at least in view of the contemporary social dilemmas concerning those without shelter.

Cixous underscores apprenticeship and "difficult" joys over alienation and by so doing opts for what I choose to call cultural ecology. Her appeal to a force of life and her overtly utopian belief that to think is to make possible, does not address, but rejects, the world of advertisement and profit intent on stamping out cultural memory. To be sure, everyone is participating in this world to a degree, even those marketing artistic or scholarly productions, including plays, books, translations, or lecture tours. It is perhaps no longer enough just to stay "outside a certain Freudian discourse with its fixation on castration"; we need to see how technology and the media can lead to the formation of entirely new subjectivities. If it can be argued that Cixous's readings refuse historical specificity, it can also be said that they themselves carry their own historical specificity. Cixous's seminars constitute a chronicle of the French intellectual scene between 1980 and 1986. They also provide an apprenticeship for the reader through finely tuned textual readings and a disengaging of the most subtle intersubjective models. But they can be dated by their post-1968 tenor, which does not lack romantic pathos. Without rejecting Cixous's attempt and the kinds of reading she advocates, one can stress the necessity of combining her world of poetic and cultural tradition with a culture of technology. The real crux of the problem would not be an either/or choice, but a mediation between the two, something that she herself inadvertently hints at in her recent *Nuit miraculeuse,* a scenario for Ariane Mnouchkine's film on the contemporary heritage of 1789.

Cixous needs to be read less against herself—less as a proper name, a cult figure whose signature can be moneyed — but *en effet* (in effect), as a force corresponding to certain shifting preoccupations of global importance, though they might be articulated, in her own style, from a French vantage point. Through her readings we sense a concern both aesthetic and ethical for the world, and a growing preoccupation with a site, a milieu, that is, with a need for new and other links with the world, the self, and, it is hoped, social collectivities.

Chapter 1
Writing and the Law
Blanchot, Joyce, Kafka, and Lispector

I want to work on texts that are as close as possible to an inscription — conscious or unconscious — of the origin of the gesture of writing and not of writing itself. Writing is already something finished, something that follows the drive to write. Such texts could be expected to be among the writer's firstborn that are not afraid to be so. Clarice Lispector's *Near to the Wild Heart* is just such a text.[1] Its title is a quotation from Joyce's *Portrait of the Artist as a Young Man*.[2]

What does it mean to work on texts that are "near to the wild heart"? Reading Clarice's text, I was struck by its extraordinary power. It is a text that has the audacity to let itself be written close to the very drive to write. At the same time, it gives the impression of being poorly written. It does not display a mastery of form or language and does not raise the question of art. It is the contrary of Flaubert. Clarice's first movement as a child was to put herself at the *écoute* of, in tune with, writing, of something that happens between the body and the world. One has to have a touch of something savage, uncultured, in order to let it happen. It is the contrary of having been so much of a student, of a scholar, that one thinks that a book is a book, and that, if one vaguely has the desire to write, one says: I have to write a book.

Clarice's text comes from within. It is written from an unformulated hypothesis that writing is something living. It is not the book as sacred object. *Near to the Wild Heart* is a kind of germination where these problems are irrelevant. It stands out by contrast with other texts, such as Flaubert's. Yet, at the same time, something makes me give Flaubert a thought, because he is one of those important beings who have a vocation — the word has to be taken in its strong meaning, in

1

relation to something of the order of a calling, and, of course, he answers it. Flaubert answered it when he was very young and said yes, definitely. He organized the totality of his material, psychological, and affective life in such a way that he became forever the lover of writing. He called it art, not writing. I said writing because I did not want to place him in a kind of unconscious pederasty. But art was his love object and it was inscribed in pederastic fashion. In a certain way, he was a monster. He made love with art throughout his entire life. In itself that would not be so bad if it were not done by a choice that excludes human beings. Flaubert was never in a relation of living and livable love with other human beings. His relation with Louise Collet was monstrous. Flaubert fixed a rendezvous with her only after completion of such and such a chapter. Living entirely in the universe of production of writing, he was one of its most arduous craftsmen. Like his successor, James Joyce, he thought of creation in extraordinary fashion. His "savage heart" can be found in his correspondence, a kind of *mise à nu* (laying bare) of a tyrannic drive, of an incredible rigor of the *bien écrire* (the beautifully written).

He is of interest as one of those beings who paid the price of their wager without concession. This presupposes that first one pays the price oneself; then one makes others pay. Is there a possibility of a half-gesture that would be less cruel? What does one have to pay to stay close to the savage heart? Flaubert did not give the answer, he died of it. We can see Joyce and Kafka appear in the same field.

Writing pushed to an absolute degree differs from that of human and mercantile dimensions. We can verify this by taking as the main question the locus of *writing* and not that of art. Flaubert advanced in this dilemma to the point of madness. For him, the question is not who but where, from where? In the course of the journey, Flaubert — like Kafka — got lost. Flaubert wanted people to burn all the papers he did not specifically authorize for publication and, in any case, Kafka was a dying man. Did Kafka finish something because he himself knew he was dying? All of his gestures were morbid gestures. Kafka's strongest writings are those that are unfinished, that he was only beginning, over and over again, and the same can be said of Flaubert.

James Joyce's *Portrait of the Artist as a Young Man* can be put side by side with Clarice Lispector's *Near to the Wild Heart*. Though Joyce is still quite young when he writes the novel, it is not his first, but a portrait of the primitive portrait. Joyce shows extraordinary formal mastery in this text, which is a kind of organized mobile that takes off from a very precise and coded architecture. Where Flaubert worked only on the sentence, Joyce goes further to work also on articulations.

Of importance for a reading concerning our *questions-femmes,* or woman's questions, is the place of origin and the object. What is a writer looking for? What are the stakes in the text? How does one search for something? The movements of the body are determined by what one is looking for and the object one seeks depends on the kind of body one has. We have to work on the first and most primitive pleasure, that is to say, on orality. Rather than give answers, we have to follow the questions, the woman-questions: How does one write as woman? have pleasure as woman? We have to be transgrammatical, the way one says to be transgressive, which does not mean that we have to despise grammar but we are so used to obeying it absolutely that some work has to be done in that direction. I find it important to work on foreign texts, precisely because they displace our relationship to grammar. I will use caution too in relation to what I call trap-words *(mots-cages)*. One has to be audacious in one's reading, so that it becomes an intense deciphering. We need not be afraid of wandering, though one should read in terms of a quest. There always has been femininity from time immemorial but it has been repressed. It has never been unnamed, only suppressed. But it constantly reappears everywhere. Of course, one finds more femininity in texts that are written "close to the savage heart," in texts that are still close to sources, springs, to myth and to beginnings of literary movements before they become institutionalized. Literature is like history. It is organized so as to repress and hide its own origin which always deals with some kind of femininity.

Joyce's *Portrait of the Artist as a Young Man:* Silence, Exile, and Cunning

The work Joyce produced in *Portrait of the Artist,* his *Künstlerroman,* his formative novel, is not without ambivalence. In one of the first scenes, he who will become the artist is in open opposition to the law and to authority. We have to look at the word "law" and render it more flexible. We have to analyze who lays down the law and who is in the law's place. In this respect, there is a difference between Joyce and Kafka. In Kafka, the law is not figured by anyone. In Joyce there are specific authorities. In the first page of his novel, the women threaten him with castration but, as in Clarice Lispector, the question of the father is important too. In Clarice's "Sunday, before falling asleep," the father is really a father/mother and everything is organized in the direction of the father.[3] Genesis takes place in a maternal and paternal mode of production. In Joyce, something analogous is related to the very possibility of the formation of the artist. Which father produces the artist? The question is related to the superego. Yet it is not always the same self that has a repressive figure.

The first two pages of *Portrait of the Artist* can be approached through a kind of multiple reading, which is what Joycean writing asks for. We read word for word, line by line, but at the same time it has to be read — because that is how it is written — as a kind of embryonic scene. The entire book is contained in the first pages, which constitute a nuclear passage. The ensemble of Joyce's work is here like an egg or an opaque shell of calcium. An innocent reading will lead us to believe that these pages are hermetic. One understands everything and nothing: everything because there is really nothing obscure, nothing because there are many referents. Perhaps Irish people would find it more accessible, at least if they know their history well. Here, we have something of a *coup d'écriture,* with many signs of the ruse of the artist. The text is presented in an apparent naïveté — like Clarice's "Sunday, before falling asleep" — but nothing is more condensed, or more allusive. It is already a cosmos.

Joyce denied using psychoanalysis in his work, yet he was impregnated by it. It is as if Joyce, though writing when Freud's texts were not yet well known, was in a kind of intellectual echo with him.

The story of *A Portrait of the Artist* is both that of a portrait being made and that of a finished portrait. The title indicates this kind of permanent duplicity. The reader is told that it is the portrait of an artist, not of a young man, which raises the question of the self-portrait of the artist, of the coming and going of the look, of the self, of the mirror and the self in the mirror.

A Portrait of the Artist is a genesis, like Clarice's text. But hers was a genesis as much of the artist as of the world, and the artist-world relation went through that of father-daughter. In *Portrait of the Artist,* one first sees a series of births, inscribed through the motif of evasion, of flight, and that is how the artist is made. The first and the fifth chapters resemble each other most. In those chapters, writing is much more disseminated, dislocated, than in the others. The successive stories of birth are stories of the breaking of an eggshell, in relation with a parental structure. In the first scene, there is a kind of elementary kinship structure. The scene opens little by little. In this story of the eye and of birds, not the real but the symbolic father marks the artist as genetic parent.

The text begins with an enormous *O* that recurs in the first pages. It can be taken as a feminine, masculine, or neuter sign, as zero. The *o* is everywhere. One can work on the *o-a,* on the *fort-da.* I insist on the graphic and phonic *o*'s because the text tells me to do so. With all its italics and its typography, the text asks the reader to listen. There is also a series of poems. The last one, with its system of inversions and inclusions and exclusions, ends in an apotheosis with "apologise."

In these two pages we have everything needed to make a world and its history, in particular that of the artist. The text begins with: "Once upon a time . . . baby tuckoo" (3). We are in the animal world. *I* begins with a moocow. Daedalus constructed his maze not without relation to a cow. It was built to contain the Minotaur, the child of a (false) cow. We are in the labyrinth. There is no sexual hesitation and the first structure puts Oedipus in place. A cow and a little boy form a dual structure. We go on rapidly to the formation of the subject through the intervention of a third term. We go through the history of the mirror stage and of the cleavage, which is much funnier in Joyce than in Lacan.

In "His father told him that story:" the colon and the organization of the sentence are important since they speak at all levels. "His father looked at him through a glass:" a window separates without separating. With mirror and glasses we are already in the complex space of the history of blindness and of identificatory images. His father told him this story. The reader waits to hear what the father thinks but at that very moment the father is seen: "He had a hairy face." This is brought about by the father's look cast upon the boy. We are reminded of Kafka's keeper of the law, who was also said to have a hairy face. Our first perception of the father focuses on the glasses and on hair.

"He was baby tuckoo": not cuckoo, but tuckoo, a failed bird linked through its double *o* to the moocow that is walking down the road. His song falls from the sky, in the guise of a failed phonic signifier.

We go on to a succession of personal pronouns and adjectives: "His mother put on the oilsheet." She functions as an anal mother. She is at the center of a moment of corporeal perceptions: cold, warm, wet, smell. The bottom of the body and the odor are feminine but the mother is on the side of a certain orality as well.

"She played on the piano," so that he would dance. The mother is equally on the side of a kind of eroticism and makes things move.

Uncle Charles and Dante (whose double-entendre of "Auntie" and "Dante" is exploited by Joyce on the side of writing) open up the value of young and old at play throughout the entire text. It can be said that the subject in Joyce is structured by a series of oppositions: young, old; weak, strong. The symbolic father toward whom one regresses through a series of signifiers is treated as "Old Father," "Old Artificer." The real father is always in rivalry with the son, expressed in such statements as "I am beating him, I run faster than he, the women are mine."

With Dante and her two brushes we enter into the world of mathematics. The number two introduces sexual difference. The two brushes are very different in this scene, written as it is perceived by the child. High and low resemble each other.

The relation between naming and not-naming has to be noted. In chapter 2 (72–86), in the scene with Heron, his classmate and rival who wants to make Stephen confess to having a girlfriend, the girl is not named. She is simply called "the girl." The motif of naming comes about in a central way, beginning with the name of the main protagonist: Stephen, which echoes the first Christian martyr, and Dedalus, a foreign name, the strangeness of which is erased but which remains unexplainable. To put oneself under the sign of Dedalus is to play the card of the signifier.

Proper names are stressed. Parnell has no first name. A Protestant, he was worshiped and called the "uncrowned king of Ireland." He died trying to lead the first Irish revolution and, at that moment, Ireland lost its exemplary battle. The men of the Dedalus family themselves — and Joyce keeps on saying it in all of his work — killed Parnell. The old, archaic, Catholic Ireland turned against him who was called its liberator. Parnell had been unjustly accused of being the instigator of the assassination of Phoenix Park. The falsifier who had fabricated the letter supposedly written by Parnell was discovered later through a spelling mistake. This (happy) mistake joins the Augustinian motif of *felix culpa.* Luckily there was a fault, so there could be redemption. Everything is owed to a fault. In a play of signifiers, Joyce works on *Phoenix/Felix* around the happy fault, which, since he hates the theological perspective, is a subversive theme. In "Phoenix" read across French and German there is also *fait nichts,* "does not do anything." Parnell is innocent. His fault is not to have done anything. The artist, however, is going to take his place in the happy, subversive fault: "I did well to do what I did." Joyce touches upon an interdict, a prohibition, the first of which is that of sexuality. We can say that Joyce's work is owed to an immense spelling error. It is nothing but orthography playing infinitely. The letter plays with the letter, from the very beginning.

"The Vances lived in number seven," has to be heard in a childish way: *in* the number itself. "They had a different father and mother." In the child's view, there is an inside and an outside. "They" includes mother and father. That is when Eileen, the feminine respondent in the undifferentiated "they," appears.

"When they were grown up he was going to marry Eileen. He hid under the table. His mother said:

—O, Stephen will apologise" (8).

The position of hiding becomes his definitive position. Is it the fact of hiding that is prohibited? The reaction — "secret," "defense" — precedes in writing the statement that signifies there has been a fault. This demonstration of fear, the necessity of hiding before the cause, refers the reader to Kafka's keeper in "Vor dem Gesetz" ("Before the Law").[4] Joyce is going to do what big people do since he identifies with them. Everyone is "they." We can deduce that getting married is also prohibited. Did Freud not say, in *Totem and Taboo,* you must not do like your father?

Yet the symbolized threat comes from the mother. At the level of the body, we have seen the father's hair. But hair does not speak. Stephen's own name appears for the first time in a reductive scene where the mother speaks for him. She announces what he will do. Throughout the whole text, Stephen will have a relation as loving and compassionate son with his mother. At some point, in a protective gesture, he is going to buy a coat for her. In other words, he covers the mother uncovered by the father, who, in Irish fashion, drinks away her coat. He covers the very mother who had forced him to cover himself. Yet the mother is a good person and not the aggressive Dante with her two brushes. She is the typical uterine mother with ten children who is repressed by her husband.

During the Christmas dinner, the scene of communion the child had desired is carried off and transformed by political arguments. In a typical Dublin scene, both clans are present. The Parnellites and the men are Joyce's father's legacy to him. Dante had been a Parnellite but has turned against him. The mother is between the two. Being on the side of submission, she tries to be conciliatory. When she speaks for Stephen, the latter goes under the table that serves him as an eggshell and whence he will not come out again.

And Dante adds:

"— O, if not, the eagles will come and pull out his eyes—" (8).

The reader does not know where the little poem "Pull out his eyes, Apologise," comes from. It substitutes itself for the wild rose but now there are eagles. It is inscribed in a terrifying threat of enucleation that cannot not be in relation with the Oedipal scene.

At the same time, there is a displacement through rhythm and we can say that the artist is being born. At the beginning there was the Verb and everything else slides surreptitiously over this dictum. At the beginning there was a scene where rhythm and music, coming from the mother, were inscribed. And the mother makes him dance. Something happens between music and the words on music. When enucleation threatens, resistance is produced in a most ruseful way. The child under the table recuperates. He appropriates what frightens him; and a division takes place between the law, the utterance of the law, and the noise that this utterance makes. At the beginning there was the noise of the word, the noise of the law. Everything is inscribed phonically, the more so as there is the couple eye, ear, and the artist is somebody who has problems with his eyesight. Joyce theorizes this problem early in his work. He analyzes his relation to language in relation to his myopia. A tremendous ambivalence is put in place. The law that horrifies him also gives him pleasure. The name of the law frightens, but "apologise" has a nice sound. The text plays obviously on the phonic confusion between "eye" and "I." "Apologise" is the last word of this short introduction and the first word with which Joyce played, which he rolled on his tongue. Quite unlike Kafka, Joyce, as a Catholic, is never done with the law. His unconscious is completely taken into the Christian space of the fault. The debate is carried out in a way quite different from Kafka, who wanted to be outside the space of the law. Instead of giving up the law, Joyce puts in place an enormous system of transgression. And there can be no transgression without law. It all remains very masculine. At the end, in *Finnegans Wake,* Joyce even managed to make of transgression his law.

In "apologise," the question is between asking and forgiveness. The mother's force is to be identified with the Church. There is a cleavage that does not coincide. The young boy is taken between two different images: his father is rebellious but he is a scoundrel; his mother is a great soul but a slave, and she asks slavery of him. He is caught in complete ambivalence toward both parents. In Joyce, as well as in his fictional characters, everything is played out in a dramatic rapport with the mother. Joyce never stops wanting to kill her since she asked for his submission. He is going to work on all that is being played out on the body of the mother and on the enormous scene where a relation to the body of woman ensues. It is most classical and not classical at all, since, at the same time, Joyce analyzes it. The question of sexuality has to be followed from one end to the other, from Eileen who is legitimate since she is named to relations with women that begin to be prohibited when they are no longer named. The boy, full of sadistic phantasms, begins to have very violent relations with women.

In addition to "apologise," in the scene with Heron in chapter 2, there is another word: "admit" (58), which means to interiorize the fault. In chapter 3, there is yet another: "amend" (135). This lexical system can be followed. Forgiveness has different forms, different colors, establishes different rapports. And the answer is always "no." The law is active in the Catholic world. It imposes upon those who resist it a negative position. Joyce's first motto reads *non serviam,* "I will not." He is obliged to begin from a refusal, from a retreat. This movement is going to be transformed into Joyce's theory of the artist. He is going to have to work on the interiorization of the fault. The three virtues of the artist's behavior—silence, exile, cunning—are related to stories of interiorization and duplicity.

Joyce situates the structure that can produce what is called "the artist" at an important archetypal level. He puts the artist into rivalry with God since both are creators. What are the conditions that produce this artist? I am interested quite generally in the structure that makes the artist write, and in analyzing it, I want to see if there are sexual differences that can be theorized as well. What structure produces the woman and the man who write? Is it as daughter, as son of the father, of a certain father that they do so? Joyce, in answer to such questions, has elaborated a rapport with castration, something inevitable for a boy. Generally, men are caught in this space; some women too, but only through identification. As Freud described it, the boy begins to symbolize from the threat of castration, from resistance to castration, and what appears, what is described in a more than illuminating naïveté, is what Joyce calls the artist. At a certain moment, there is an encounter, and a law is interiorized in a certain mode. It has to do with inhibition, with the staging of a limit right where Stephen's body is small, weak, and marked by bad eyesight. There, at once, a physical weakness, the system of prohibitions, and the violence of history produce prohibiting knots. It is at these very points of encounter that something will disengage itself and produce the artist.

One should keep in mind the primal scenes from Joyce's *Portrait of the Artist,* Lispector's *Near to the Wild Heart,* Kafka's "Before the Law," and Blanchot's *The Writing of Disaster. Near to the Wild Heart* is the portrait of the artist as a young woman. It is a primitive, archaic, unique text. When Clarice was seventeen, she did not write the portrait of the artist; she wrote the portrait of the subject in formation, a feminine subject that reveals at the same time all the traits of the artist. It is the portrait of someone abnormal—that is, of someone who is outside norms and who continuously gathers moments of the real, just the way Stephen had done it under the name "epiphanies."

I want to put Joyce's primal scene side by side with Clarice Lispector's from *Near to the Wild Heart.* Clarice's scene, on the side of a feminine fault, also

WRITING AND THE LAW □ 9

begins with a relation to the father, soon after the latter's death. In Lispector, the father always has to be dead. There is going to be a scene with a real aunt in relation to the story of a theft.

On two different sides of sexual difference, *Portrait of the Artist* and *Near to the Wild Heart* stage the same scene. Young Stephen's fixation on language is the main element of the text that is marked by a succession of short poems punctuated by the word "apologise." Clarice is into chickens and worms, Joyce into roses and eagles. The system of thought of the young artist is put in place. From thinking about things the artist ends up understanding them. Joyce says this along these lines: If one reflects on words, if one warms them like a hen, one ends up understanding them. The little boy is constantly before a secret constituted by signifiers or by words. Over hundreds of pages, for Stephen Dedalus it is but a question of enigmas. Where there is a primal scene, there are also primal words, since the two are equivalent. The words hold back, they bind the future artist as young man. On the first page, the subversion of the law in the form of ambivalence, fear/pleasure, had taken place. When Stephen hears the threat:

> "Apologise,
> Pull out his eyes"

he is afraid, yet he feels an auditory pleasure. What the law says frightens but its noise is pretty. Joyce is fixated by the noise of the law. He is someone for whom the secret is audible, which is not the case of Blanchot or of Kafka. Joyce writes to the ear, whose secret he tries to surprise. This goes with the fact that he is very myopic. And, with his poor eyesight, the question of the law always returns. A drive is displaced because at that very moment the look is related to something specular. There is insistence. The look is in relation with space and opens upon a system of meaning that allows appropriation in distance and is the closest to symbolization. The sense of smell is the most primitive and relates to objects close up. The more one is elevated intellectually, the less one smells, the more one sees, farther and farther. One enters into an intellectual dimension. Hearing is much closer to the body, to the ear. In this way, the artist is quite explicitly in relation with femininity. At a certain moment when he goes over to the side of creation, or when, after all the emotions of childhood, he begins to be the one who produces, the metaphoric systems alluding to the soul of the artist as the Holy Virgin keep recurring. Femininity is all the stronger as it surges in an imaginary, Catholic space. The ideal figure of the Virgin is not an archaic, primitive femininity but a much reelaborated femininity, that of the Virgin Mary as desired by the artist.

Near to the Wild Heart: **How Not to Appear before the Law**

I am going back to my chickens. The first pages of *Portrait of the Artist* are the embryo of the whole work. In *Near to the Wild Heart,* the phonic obsession is magnetized by the words "never" *(nunca)* and "yes" *(sim)*. When Joyce wrote *Portrait of the Artist,* he was a sly old fox, while Clarice was seventeen years old when she wrote her text. The dinner in the third chapter of *Near to the Wild Heart* can be related to Joyce's Christmas dinner, where what should be a scene of orality is symbolized right away. Orality is displaced, carried off, through a great political struggle in a story where politics and food clash. In Clarice, the scene of the meal turns around chickens. We have a certain story of cannibalism that she experiences when she is eating the chickens to whom she gives the names of daughters. She epiphanizes a certain femininity in the chickens. They are body. In Clarice's writing about the naked chicken, there is a strong feeling of sacrificial, erotic violence. The scene is all the stronger as it happens between the father and one of his friends, that is to say among men. Suddenly a naked chicken lies on the table and Clarice notes:

"The father and the man were drinking wine, and the man was saying from time to time: I cannot even believe that you have found yourself a daughter" (20). We are on the side of elementary formation.

A few pages later, the reader learns that Joana is an orphan and that she is now at her aunt's. With an artist or a writer, one has to think of the structure that gives birth to, that produces, the strange being whose life is divided and who lives in a kind of duplicity, permanently torn between living and writing. The question was lived mortally by Kafka, but the necessity of a choice is always present. To write is a more or less solitary activity. For Kafka, it was total solitude. For Joyce, three main words — silence, exile, cunning — are the development of the theme of isolation and of a solitude needed to write.

Writers inhabit both the living and the writing worlds. They navigate with difficulty between the two, of which one will always be emphasized more than the other. To be the inhabitant of two worlds brings about a feeling of betrayal. Every exile cannot but think this way since one cannot change countries without being from two countries. This double appurtenance, this double locus is going to lead to the theme of betrayal, a dominant problem in Joyce. It is put into place by the institution of a double world.

The two worlds — of presence and absence — are formalized. They name, yet are lived, inscribed in the body. In *The Uncanny,* Freud tells us that death is a late discovery of mankind. Writers carry within themselves their own disquieting strangers, like Kafka who felt that he had been on Mount Sinai and had experienced another world. The variable of this structure is that death is lived necessarily as if it were one's own. The supreme case is to have made the experience of one's own death, of one's own castration. It can be played like the death of the other, but of an other so close that it is interiorized. In any event, it is being played in relation to a certain loss, which then has to be sublimated.

Clarice inscribes the death of the father. The latter is at the origin of the movement of reconstruction, of a writing as resistance to castration. This is the thematic of Freud's *Totem and Taboo*. For the boy, the threat of castration is of an extreme simplicity, as we can see in *Portrait of the Artist:* If you do not behave so as to be forgiven, the eagles will come and pull out your eyes. For Clarice, the threat of castration is displaced and symbolized rather late through the loss of the living phallus, the father. In *Near to the Wild Heart,* in a chapter entitled ''The Aunt'' (that is, after her father's death), she has to succeed in interiorizing a certain reality of that death. In an extraordinary scene, Clarice takes refuge from her aunt and her vulgar femininity. She tells the story of the latter's breasts, enormous and fatty, that look at the girl as if they were about to swallow her. The little girl runs toward the sea. In a moment of savage communion, she arrives at the following thoughts:

''Her happiness increased, it united itself in her throat like a sack of air. She understood that is was over with her father. That was all'' (32).

And Kafka? After all, his father was not dead. Kafka's story is obviously written in relation to his father, but human beings are not made of blocks of cement. Kafka was composed of his father, which was not very amusing because the latter was a tall, thin man whom he could not contain. He dies from his father, but an interiorized father. In Clarice, the father-daughter relation is mediated by the sea. The chapter ends with a short poem the father had made up when she had said to him: But what am I going to do now? It reads as follows:

> ''Daisy and Violet knew
> One was blind, the other lived very crazily,
> The blind one knew what the crazy one said,
> And ended up seeing what no one else saw'' (40).

That is the father's testament.

The chapter entitled ''The Bath'' begins with these words:

''At the moment when the aunt went to pay for her purchase, Joana took out the book and stuck it carefully between the others under her arm. The aunt turned pale'' (42).

In the street, the aunt tries to make Joana feel guilty:

'' — Do you know what you did?

— I know . . .

— You know . . . and you know the word?

— I stole the book, isn't that it?'' (42).

And in answer to the aunt's question about whether Joana thinks that one can steal, she answers:

''I can.

— You?! — screamed the aunt.

— Yes, I stole because I wanted. I will only steal when I want.''

This scene can be put side by side with Stephen's. The little girl in this scene does not enter into the space of the fault. Clarice puts herself in a special rapport with the story of forgiveness. In the scene that follows, the little girl, glued to the door, hears her aunt complain to her uncle, saying: "She is a viper" (44). In a truly comic scene, the aunt opposes Joana, the artist, and Amanda, the daughter of the house. The uncle claims that Amanda would also be capable of stealing books. But the aunt continues to scream that this is different. Even if she did, she would remain a person.

The power of Clarice's remark, which reveals her moral law, has to be underlined: It is not bad because I am not afraid. She is not under the spell of transgression, while in the Joycean dilemma, nothing can function without transgression. There must be law so it can be transgressed.

Joyce — and all that comes through him — is going to say: Tell me no. Whereas Clarice — and this marks the totality of her text — does the contrary. Clarice does not respond to the calling of the law. Her relationship to the inside of the law is different. She does not enter though the aunt with her big breasts would like to make her do so. Clarice produces the inverse of this gesture. Her aunt tells her: Do you know what you did and what it is called? The sentence goes through an entire system of naming. Joana, the protagonist, is not ignorant. Yes, she knows that in a certain vocabulary and in a certain world, it is called "to steal." There is a displacement of values — something more than simply Nietzschean — or a reversal, but elsewhere. Joana does not appear before the law.

When Stephen says in chapter 5 that it is as Icarus that he will leave Ireland, we may think, on the one hand, that he will fall into the sea, and on the other hand, we may read it as an allusion to the trajectory of the Luciferian fall. Lucifer is the one who said no to God. He is the creator as anticreator, the rival. Is he not the son? The equivalent of the relation Lucifer-God is the already human character of Prometheus, who is announced in the first page with the appearance of the eagles. Prometheus's eagle did not tear out his eyes but his liver. Joyce plays as if he were mixing the cards of mythology. There is some Prometheus in the motifs of punishment, of the eagle and enucleation. Under Prometheus and behind the eagles, Oedipus appears. We could speak of a composite myth, the way we could speak of a composite kinship. According to Marx, Prometheus is the first martyr of the philosophical calendar. One could say that Stephen Dedalus is the first martyr of the literary calendar. Joyce touches on this kind of subversion with a Promethean character who resists but does not give in. Hephaistos introduces a supplementary link since he had been forced by Zeus to chain Prometheus to the Caucasus. The scene is cruel, because, in a certain way, Hephaistos likes Prometheus in whom he sees himself. The motif of the chain, of links and of linking, is introduced. Hephaistos is taken in the chain of chains, be it the conjugal chains he tries to protect, or the weave of the net in which he captures adults. He is someone who forges.

If we look ahead to Kafka's texts, we see that links are everywhere. They are Kafka's very drama. We can see it in the famous story of his impossible engagements. Kafka spent his time getting engaged and disengaged, indefinitely. He was playing with his own life and death. His major engagements were those he tied and untied the most, as the one with Felice, a kind of first *felice culpa*. Felice Bauer, whose name, across German, insists on peasant and construction, marks Kafka's texts under the initials F. B., which one finds constantly in *The Trial*. Through these engagements and disengagements, linkings and unlinkings, something important is going to be played out in relation to the law. As with Joyce, though written quite differently, the statement that can be read in filigrane throughout Kafka's adventure is: Tell me no. Kafka needs someone to tell him yes in order to be able to say no. The most solid person in this respect was Felice.

Kafka's last tragic scene took place just before his death. His last fiancée, Dora Diamant, was nineteen and Kafka was forty-one. It was a completely incestuous relationship. We have been told that Kafka wanted to live until the very last minute. He was so caught in the death drive that at the moment of agony which lasted several weeks, he was overcome by a terrible desire to live. In his last moments, he did what he had done during his entire life; that is, he asked Dora's parents, since she was so young, if he could marry her. He wrote to Dora's father who, as an orthodox Jew of the Hassidic sect, venerated an old, saintly rabbi. The father showed the rabbi a letter in which Kafka asked: Will the marriage take place? Before this sphinxlike question, the rabbi shook his head. The answer came back descriptive rather than written, the supreme mark of Kafka's destiny. At that moment, he had all he ever wanted. His demand for ''no'' and exclusion had its ultimate answer.

Compared to Joyce, the difference would be in the way the artist says no. Joyce hears real and not imaginary voices, voices of authority — like his father's — which call him and make certain propositions to him. In *Portrait of the Artist,* the most obvious example is the proposition the rector makes to induce Stephen to enter the Jesuit order. He *is* chosen. It is an enormous proposition of legitimation. Yet after a slight manifestation of seduction, he refuses.

There are also several scenes of exclusion. The first one takes place when he hides under the table. Another defensive exclusion occurs right afterward, during a childhood scene at school. The boy constantly describes himself as the little-young-weak one, he who always remained on the edge:

''He kept on the fringe of his line, out of sight of his prefect, out of the reach of the rude feet, feigning to run now and then'' (8).

This marks the beginning of the theme of appearances. There is an explanation:

''He felt his small and weak body amid the throng of players and his eyes were weak and watery'' (8).

The first violent interpellation is:

'' — What is your name?

Stephen had answered: — Stephen Dedalus.

Then Nasty Roche had said:

—What kind of a name is that?

And when Stephen had not been able to answer, Nasty Roche had asked:

—What is your father?'' (8–9).

All the elements are here. The question of appearance, of its value, opens the system of a vicious circle or of a double-bind. In this classical scene, we can see the defensive position of the little weak one who only pretends he is running. At the level of the body, he makes a simulated gesture in order to pretend that he is part of it, in order not to be interpellated any more. Difference is marked by a negative sign. He is less strong, weaker, smaller. Everyone has known such power relations. They are the first inscriptions of a threat of castration, of an exclusion inscribed spatially. We are on the edge, at the outer limit, which is going to be the metaphor of something that will be the exclusion caused by inverse reasons. He is excluded as corporeally weak. But he is on both sides of the barrier. Intellectually stronger, he is the one who is most threatened. He who is below can be looked at, he who is above cannot be seen. He disappears, becomes invisible. He who knows more, who has a greater score, cannot be understood. Literally, he cannot be included since he is in excess. When he is below, he can be caught and understood by images in the order of representation. But he becomes unrepresentable when he begins to exceed the limit.

Kafka's "Before the Law": How to Go before One's Door

In *The Passion according to G. H.*, Clarice uses the metaphor of cutting meat into small pieces to produce form. There must be form but there also can be something formless that can be given a positive value. What has no form totalizes, and the unlimited suscitates the necessity of making distinctions. How can it allow for otherness? It is all and nothing and has to be organized, which does not necessarily mean to lay down the law. It can also mean to shape a body. Form is needed in order to give it to the other.

A text calls for, provokes, calls for a certain reading. In ''Before the Law,'' in two pages, Kafka, the hunger artist, wrote something immense. The text is but writing, the sublimation of a paradox. It is not the *body* that prevents the man from the country from going through the door, but the *word*. The law is but a word, not a real being, and from this Kafka draws certain effects. In his diary, on November 6, 1913, we can read: ''Whence the sudden confidence? If it would only remain! If I could go in and out of every door in this way, a passably erect person. Only I don't know whether I want that.''[5]

The text is situated in a space where the distinction between reason and madness is impossible. We are in a paradox, where when we think one thing, the thing itself thinks the opposite of what we think that it thinks. What does it mean to be outside the law or to be in the law?

Let us take what Clarice called, in her novel with the same title, "an apple in the dark." We can imagine that it is a candle. With the "apple in the dark," we go into the labyrinth. The first narrative of a series of interdictions is the story of Eve and the apple. The poor man from the country is before the apple, except that there is no apple. In Kafka, it is a question of differences. The story takes place between city and country, nature and culture, while knowing that the opposition never has an absolute value and that nature and culture are always in contact and in exchange. One has to shuttle back and forth beween the enunciation — the statement — and the locus of reading.

Does the law come first? There is already an implicit paradox in the fact that the text begins with "Before the law." The text says it, and imposes on the reader a law that consists in making it impossible to put into question the existence of the law.

From the beginning, we are interpellated by the word "law." Kafka's genius is to put everything in place in the first three words. Then, with the man from the country, we are going to wait before the door and learn to be patient. We become old and deaf. We share the destiny inaugurated by the word "law," while throughout the text, we are in a relation of desire along with the man who wants to enter the law. We are not supposed to ask him what the law is. The law is treated like a place one thinks one is going to enter. From the beginning, we are prohibited from going in, and from asking ourselves what it means to enter the law. The law is inscribed as spatialized, localized, even if it is so in an indefinite way. If, instead of "law," I would say, with echoes of Clarice, "before the apple," I would not be so crazy. But, in fact, I should say "before the word." Is the man before the law not already *in* the law? The man arrives, desiring to enter in the law. His desire already belongs to the law. It does not come while he desires to transgress the law. However, to want to enter into the law is transgressive. The man from the country is in this strange situation where from the moment he wants to enter in the law, he is not there. In order *not* to transgress the law, he has to remain in the immobile situation before the law. One has to want to enter. It is enough to become mad and deaf.

To whom does he address his desire to enter the law? To the guardian, to the *Türhüter*. Etymologically, *hüten*, "to keep," is also *bewahren*, as in *wahr*, "true." The keeper is posted before the law in order to maintain its truth, in order to keep it for himself. One falls into a terrifying microscene where, as in every story, one finds oneself answering the question of the man from the country with: What do you want to know? But he does not know what he wants to know. This sends us back to a childhood scene: Why? — Because! What do you want to know? A cruel question, the answer to which is: I want to know.

What are the evident themes? The text begins with: "Before the law stands a doorkeeper." *Türhüter*, "doorkeeper," is in one word, which doubles the effect of the keeper.

"To this doorkeeper, there comes a man from the country and asks for admittance to the Law."

The story takes place between two men, the doorkeeper and the man from the country who is marked by his origin. He will never get over coming from the country.

The text is in a glacial present tense that carries us into the level of something eternal, definitive: the text is the law.

But the keeper tells the man from the country that he cannot grant him entrance. The text is about entering. The door is not there, except in its composition with the keeper. The man asks to enter. It all remains very abstract.

The game of entering and not entering which will be solved with a "You have not entered!" reminds us of the Biblical exclusion from paradise, an echo of which is going to be played out again in the story of Moses, who loses something before entering. You will not enter into the Promised Land because you were not already there, or, to put it another way: You would not look for me, if you had not already found me. This is the reassuring motto of the Christian quest. Judaism is much more tragic. Christ came and he remains to be found. Moses' law is: you will not enter because you are not in it. The man from the country is Moses' imperceptible double. "You will not enter into the Promised Land" promises negatively and positively. It promises that he will not enter, but it promises the earth. Moses, contrary to the man from the country, saw it from a distance. It is a story to be put side by side — though at opposite ends — with Moses' story.

The keeper does not tell the man from the country that he will not enter. It is less a question of entering into an outside than into an inside that is difficult. There are three points of view: that of the man from the country, Kafka's, and ours. In his diary, Kafka lets us know that he insists on "entering." Nothing is inscribed in a nonparadoxical way. The entrance is not that of Moses. It is not a question of entering into a forbidden place, because that would be related to desire. But we do not know if there *is* an inside. In an arrested and terrifying movement, reducing the space between the two men, the text relates that there is no inside. It is the story of a man and the law. Perhaps the drive to enter is similar to that of wanting to enter the body of the mother. But the similarity is at the level of the drive only, because the object is not feminine. The law, *das Gesetz,* in German is neuter and we have to stay with the word.

The relation between the two protagonists, described in concrete terms, is going to last a lifetime. The positions of the bodies are important. The keeper, described physically with his fur coat, is before the law in such a way that he has the law behind him. The man to whom the keeper assigns a place before the door, on a little stool — an inverse description of the Oedipal enigma — arrives upright, then sits down, shrivels up, and finally reverts back to childhood, even from the point of view of language. He does not know if darkness is inside or outside. But he recognizes a glorious glimmer, somewhat of a contradiction, that eternally shines forth from the door of the law. Here we have a key for the use of tenses. The man is in eternity.

"Now he does not have very long to live" is paradoxical. If he sees eternity, is he still alive? These two sentences hint at the question of mortality and immortality. At the moment of "nun lebt er nicht mehr lange (now he does not have much longer to live)," there is no more separation between life and death. The sentence tells us that we are already in eternity. All is concentrated in the one and only question he did not ask. The man is already in a state of rigor mortis and his body is stiff. The difference in size between the two is modified to the disadvantage of the man from the country.

"What do you want to know? You are insatiable."
The man's essence is insatiability.

"All aspire to the law. How is it that all these years, no one has asked to go in?"
The man himself happens to enunciate the law as a universal utterance. And he obeys the law. One can ask the question of what he asked himself without asking the question. He is at the end of his life. Am I the law myself? Perhaps only *I* asked to go in. What anguish! And what if he made a mistake? He is going to die reassured.

"The keeper recognizes that he is already at the end."
Not only because he goes out like a flame but because he did ask the final question. He approached the truth of the law in the very terms of the law: If everyone, then why me alone? He is crossing the extreme limit. The following question can be asked only if there is still some breath left: Did I make a mistake? This would question the scene of the law, which cannot be separated from the law. Worse, perhaps, he could not say: If there is only I, then I am wrong because truth is universal. But where could the error be? In the door, in the moment, in the keeper? There has been no doubt until now, but it occurs with the *doch* (but). The keeper recognizes that the man is going to die, for one cannot doubt the law during one's lifetime. One cannot doubt death, since one is no longer here to doubt it.

"The doorkeeper recognizes that the man has reached his end, and, to let his failing senses catch the words, roars in his ear: 'No one else could ever be admitted here, since this gate was made only for you. I am now going to shut it.' "
The man from the country arrives and the keeper leaves: "I am now going to shut it [*ihn*]," that is to say, the entrance. He can only *close* the entrance, since there is nothing inside. The *ihn*, "it," is the key to the text. It means that the keeper himself cannot say anything about the inside. He cannot say but what he knows, that is to say, the entrance.

I come back to the main threads of interpretation.

At the level of the dilemma that can be read throughout the text, we begin to see in the last conversation that the law is forbidden. It prohibits because it is prohibited. What the man wants to know touches on the law itself. It is prohibited like everything that is inaccessible or unapproachable. This paradox can be found in everything of the order of defense. There is no gesture of defense that does not have this kind of ambivalence, that does not push toward the outside and the inside, that does not have this double trait: to defend toward the inside, while defending against the outside. From the very beginning, the movement of the text itself is: You will not enter. It is prohibited. There is a no-trespassing sign. The law prohibits and is prohibited.

But the secret of the law is that it has no material inside. The text is diabolical and puts down the law of the reader. One cannot contest that one is before the law, even if one does not know it. The law cannot be defined. It is neither man nor woman. It is known only as a verbal construct and is designated to come and go, in relation with a concrete object, be it the apple or the mother's body.

The imperceptible *tour de passe-passe* (sleight of hand) of this text is that it begins with a keeper and it ends with: "This door was only meant for you." Hence, I, the keeper, was only for you, since there is not one without the other. In a very definite way, everything happened inside the man from the country.

The law especially defends its own secret, which is that it does not exist. It exists, but only through its name. As soon as I speak about it, I give it a name and I am inside Kafka's texts. The law is before my word. It is a verbal rapport. The entire force of the law consists in producing this scene so that it be respected. How? The police force is concrete and we are on the side of the state. "Before the Law" is a story of symbolization in relation to the unconscious since it does not have recourse to the police force. From the beginning, we have a mechanism that says: It is possible, but not now. The text raises the question of a narrative instance. Like Kierkegaard's Abraham, Kafka's man came to his rendezvous with the law alone, with his provisions. The door is open. The system of repression is put in place. He leans forward to look inside but he does not see. We are not told this because the keeper begins to speak. The man thinks the law. The reality of the law is in the keeper who acts and prohibits. Hence, he also institutes the possibility of trangressing. The scene is comical. The keeper is seen like the father in *Portrait of the Artist:* he is hairy, with a beard and a long nose. The keeper opposes the man's desire verbally and there is no bodily struggle. "You can enter if you want," translated into elementary Freudian terms would read: "If you want, you can." But Kafka would say: I can but do I want to? I can go in and out of all the doors but am I sure that I want to? Kafka expressed it as a desire, but a split desire. The man from the country desires himself as wanting. True desire is: I can and I want. The keeper's presence splits the man's desire into: If only I could want what I want. This is the instance of the law. Nothing prevents me, except the law transformed into the self. *I,* the law. That is what psychoanalysis calls the superego, which is an inner instance. The law is *in* the man so how can he enter the law? The law is the divided desire inside him. There are antidotes to this; for example, apples and oranges à la Clarice.

In Kafka's text, there is a monstrous opening without inside. Something has to be opened. If the law existed, the man would have entered. The stakes of his desire were situated between the opening and closing of something that does not take place. The entrance is the very step the man does not take. He did not come to enter but in order to ask for entrance. But the law is truly a French *pas,* which is both a step and its annullment, a step-not. It opens or closes. Everything happens in relation to an originary given, to the law of the law: I exist. The definition of the law can unfold only in relation to the question of the origin of the law. In order to get out of Kafka's text, we must ask: Where does the law come from? and not think that it has always been there.

Blanchot, *The Writing of Disaster: Nothing Is What There Is*

In Blanchot's *Writing of Disaster* there is also an important primal scene. Blanchot, Kafka's phantom and vampire, preys upon the latter incessantly. However, he distilled something and pushed the Kafkaesque dilemma toward an algebraic formulation. Blanchot, who is not without psychoanalytic knowledge, has a different style. The passage I chose to read on page 72 is taken up again on page 114.[6] The second version becomes a remainder through a kind of explosion, or decomposition, hence through a kind of analysis. The scenes could be juxtaposed, critically, to Clarice's text "Sunday, before falling asleep." The second, exploded version contains certain small motifs that are like signifying, partial objects, for example, a tree, reminiscent of what we read in Clarice's story. We can distinguish between common and differential elements in both texts and make a kind of montage with the different images of the body. In Blanchot, a child is standing upright while lifting the curtains, and looks out of the window. In Clarice's "Sunday, before falling asleep," the child is in bed, looking out of the window. In a system of relations between body and self, self and world, there are differences and similarities. In the first version of the primal scene, Blanchot directs himself to "You who live later." With Blanchot, everything is always posthumous. The scene reads:

"(A primal scene?) *You who live later, close to a heart that beats no more, suppose, suppose it: the child — is seven years old, or eight perhaps?*" (translation modified).

"Suppose it" refers to the heart. But afterward, there is a colon. And then there follows the child. The text is being organized around the child and the heart. There is a masculine, grammatical chain with *le* (the and it). However, Blanchot does not say "the boy." The originary scene takes place when the child is about seven or eight years old (hence late), but the child, masculine and not masculine, is still on the side of a certain neuter.

"*What happens then: the sky, the* same *sky, suddenly open, absolutely black and absolutely empty, revealing (as though the pane had broken) such an absence that all has since always and forevermore been lost therein — so lost that therein is affirmed and dissolved the vertiginous knowledge that nothing is what there is, and first of all nothing beyond.*"

The short text, located in the middle of *The Writing of Disaster,* is also the heart of the book. The entire book does nothing but retell this scene referring to the writing of disaster. We see here a disaster, as dis-aster *(dés-astre),* as that which is without *astres,* without stars.

''What happens then: the sky,'' has to be questioned at the syntactical or gram-matical level. Of importance is the interpellation of the sky, a matrix that is dis-seminated in the whole paragraph. The sky, *le ciel,* by disseminating itself in expressions like *s'y est, s'y affirme,* signals its own annullment as *''s'y.''*

A primal scene always refers to the parental coitus. *Finnegans Wake* can be read as a primal scene. People do nothing but listen at doors while something is happening. Therefore we are voluntary or involuntary witnesses, something that is difficult to analyze, but a sign of destiny for us. The child is always in the position of a third, excluded term, behind doors or behind the window. There is usually a displacement toward the look, since in the originary scene, something not seen is given to be seen, or something that is not to be seen is staged.

Blanchot writes the scene with a question mark: ''A primal scene?'' Is it or is it not? What is it? In Blanchot, something is happening that is nothing. We are at the limit of a ''happening,'' of presence and absence.

We have to recall the conceptual frame. In a classical analytic space, the dis-covery of the nothing takes place in a formidable scene for the child which is the impossible discovery of the mother's castration and the entire articulation of the mechanism that is going to be described in the constitution of fetishism. When one says ''the discovery that the mother does not have a penis,'' one already states it in Freudian way. One discovers that she does not have something. Obviously that is not the way it is said in Blanchot. That would be too simple. It is not written in the form of lack. Very subtly, two coordinates are at work: the originary scene and the mother without a penis. All illusions have to be kept.

A theme, borrowed from Kafka, keeps recurring in Blanchot:

''Absolutely black and absolutely empty, revealing (as though the pane had been broken) such an absence that all has since always and forevermore been lost therein.''

The utterance is paradoxical. There is not nothing, there *is:* nothing. At the end of the text, if, as Blanchot suggests, the flood is infinite, what does the reader do with ''He will weep no more''? Is it to be read as an opposition? No, because the flood is not of the same nature as in ''He will weep no more.''

According to Freud, it is from the discovery of the absence of the mother's penis that fear of castration and masculinity are constituted. Something is being symbolized where there is interiorization of the threat of castration and resistance to castration. Something is being symbolized there. Resistance to castration is often figured in the form of petrifaction, as in the story of Medusa. Here, in Blanchot, to the contrary, we have an infinite *flood.* It cannot not be heard on the side of femininity. On the side of masculinity, it could be heard as an endless ejaculation but that does not mean anything. Hence, it can be said that it is really a resistance to castration put in place by a kind of femininity.

"He says nothing. He will live henceforth in the secret. He will weep no more." "Says" is a present to be questioned. Henceforth, he will live in secret, indefinitely. If one moves in the direction of writing, a lot can be said about the various floods and their drying up. "He says nothing" and "He will weep no more" are related to dessication and can be associated with the secret. What is before the secret but helps keep it? He says nothing because he cannot. He is somewhat in the same situation as Kierkegaard's Abraham. What he has to say is unspeakable and inaudible. Beginning with the space of misunderstandings, on the side of the parents, he is being comforted for something that has no consolation. He is considered by others to be afflicted with grief, while he is submerged by joy. The experience he has had in the primal scene cannot be transmitted. Where does it lead? Either one is in the space of Abraham, on the side of the knight of the absolute, of the unique experience — hence we cannot understand either, and that is part of the paradox — or one is prey to easy symbolization and the material constitution of the space of exclusion. In *Portrait of the Artist,* the scene is constituted ambiguously. The experience of the artist is not absolute but belongs to a level of communication. Artists are supposed to communicate, at least among themselves. Dedalus, for example, can communicate with the Ancient Fathers.

Most often we do not deal with the law but only with its representatives, its incarnations and figures. All of *Portrait of the Artist* occurs in a classical Oedipal space because there is someone who laid down the law for him who puts down the law. Generally we are before a hairy father and an aunt with brushes. But in life we encounter representatives of the law who are mistaken for the law because we do not look behind them. The force of Kafka's text is that he does not deceive the world. The first sentence reads, "Before the Law. . . ." There is a representative of the law, hence we have an Oedipal scene and the space in which it is inscribed which begins with the law. But we do not see the law that is *behind* the text.

If we come back to Blanchot's primal scene in *The Writing of Disaster,* the look is related to respect for the law, to the nonvisibility of the law: "Nothing is what there is" (72). It is also a story of respect. The child leads us through the window and into the garden:

"The child — is he seven years old, or eight perhaps? — standing by the window, drawing the curtain and, through the pane, looking. What he sees: the garden, the wintry trees, the wall of a house."

The child looks up toward the sky. The narrator sees what the child sees: nothing *(rien)*. He sees the sky and then the same sky. He respects the sky, he looks *(re-garde)* in the sense of keeping, of appropriating the sky. In this text, which is a sequel, a kind of commentary on Kafka's "Before the Law," what *happens* is that the child has seen the law. He has seen "nothing." He has seen the sky, absolutely black and absolutely empty.

"The sky, the same *sky, suddenly open, absolutely black and absolutely empty, revealing (as though the pane had broken) such an absence that all has since always and forevermore been lost therein — so lost that therein is affirmed and dissolved the vertiginous knowledge that nothing is what there is, and first of all nothing beyond"* (72).

This is what Blanchot wrote on the tomb of the man from the country who did not die seeing nothing, but who died of seeing "Nothing." He died from wanting to see something that was really nothing. And the child, not yet all shriveled up, at the age of seven or eight, pushed the keeper aside and looked. He saw the law, even the sky. Can one say that he did not die of it?

"The unexpected aspect of this scene (its interminable feature) is the feeling of happiness that straightaway submerges the child, the ravaging joy to which he can bear witness only by tears, an endless flood of tears."

He cannot be a witness other than through tears. He makes his testimony through his tears, through a kind of sexual gesture and also through writing, but a silent writing. He cannot bear witness through words because that is what the law does. "An endless flow of tears . . . he said nothing." Is he dead or not from having seen nothing? He is like someone who does not live. He says nothing. He does not say "nothing." Silence, as we know, is the metaphor of death. "Hence he will live in secret." He keeps the secret and is kept secret. "You who live in the future" is a reading among many. All this to say that in a certain way it is possible to see the law. I need a basket full of quotation marks not to be, henceforth, in the secret of the law which is ordinary, black, absolutely empty, and which is nothing. But Blanchot's child is a masculine child. For him, there is not nothing but nothing is what there is.

If I go back to Kafka, I read: "Now he has not very long to live." The short sentence cannot be replaced. He comes from the country and is insatiable. But let us go back to a general philosophical territory. On a philosophical level, the text is about respecting the law as an expression of the moral law, or of the law as moral. If the man had wanted, he could have entered. He would have transgressed but obeyed the law in a different, negative way. But he does not and thus puts down the law for himself. He decides to wait to receive permission, instead of granting it to himself, something he could have done. The mechanism of the law is to ask us to lay down the law. If we do not, as we can read in Joyce, "the eagles will come and tear out our eyes."

One arrives at something enormous, unthinkable. One knows nothing about the law. One can only respect the law, that is, be content with knowing nothing. All human beings have been exposed to this. Not to know anything is difficult. By definition, humans, children of cows, as Joyce tells us, are curious about the origin, about the inside, the belly. Hence the importance of the gaze in relation to the body. The body starts close to the ground then gets up and looks into the distance, toward the inaccessible. It occupies a moral position. But it is also the body's erect position that plunges us into the abyss of the sky. The law is related to *non-savoir,* to not-knowing, but the originary scene is related to a desire to know. Curiosity is a feminine fault because men who respect themselves do not have that vice. The man from the country had this kind of feminine curiosity. Respect implies a distance from the law. The trace of femininity in the man is that he *wants* to know. He does not, since he is from the country, respect the unthinkable fact that nothing is what there is to know. He thinks — and this is rather comical — that there *is* something. He *imagines* the law which means that he is always outside the law. He has always wanted to see God face to face, as if God had a face. The supreme respect, the pure law, would be more than to accept. It would be not to know in Christian terms, but to be in a kind of quiet knowledge, without feeling anxiety.

If we are like the child, and look from the tomb of the unhappy man, we see the sky. Blanchot writes in the perspective of a certain knowledge, with a memory of philosophical and psychoanalytic references. The text can be read as a metaphor of a primal scene. And the sky is empty, absolutely black. It cannot not be put in relation with a traditional background that surrounds the dilemma of the moral law the way it has been analyzed, unfolded in texts by Kant and taken up again by Heidegger. We have to recall Kant's sentence dealing with the origin of the moral law. He writes his own relationship to the moral law as the starry sky above his head and the moral law in his heart. This produces feelings of moral respect. Admiration and fear produce a moral feeling of respect. What is extraordinary in Kant is the mention of the starry sky.

In *The Writing of Disaster* Blanchot writes of a sky without stars. It is the critique, the passage to the limit of the Kantian or Freudian moral, but it is not at all immoral. Blanchot's strength is to have said not just "the sky," but the "*same* sky," "absolutely black" and "absolutely empty." It is a kind of philosophical profession or a poetics of atheism. What he sees is of such absence that "everything has always lost itself in it and has been lost forever." If, for example, he had seen the stars — because Blanchot does not say that he sees God, he is not mad, he is a philosopher, hence he sees something sublime. If he had seen the stars or a satellite, if he had had an Einsteinian vision or if he *had* seen God, the world would have had its limit. Of course, what he sees is, as he says, "nothing." Henceforth he will have to live knowing that there is nothing beyond. He tolerates what is intolerable for the human imagination, that is to say the absence of limit, or of limiting transcendence. Why is this despair? We all know that civilization, limits and laws, are practical. We need them. If the law is not imposed on us, we have to impose it on ourselves. Is it possible not to lay down the law for ourselves? In other words, can we live without law, and if so, what does it mean?

One has to begin with the first three words in Kafka's story. In fact, we do not think, say, or articulate anything that is not "before the law." In banal psychoanalytic terms, one would say that it is symbolization, in the name of the father, that is the law.

Philosophy, psychoanalysis, have worked on the history of the origin of the law, of morals. Freud studied these problems in texts that are at the basis of his whole edifice, like *Totem and Taboo*. Kant produced a gigantic work on this question: Where does the moral law, outside the police and the armies, come from? He worked philosophically, preanalytically, in a passionate search, and arrived at an impasse because he was not a theologian. For him the law was not given by Moses and the moral law did not depend on God. It had to be in relation with a finite human being. He arrives where we would also arrive if we followed the path of reason. Going back from generation to generation, we arrive at Adam and Eve and there everything breaks down. Every time one breaks down with Kant, one ends with the aporia of: "There is neither origin, nor beginning." There is no first example; all is pure, immediate. And Kant's conclusion is well known: There is pure law, pure moral law.

There is a gap between Kant's and Kafka's texts. Kafka asked the real question of a law that was only for him, while Kant, turning like a rat in a labyrinth, had to send everything back into a reflexive mode. One cannot say that respect for the law is only intimate. The law is here to be respected the same way that radishes are here to be eaten. Kant turns in circles he can close only through a categorical imperative. For him, it is yes or no and those who say no will be decapitated.

Freud took up this problem and arrived at the same impasse. Working on the origins of the prohibitions upon which civilization is founded, he invented the story of the murder of the father, both a Freudian hypothesis and a phantasm. It is the murder of a very heavily symbolized father—Freud did not choose to explicate the original fault—which leads to the formation of the subject, subjectivity, and repression.

In *Totem and Taboo*, Freud tells a story that is forever unfinished. We barely come upon the father, and then upon the moral place of the father, and, quickly, we fall into remorse. Freud touches on fascinating and terrifying problems resembling Kafka's as well as Lispector's. From what moment on can we say that a gesture is bad? Generally, this is not asked since the law is affirmative. The law first designates something and then limits it right away. Freud is turning interminably around the question: What if one says that the murder of the father is bad? He declares that at the origin there is the murder of the father. Then there is punishment, fault, guilt. But to feel guilt, one needs a feeling of guilt. Where does it come from? Freud cannot break out of the closure of guilt. Kafka and Blanchot do not leave it either. Explicitly, I have seen only Clarice Lispector produce utterances that do not deal with the law or what goes with it, that is, transgression. She does it, as we have seen, in the episode of theft by putting herself at the origin of what could be the law. She herself decides the value of such and such a gesture.

She had the incredible strength to resist the ready-made in the world with its finished laws ordered by a system of moral values, hierarchized into good and bad. The ready-made laws are always hierarchized from an anthropomorphic point of view, instituting a god, then angels, men, women, animals, plants, always in a descending order. Clarice dehierarchizes. She does not accept that the law is systematically anthropomorphic. It is always andromorphic. Clarice takes as law, the law of the living. She takes it "as" the law. Because there is an absolute without law, all depends on the content one puts into the word "law." Clarice infuses this word with a content completely subversive in relation to what has been transmitted by it since time immemorial. The secret of the law, of the categorical imperative, of the Oedipal prohibition, and of all the laws under which we live, is that there is no secret, there are no stars. If the law tricks us, it is because we internalized its interdiction. We are always inside the social, and history began before us with the law. We are inside the narrative of the law and we cannot help it. The law tells us a story. Is there an author? That is the question. Given a masculine consensus, I have to say that the author of the law, transmitted from father to son, is "they." Blanchot's story is exemplary. He saw that there *was* nothing. And since he was a boy, he died of it. After having shed all the tears in his body, he precipitated himself into the silence of the law and into the secret. And he has a lot to cry about. Kafka's man from the country kept on thinking that there was somebody or something inside. He thought there was an inside. Blanchot's little boy has seen nothing and does not betray. He obeys nothing. The horror of his fate is expressed in the last sentence: "He will weep no more." He sees that there is no transcendence. One cannot wait for the law to fall from the sky. He has to be autonomous and make someone lay down the law for him. There is, of course, something supreme, something difficult, that is to say, love, about which he says nothing. He leaves others with these illusions. He only knows that there is no starry sky, no sublime origin of morals. He says nothing and lies. He does not say anything of the truth but spares others. He keeps the secret for those who have not understood him yet, but his fate is sealed. He will not cry anymore because he has no grief. The sole passion of his life will have been this feeling of ecstatic happiness, once and for all. That is because in Blanchot, we stay in the space of the classical moral law and of the categorical imperative.

But there are always variants. In Kafka, it is not as clear as in Blanchot where it is written in a kind of a scintillating black and white. In Kafka, everything is very ambiguous. The man is insatiable and he still cries. A key for understanding is given too late. There are continuous slippages. It is either as if Kafka could not tolerate such cruelty or as if he told himself the story.

Clarice Lispector completely displaces the dilemma. She never did enter the world of the law as it is described here. This does not mean that she is absolutely without law. If we look at the different positions, we can say that where Blanchot discovers that there are no stars in the sky and that he is going to be his own executioner, he stays under the influence of the starry sky. But he does not even have the stars to console himself. He is in the enigma of human destiny, which is one of being in the law without knowing why. He is not an atheist, he is nontheistic. Like Freud and other men, he is still inside the closure.

Without theorizing, Clarice Lispector says that there are no laws other than those imposed on us by institutions, religion, morals. At seventeen, she already writes that she is going to stay far from this kind of thinking. She says in *Near to the Wild Heart* that it is bad to steal if one steals while being afraid. It is bad to steal inside the law. She refers stealing back to the word with its negative connotation. To steal without fear is not to steal at all. She is not on the side of delinquency but, to the contrary, on the side of a critique of metaphysics. This is carried to its extreme refinement in *The Passion according to G. H.* In *The Passion,* we can read her legal tablets. They are those of another law. This means that without being regressive, there can be another law, of the order of the living. Clarice is neither mad nor under an idealistic or aesthetic illusion. She fully recognizes the death drive. She deconstructs. She is neither crazy nor idealistic. She does not reject a current vocabulary but goes through it. That is why, in *The Passion according to G. H.,* there is a step-by-step deconstruction of morals and of metaphysics. Otherwise she would be in magic or in madness. But she says — and this is why her gesture is so important — that we are not hysterical, or mad, or anything at all, if we do not legitimate the system of moral laws that is in reality already a system of political laws upon which civilization, as Freud had described it, is founded. One has a choice between the moral law, the asylum, or being asocial. Or one can have recourse to another logic altogether. Where morals are concerned, everything has always been done in the name of reason and reason did not fall from the sky. It is the very discourse of half of humanity. But one can have another reason, another logic. One can have interest in something that again does not interest half of humanity. There is a kind of creation of the world, a cosmos having nothing to do with the classical creation that is immediately hierarchized. Clarice obeys the laws of the living, of pleasure, in a very realistic mode. She never ignores the limit, death or pain. She is not a partisan of excess. She embodies another economy. That is what is of interest to women. One can ask the question of why this happens and why half of humanity continues to be caught in the vicious circle described so remarkably by Kant and Freud. Why do they say that everybody thinks that way, and why do they include everyone? Is there really something else, something that could be called feminine and that disengages itself from the Kantian or Freudian structure? One has to come back once more to the old question of libidinal economies. All morals must go back to these questions. There is such an attachment to the moral law and to what it may represent as cruel, intolerable, rationalizing, including the imposition of all that is nonexistent, such as "nothing is what there is." Such an economy is in relation with a certain need, for if it were not it would be inexplicable. For most men it is not possible to think, to want, to desire a life that would not be structured by the moral law and by its functioning of prohibition that supports sublimation, restriction, immobility, and all that can be seen in Kafka's text.

I said that the system of putting a keeper in front of the law the secret of which is life, the secret of which is that there is no secret, is symbolized perfectly in the scene where a sentence is placed like a legend to a vignette. There would be 'a legend before the apple that says: ''You will not go in.'' It is the other side of the law because if you touch, you will discover that the apple has an inside and that it tastes good. You will go over to a pleasure that goes through the mouth. Such a feminine libido is stronger than anything and Eve will go in. The law in Kafka says: ''You will not enter,'' because if you do, you will discover that I do not exist. One has to do everything so that the law will be respected, so that one stays in front of the word, so that the word will be the law, as it says in all the books. But it has to be a ruseful law because there are always men from the country with a little bit of femininity who feel like going in to see nevertheless. But the word is always stronger. That is why men were believers and women were witches. Something happens constantly at the level of the body that is related to libidinal economies. True, men know how to sublimate, they have a libidinal interest in sublimation, and women do not. That is where we women have our political problems. These are real differences. There is something of the other that cannot be transmitted unless there is a political revolution such that a masculine man will let go of his phallic position and accept, even without understanding, the possibility of something else.

1980–81

Notes

1. Clarice Lispector, *Perto do coraçao selvagem (Near to the Wild Heart)* (Rio de Janeiro: Livraria Francisco Alves, 1963). All translations mine, with the help of Claudia Guimarães.

2. James Joyce, *A Portrait of the Artist as a Young Man* (New York: Viking Press, 1969). Cixous's reading deals especially with the opening passage, 7–10.

3. See ''Sunday, before falling asleep,'' in Hélène Cixous, *Reading with Clarice Lispector,* ed. and trans. Verena Andermatt Conley (Minneapolis: University of Minnesota Press, 1990).

4. Franz Kafka, ''Before the Law,'' in *The Complete Stories,* ed. Naham N. Glatzer (New York: Schocken, 1983), 3–4.

5. Franz Kafka, *The Diaries, 1910–13,* ed. Max Brod, trans. Joseph Kresh (New York: Schocken, 1948), 307.

6. Maurice Blanchot, *L'écriture du désastre* (Paris: Gallimard, 1980), 117 and 176; trans. Ann Smock, *The Writing of Disaster* (Lincoln and London: University of Nebraska Press, 1986), 72 and 114–15.

Chapter 2
Grace and Innocence
Heinrich von Kleist

At the heart of my reading, there will be the question of confidence. What is confidence and what is its value? I am also thinking about something else that, seemingly very far from this question, belongs to it. I am going to work on love, on who loves whom, not in a kind of way but at the summit, at the apogee, where it is possible to speak of an economy of love in terms of the gift.

This kind of love is related to a movement that can be read in Heinrich von Kleist, Clarice Lispector, Torquato Tasso, and others. It appears only at the summit, at the *term* of a movement. I say "summit" but I could also say "depth." We can hear in this metaphor the inscription of a journey, with implications of distance, proximity, and displacement of a self toward a *you*.

In Tasso, there are two quasi-archetypal protagonists, Tancredi and Clorinda. *Jerusalem Delivered* is derived from one of the great narratives that succeed the medieval quests. We can read in it the same equivalences as in the stories of Perceval and Galahad. The story opposes two camps, the Christian and the pagan, and deals with limits of culture that cannot be treated without reflections on racism. Tasso's world is completely divided. The pagans are on the side of the condemned, they are the unfaithfuls. The Christians are, of course, the faithfuls. But there are also some unfaithfuls among the Christians, and vice versa.

Tancredi, absolutely noble, is the faithful of the faithful. The jewel of the Christian army, he is lost in love for Clorinda, the mysterious other, a sumptuous warrior and his opposite number in the pagan camp. Tancredi does not know he is pursuing a woman until the moment Clorinda takes off her helmet in a clearing. From then on, hopelessly in love, Tancredi searches for the other.

The story raises the question of love's reason. On the one hand, there is Tancredi who alone is capable of loving Clorinda, not in the sense of a *coup de foudre*, of being lovestruck, but as necessity of corresponding libidinal economies. The text incessantly questions the relation to castration and the exchange of masculinity and femininity.

On the other side there is the classical, heterosexual couple, Rinaldo and Armida, in which the woman functions as seductress in a space of classical femininity. By contrast, Tancredi's and Clorinda's sublime masculinity and femininity show analogies and differences with Kleist's Achilles and Penthesilea. But in Kleist, at the end, there is a break in confidence.

If we follow Tancredi and Clorinda across the universe, we come upon an opera by Rossini called *Tancredi*. In this displacement, Clorinda becomes a woman without armor, Amenaida. Rossini's idea to have Tancredi's voice carried by a mezzosoprano is important. Tancredi is full of woman, though he is a man. It is a *coup d'inconscient*, a stroke of the unconscious, because Rossini only practiced the inscription of femininity, without theorizing. In the relation between femininity and masculinity, he makes something mysterious appear that goes beyond anatomy, the common ideology, and classical definitions, and that raises the question, What is the other?

Why music? Music, closer to the unconscious, to drives, has an advantage compared to the world of speech; it escapes the compulsory enslavement of man and woman. In music, there is a law that does not speak, there is no interdiction about woman and man. No one is offended when Tancredi is sung by a woman. If one tried to write a book this way, critics would be up in arms. As Clarice Lispector would say, certain things are dangerous for the social, cultural, and political organization. But since music is not tied to speech, it is probably considered to be an inoffensive cultural space. In music, events are much closer to our reality. One should be able to write the way one sings. Through Rossini, Lispector, and Kleist, we can meditate on the language of words and on the ensemble: language, silence, music.

In a letter, Kleist writes:

Nur weil der Gedanke, um zu erscheinen, wie jene flüchtigen, undarstellbaren chemischen Stoffe, mit etwas Gröberem, Körperlichen, verbunden sein muss: nur darum bediene ich mich, wenn ich mich dir mitteilen will, und nur darum bedarfst du, um mich zu verstehen, der Rede, Sprache, des Rhythmus, Wohlklangs, usw. und so reizend diese Dinge auch, insofern sie den Geist einhüllen, sein mögen, so sind sie doch an und für sich, aus diesem höheren Gesichtspunkt betrachtet, nichts, als ein wahrer, obschon natürlicher und notwendiger Übelstand; und die Kunst kann, in bezug auf sie, auf nichts gehen, als sie möglichst *verschwinden* zu machen.

[It is only because thought, in order to appear, similar to these fleeting, unrepresentable chemical substances, must be linked with something coarser, more corporeal: only for that reason I have recourse when I want to communicate with you, to speech, language, rhythm, sound, etc. and no matter how seductive these things are, insofar as they envelop the mind, they are, seen from a higher vantage point, nothing but a real, though natural and necessary, evil; and art can, as far as they are concerned, do nothing but make them *disappear* as much as possible.][1]

Similarly, Clarice Lispector says in *Agua viva* that if one has to write, at least one should not let the words squash what is between the signs. Kleist also notes that, at times, the tree hides the forest, a metaphor implying that form hides the idea. It can also function as metaphor for the phallus and hide another libidinal economy that does not have limits like a tree trunk. And, furthermore, it is also — and that is where Clarice Lispector would go a step further — the danger of repressing the tree *at the same time* as the forest. Kleist makes an incisive critique of seduction. He continues to insist on the necessity of transparence, of the greatest lightness possible in language, so that what he calls the "idea" may appear. Kleist would like to be able to compose a poem by extracting from his own heart the very "idea" that inhabits him in order to deposit it with his hands into the heart of the other. Kleist's mad desire is similar to that of Clarice, who insists on making the hand appear in her text. Clarice wants things to circulate from hand to hand, from heart to hand, from blood to blood, and go to the other side of the poetic bark (*écorce*) without which, paradoxically, she cannot do but beyond which she wants to go.

I already spoke of silence, whether on the side of hysterical aphonia or on the side of a strong silence, like Abraham's. At the summit, at the extremity or at the root of language, we can hope to attain silence as the ultimate refinement. It could be defined as a passage to the infinite of words, or of concrete language. If the infinite exists, it does as non-existent. The passage to the infinite is a disappearance, an infinite distancing from the finite. I am speaking of the movement of Kleist's puppets and of Clarice's thought gathered in her statement: "In order to understand my non-intelligence, I had to become intelligent." At the limit of comprehension, one begins to understand noncomprehension. This may be felt as a threat. We can think it in terms of the other, a term that has been utterly banalized. The other is always familiar, reappropriated. But if we pursue the notion on the side of a more philosophical rigor then the other *is* the (incomprehensible) other. Clarice works on this continuously. She asks, What is "not me"? The question can be read in Lispector as well as in Kleist.

Where does the other begin? Is it possible to have a relationship with something *truly* other, something so strange that it remains so? The question can be asked otherwise. For example, what does the sentence "If you eat this fruit you will die" mean for Eve who is in a place where there is no death? That is the very question of theology and of philosophy. How can someone who does not know what sin is become a sinner?

The universe of "man" managed to explicate how from innocence one could become guilty, and even how someone innocent can be guilty. That is the very foundation of the law and the space in which we are caught, interpellated, but whence we need to be disengaged because we are not really taken in by the law a priori. How? Obviously not by staying in the innocence of the child who is not yet born. We are not without a certain kind of knowledge. That is why I chose to work on Kleist. There is something important that can easily be forgotten either through idealism or inattention, that is, that there are *two* kinds of innocence. There is a first kind of virgin innocence and then there is another, a second innocence, neither pregiven nor paradisiacal but one that has been found again. Or rather, it can be regained though it is constantly being threatened or being lost again. Innocence is not a heritage that can be invested or kept. It can be saved, or regained over and over again.

I want to work on what I would call an *economy of innocence*. We need to focus our attention, lightly but intensely, on a point where the second innocence exists only in relation — ever so slight but always there — with the possibility of its opposite. That is why I keep on saying that Eve does not know what a fault is.

"On the Marionette Theater": The Swing of the Pendulum

I will take up the schema of a convex and a concave mirror. In a convex mirror, the image is symmetrical to the object. As the object appears in a convex mirror, the image also moves away, disappears; but then reappears inverted.

The disappearance is related to the fact that we leave the visual frame at a moment when the image is so large that it exceeds our field of vision. At the moment of its disappearance, it is inverted. I am interested in understanding this metaphor, which is the conclusion of Kleist's text "On the Marionette Theater." The metaphor is expressed as a reappearance following an infinite disappearance. The infinitely large image does not exist for us. It is visible only because it is infinitely blown up. In translating something of this optical experience into symbolic terms, one could say that reversal or return are possible in infinity, because the latter is neither positive nor negative but indifferent.

Innocence is being lost little by little, transformed into non-innocence. The same would happen with guilt. As long as we are on the trajectory of the visible, we are more or less innocent or guilty. Certain feelings lend themselves especially well to such nuances. If we go to the end of guilt or innocence, we see that an infinitely strong guilt does not exist because it exhausts itself. It can only turn into its opposite. I will take another example from the question of confidence. If a relationship based on confidence begins to be tarnished, confidence can be lost as long as there is some left. It can only reappear at the moment when every relation of confidence, *including* that of the loss of confidence, has been lost. In an amorous relation, the passage through zero must have been completed before another confidence can reappear.

The mirror is a metaphor — but not a gratuitous one — that operates throughout the "Marionette Theater." The dialogue between two people produces supplementary effects of meaning. Everything is summarized in the last lines, since the story is a kind of demonstration. The text begins with a dance scene. We have to work on the music mixed with words and see how music carries the text away. We end up on the other side of the human beings with a puppet, or God, but stripped of theology and religion as in Clarice Lispector. For Kleist the puppet, God, or matter are the same thing. At the heart of the "Marionette Theater" is a story of castration.

The textual construction is astonishing. It is pendular, made of small, symmetrical pieces. It swings incessantly from one interlocutor to the other. It is a marionettelike text, hence well balanced. Kleist makes a very direct critique of narcissism. By contrast, Clarice performs an ongoing one. Her bear — more refined and more elaborated than Kleist's in this story — is the cockroach in *The Passion according to G. H.*, where a relation to the other as animal takes the form of a passion. In Kleist, a quasi theorem makes the text look older and more rigid. The schema has the shape of a key and turns like one.

In the "Marionette Theater," in the part of the story organized around a center, there is a dialogue on the mystery of dance. Then there is a second moment in the text with the story concerning the young man with a thorn in his foot. The articulation of the two stories occurs around the sentence:

"I said that, regardless of how cleverly he might present his paradoxes, he would never make me believe that a mechanical puppet could be more graceful than the human body."[2]

The sentences beginning "I said that" and "He said that" reproduce the movement of the pendulum in the text:

"He said that it would be impossible for man to come anywhere near the puppet. Only a god could equal inanimate matter in this respect; and here is the point where the two ends of the circular world meet" (241).

The center of gravity is located between the two scenes. There follows the story of the young man, which, in turn, solicits an answer from the interlocutor: "At this juncture" (242) introduces the story of the bear. The answer is binary, even ternary, since, between the two poles, something else articulates them. Similarly, the story of the young man articulates the story of the puppet and that of the bear. The puppet is made equivalent to God. In the middle, the man, following the movement of the text, tells the same schema as the concave mirror.

The text begins in a classical mode, like a story by Diderot. Kleist invokes the art of the story, which is also a trompe l'oeil. It is his way of banalizing the extraordinary. We start with a dance scene. With the first paragraph comes the astonishment: Why does the first dancer of the opera take so much pleasure in going to see the puppets?

"[He] let it be known quite clearly that a dancer who wanted to perfect his art could learn a thing or two from them" (238).

The reader is supposed to go from astonishment to astonishment. The first dancer acknowledges that he has things to learn from the puppet. The German vocabulary in this sentence is quite suggestive: "ein Tänzer, der sich ausbilden wolle, mancherlei von ihnen lernen könne." "To perfect his art," in German *ausbilden*, refers to the image, *Bild*. There is an idea of entering an apprenticeship in a quasi-Socratic exchange:

"He asked me if I hadn't, in fact, found some of the dance movements of the puppets, particularly of the smaller ones, very graceful" (238).

Very discreetly, the important word "graceful" happens upon us. The whole semantic field of grace infiltrates the text surreptitiously in a way that would be just a simple qualifier of dance.

"A group of four peasants dancing the rondo to a quick beat could not have been painted more delicately by Teniers."

We are on the side of delicacy. Grace infiltrates slowly:

"I inquired about the mechanism of these figures. How was it possible to manipulate the individual limbs and extremities in the rhythm of movement or dance without having a myriad of strings on one's fingers?"

Answer:

"He answered that I shouldn't imagine each limb as individually positioned and moved by the operator during various moments of the dance."

In the short paragraph, all the threads have been gotten rid of. One is unbinding something, that is, the puppet.

"Each movement had its center of gravity: it would suffice to control this within the puppet; the limbs, which are only on pendulums, follow mechanically of their own accord — without further help."

The text stays in the most simple demonstration, but the interlocutor adds, speaking of the line that had to be described by the center of gravity:

"But, seen from another point of view, this line could be something very mysterious, for it is nothing other than *the path taken by the dancer's soul*" (239).

Following the line, one arrives at the center of the dancer's soul. The operator, to put his puppets in motion, has to identify with the ideal dancer or with a puppet. He has to remain at the center in order to produce a rhythmic and harmonious pendular motion. The dancer says that one has to know how to position oneself at the central point, at the focal point of the mirror, or at the center of the movement of gravity, in order to produce a movement. And he adds that this is "somewhat like that of numbers to their logarithms or the asymptotes to the hyperbola."

The center of gravity, the asymptote, is the point where the curve brushes against the x and y axes, before the hyperbola. We can see the movement that, from a center, never reached but only brushed against, goes to infinity. In the mirror, the passage to infinity goes through a point of disappearance. By contrast, Kleist says:

"And yet he believed that even the last trace of human volition to which he had referred could be removed [entfernt] from the marionettes" (239).

Through his commentary, the dancer removes, little by little, the operator, to speak of a technique of propulsion of the puppet that would eliminate the human factor. The latter, of course, is always subjective, even when the operator is experienced and knows how to be situated at the center of gravity. There is always a factor of error. At that moment we go toward the mechanical machine or the robot:

"I expressed my astonishment at the attention he was paying this species of an art form intended for the masses."

We move away hyperbolically from the articulation between puppet and operator.

"He smiled and said he was confident that if a craftsman were to make a marionette according to his specifications, that he could perform a dance with it which neither he nor any other skilled dancer of his time, not even Vestris herself, could equal."

With the allusion to a real dancer of the period, the look intervenes that becomes more and more insistent.

"I said nothing and looked down at the ground. Then he said:

'Have you heard of those artificial legs made by English craftsmen for those unfortunate individuals who have lost their limbs?' "

The conversation seemingly continues by association but the latter is always in the mode of propagation of the same line. From the legs of the dancer, we go on to mechanical legs.

The movement of the automaton can also turn out to be that of the false automaton, as, for example, in the stories of Edgar Allan Poe, or those of Vaucanson, crafted together with mechanical wheels. At that moment, we have a coarse imitation of the human body. But Kleist tries to show difference, rather than sameness. His insistence leads us to the most important point, about which the dancer speaks continuously — that is, grace. And nobody could call an automaton graceful. With Kleist, we are in the field of grace. From his text, it is possible to extract a definition of grace in banal terms, as when we say that a person has grace, as well as a quality in the body related to what we could call grace as a spiritual feature. After having been told this, lightly and gracefully but never directly, we have arrived at a point of intersection between corporeal and spiritual grace. The two intersect and one cannot exist without the other. In the automaton, a coarse interruption of movement pervades. But with the marionette, motion is continuous. From bodily grace, the text leads us to spiritual grace when the marionette is freed from its threads. Human intervention becomes less and less necessary. Supreme art does away with the operator. All is happening in the most supple manner. We continue along the same line, from the legs of the dancer to mechanical legs, and arrive at the story of an amputation that, in turn, leads to a scene of castration and the mention of the unfortunate people who have lost their limbs.

A mocking answer shows that the narrator is ironic, hence not graceful, and the reader sees what kind of effects this will produce.

"I said, somewhat lightly, that he had, of course, found his man. A craftsman who could make such a remarkable limb could surely construct an entire marionette according to his specifications."

In other words, anyone can easily be replaced by a prosthesis.

"'What are the specifications you are thinking of presenting to his artistic skill?' . . . Symmetry, flexibility, lightness — but of a higher degree; and particularly a natural arrangement of the centers of gravity. . . . First of all [the advantage] would be a negative one, my dear friend; and that is that it would never behave *affectedly*."

There is only one grace, but in French there exists a slippage from grace to graces, as in the derogatory expression, *faire des grâces* (to make graces), and that is what is happening here. Kleist's story can be put side by side with Clarice Lispector's text, "Sunday, before falling asleep," where the youngest daughter falls from grace:

> "The youngest daughter insisted upon sitting on one of those high stools and Father found this amusing. This was great fun. Then the child would demand more attention and it was no longer quite so amusing.
>
> [A filha menor quis se sentar num dos bancos, o pai achou graça. Ela então fez mais graça e isto já não era tão alegre.]"[3]

In Portuguese, we went from grace to more grace; in French we can go from grace to graces. Yet there is truly only grace.

Brushing *(frôlement)*: Clarice and Kleist

In one of Clarice Lispector's chronicles, "Because they were not distracted," we also begin with what we could call the very extremity of lightness:

"There was the gentlest ecstasy in walking out together, that happiness you experience upon feeling your throat rather dry and upon realizing that you are so astonished that your mouth is wide open: they were breathing in anticipation of the air ahead of them, and to have this thirst was their very own water. They walked through street after street, conversing and laughing; they conversed and laughed to give substance and weight to the most gentle of ecstasies which was the happiness of their thirst."[4]

At this moment — a moment of grace — they talk and laugh in order to give matter and weight to what has none.

"Because of the traffic and crowds, they sometimes touched, and as they touched — thirst is the grace, but the waters are the beauty of darkness — as they touched there shone the brilliance of their waters, their throats becoming even more dry in their astonishment."

As in Kleist's text, we begin with grace and end with a loss of grace precisely "because they were not distracted." An infinite lightness touches that which is without mass, volume, or weight. Everything is happening on the side of the soul, though it is also materialized through the body. The protagonists are in the *lightest* relationship possible to a graceful object, here ecstasy, that is, the joy of their thirst. The sentence begins with a present participle, seemingly so that the subject does not weigh in the materializing gesture of conversing and laughing. The repetition of "they conversed and laughed" marks the intervention of narration. The spiritual nature of the gerund is being materialized. To converse and to laugh barely touch on matter but something sonorous is going to crystallize, like a wave. In the first paragraph, there is grace. How is it lost in the second paragraph?

"Until everything transformed itself into denial."

The beginning of the second paragraph is an adequate and cruel definition of the loss of grace. Everything was transformed when they consciously *wanted* the joy they already had. The development bears on the sin of wanting and not on what is happening:

"Simply because suddenly becoming demanding and stubborn, they wanted to possess what they already possessed."

This refers the reader to the episode of the young man in the "Marionette Theater," or of the little girl on the bar stool in "Sunday, before falling asleep."

I come back to the passage on the marionettes in Kleist's text. The advantage of the marionette is that it never becomes affected. Affectation appears in the soul at a point other than that of the center of gravity or movement.

Kleist offers a comical criticism of the famous dancers:

"Take, for example, P., the one who dances Daphne," he continued. . . . "Her soul seems to be in the small of her back. . . . Or look at young F., who dances Paris. . . . His soul is located (and it is a fright to perceive) in his elbow."

When the dancer's soul is not where it ought be, the spectacle is grotesque. But why does Kleist put it in the vertebrae and in the elbow? We have to note the scenic element. The people mentioned are in reality great dancers, whence a double implication: that of the limit of the human body, doubled by subjectivity, and the fact that these are two scenes of seduction. It is because P. blew it that all of a sudden she no longer looks like a dancer but like a statue. She loses her human quality and becomes deformed, immobilized in her gesture when she should be all movement. Situations of seduction lock people into the least graceful of bodies.

Kleist questions the limits of the human body. We know that dancers or acrobats from Far Eastern countries push their lightness toward the side of Kleist's marionettes. But at the same time, there is a difference between our bodies and that of the marionette. If the latter were not held by a thread, it would fall. It would be in what we call a free fall.

To get to a supreme lightness — and the same holds true where language is concerned — we have to struggle not against the laws of the body, but against human laws *governing* the body. We are not into free falling because we do not *want* to fall. We respond to external constraints with a weight. We can stand up. We answer an inner constraint with the tensing of muscles. During dance exercises, we respond to the calling of a weight with another weight. What does the puppet do? It responds to external constraints by giving in to them and without tensing its muscles. We arrive at a paradox, which is that the puppet has no inner constraint. This can be understood positively or negatively. Negatively, because it implies that it has no inside; positively because it has no constraints. The puppet does not really dance. To dance is already to *want* to dance. The puppet is simply in harmony with external constraints. Humans can never get there except in brief moments, in hundredths of a second and quite exceptionally. We live the tensing of our muscles as spontaneous. Slaves to the spirit that keeps us upright, we are struggling against external constraints. Someone who faints no longer controls fainting. Kleist works on pushing back as far as possible any control or mastery, or what, in Clarice Lispector's chronicle, was called "wanting." Clarice had urged a minimum of "wanting," instead of a wanting that does not even know that it wants. Kleist develops this in the second paragraph of his story.

" 'In addition,' he said, 'these puppets have the advantage of being practically weightless. . . . The force which raises them into the air is greater than the one which draws them to the ground.' . . . Puppets, like elves, need the ground only so that they can touch it lightly and renew the momentum of their limbs through this momentary delay. We need it to rest on, to recover from the exertions of the dance, a moment which is clearly not part of the dance. We can only do our best to make it as inconspicuous as possible" (241).

The moment disappears because it is not a moment of dance but a human moment.

I must return to the notion of paradise:

"Such mistakes are unavoidable," he said, "now that we have eaten from the Tree of Knowledge. But Paradise is locked and the cherubim behind us; we have to travel around the world to see if it is perhaps open again somewhere at the back."

Kleist insists on a place we have left and that has been locked behind us. We have arrived at a point where we can understand that it has been a question of grace throughout. We are now going in the direction in which we should go to find ourselves again in paradise. But since this side is locked, we have to approach it from the other side.

When we begin to lose confidence, we cannot find it again. When we begin to lose this ultralight spiritual weightlessness, something that has no name, (though perhaps we could relate it to confidence), it is useless to imagine that we can go back to find it again. There is *no* turning back, or as Kleist would have it: "But Paradise is locked [Doch das Paradies ist verriegelt]." What can be done? We have to advance. As one cannot go back in time, one cannot go back to lost confidence. But one can continue to advance along the trajectory of loss.

Kleist's cherubim is behind the door, like Kafka's keeper. We can go straight ahead, but straight lines are curved, except in theoretical geometry where everything is only abstraction. To go around the world is both metaphor and reality, since paradise is locked. It is possible to think that we will come back to the same point on the other side. But we do not know if we will find an opening on the other side.

There are two reasons why we were expelled from paradise: sloth and impatience. Contrary to Kafka, in Kleist the door is locked. He tells us clearly that there is no turning back. Paradise *is* there but we are no longer in it. We could go back but we do not, for reasons similar to those for which we have been expelled, such as impatience. We would have to follow the tiring trajectory suggested by Kleist. Kafka says the same thing but without locking the door. Kafka is rather on the side of impatience and sloth. He does not risk. Kleist indicates that there is a possibility, though we will never be the same again. We will be those who have lost paradise and who have gone around the world. That is Kleist's dilemma. It is also ours today.

Both types of grace can be good, the first as well as the second, but I do not want to enter into the problem of loss. I am not on the side of necessary loss and castration. Yet I insist that *both* types of grace have to be thought through, the one we were given and the one we find after having lost the first.

We need to recall that there is a double movement in Kleist's text, on a material and a spiritual level. On the material level, we have to rest on the ground. On the spiritual level, there is a question of a certain moment of "rest" or of pause *which would not be part of grace*. We cannot do without the following reflection:

"I said that, regardless of how cleverly he might present his paradoxes, he would never make me believe that a mechanical puppet could be more graceful than the human body.

"He said that it would be impossible for man to come anywhere near the puppet. Only a god could equal inanimate matter in this respect; and here is the point where the two ends of the circular world meet" (241).

The ends of a straight line that seem to be infinitely apart will end up touching after going around a spherical world.

"It seemed, he said . . . if a man wasn't familiar with that first period of all human development, it would be difficult to discuss the later ones, not to mention the final one."

Now we arrive at the other tip of the scale with the story of the young man who goes through a scene of absolute cruelty:

"I told him that I was well aware of how consciousness could disturb the natural grace of man. Before my very eyes, one of my young acquaintances had lost his innocence, all because of a chance remark, and had never again, in spite of all conceivable efforts, been able to find his way back to its paradise."

Innocence is the very locus of paradise. Kleist here is close to Clarice Lispector for whom innocence constitutes paradise, or a place of absolute bliss.

Then comes the story of the young man as told by the narrator: "About three years ago, I related, I was at the baths with a young man . . ." The principal part is given to the narrator who, in German, comes at the beginning of the sentence: "Ich badete mich." The young man has a complementary part. By reversing the construction in translation, one reverses the accent on innocence or guilt:

"Who at the time was remarkably graceful in all respects of his education. He was about fifteen years old, and only faintly could one see in him the first traces of vanity *[Eitelkeit]*—as a result of the favor shown him by women."

Fatality is already here because vanity is non-grace.

"It just so happened that in Paris we had seen a statue of a young boy pulling a thorn from his foot."

The text alludes to many sexual symbols. Every reader is supposed to recognize the statue:

"[The young man] was reminded of the statue while he looked into a tall mirror."

Eve and the young man don't have the same story. The young man is preoccupied with his foot, Eve with her hand. The object is not the same either. Eve's is a fruit; the young man himself is an object itself.

There is neither fault nor absence of fault. A certain mechanical sham is at work because the *narrator* is telling the story. The reader is supposed to think that the narrator does not make a gift to anyone, not even to himself since he seems to relate the bare facts:

"Only faintly could one see in him the first traces of vanity."

The narrator picks his boy at a well-known age, in his sixteenth year, virgin and all, and includes himself as subject and object of desire. Before the story of the mirror—noted by the narrator, as in a biographical narration—there happens a distant, light mutation of puberty and the first signs of vanity. Vanity is the opposite of grace. Obviously, the scene is one of narcissism. Is Narcissus guilty or not? Yet that is not what the story is about. This Narcissus who bears no name is going to fall not into water but into the mirror, and there he drowns. He is losing his balance, something that is in a harmonious, precise relationship with itself, like the movement of the marionette. The young man is leaning toward vanity. He is going to fall into an absolutely mortal mode. Kleist exploits the scene admirably. The look comes from someone else, and not from just anyone. It comes from the favors of women. The boy who was pure boy is being altered by the favor of women. An entire play develops in this brief scene. It is the more than equivocal story between a young man and an older man, a complex erotic rapport where the stake is the rivalry for women.

In Clarice Lispector's "Sunday, before falling asleep," the little girl's loss of grace is determined in a scene where she is trying to please her father. Clarice raises the question of whom one wants to please. Are the stakes homosexual, heterosexual? Clarice describes grace. Kleist describes someone who is already losing grace. What makes the reader resist the young man's loss of grace is the violent intervention of the narrator upon him. Yet he has power over the boy only because the latter gives him the power.

"[He] told me what he had discovered."

Grace is not lost all at once. It is on the way to being lost. When he makes his discovery known, it is already too late. When he discovers in the mirror not himself but something else that, moreover, is a statue, a work of art, he is already alienated, altered. The question of the look is important.

By comparison, in Clarice Lispector's "Because they were not distracted," we can read:

"Because of the traffic and crowds they sometimes touched." Yet there is no internal cause. The protagonists did not look at each other in the first paragraph though, as Milton would have it, the snake, represented by the system of mirrors, was covered with brilliant scales. At the end of the first paragraph, the snake is already in place:

"As they touched there shone the brilliance of their waters, their throats becoming even more dry in their astonishment. How they marvelled at finding themselves together!"

We move toward the second paragraph. First the protagonists bathe in and slide insidiously into something that constitutes the root of a reversal, that is, a consciousness leading through speculation. It is the danger of the image. Does that mean that one should never look into a mirror? Certainly not. But the mirror deals nevertheless with reproduction, repetition, with a doubling and imitation. In any event, Kleist's young boy is no longer himself since he resembles another. He may look lengthily and innocently, but we do know that the mirror is irresistible.

In Kleist as in Clarice Lispector, catastrophic effects are produced by the appeal to the Father or the request that something be legitimized by the Father. The young man falls into a trap that consists in having legitimized something that needs to remain intimate and belong only in secrecy.

We could allude to Medusa, the woman whom man is not supposed to look at for fear of being petrified, and who could be placed in a symmetrical rapport with Narcissus. Again, all takes place in the space of the dangerous look. This could make us say that the look is more dangerous than touch, because it produces doubling and refers to the Platonic dilemma where everything secondary is always inferior in relation to the primary. But here we speak in terms of a double because it triggers a mechanism of reappropriation and overestimation that does not exist without the image.

The young man's actions are symptomatic of a path of loss. He tries to imitate a statue. He did not see *himself* in the mirror, but another. The monstrous intervention by a third masculine, overdetermined by women, makes it all the more difficult.

"But—I don't know if it was to test the security of his grace or to provide a salutary counter to his vanity—I laughed and said that he must be seeing things!"

To laugh and to say those words is more than an execution, it is a violent process of alienation. The narrator drives the young man mad and sends him over into absolute vanity.

The second and third attempts by the young man are ambivalent. They mean that it was to be predicted, as the narrator says, that he would be "unable to reproduce the movement." At the same time they mean his innocence and a touch of belief. "He stood in front of the mirror for days," until the complete and irreversible loss of grace. He goes on to complete exhaustion. But it is a negative exhaustion. He does not go over to the other side of the mirror and he dies of it.

"An inconceivable change came over the young man."

The narrator had not foreseen the consequences and will have understood the process of the loss of grace only in the last paragraph, which sheds light on the entire story.

All of Kleist's marionettes have threads that we can choose to let go or not let go. I would like to put myself in a rapport with these marionettes that would be like a brushing or a slight touching, with as much lightness as possible. The texts read each other. A space that answers all of Kleist would be in relation with all of Clarice Lispector. Our memory has to be vigilant on all sides.

The thematics of my reading deal with innocence, or with what I would call a *second innocence*. There are at least two types of innocence. I could speak of a virgin innocence and of an innocence regained, even if it seems tautological. Is there a nonvirgin innocence? Yes, I think so. I want to study innocence according to G. H., C. L., H. K., like Clarice Lispector who, in *The Passion according to G. H.*, in her brilliant and light way of writing, uses only the initials G. H. At no point do we know if G. H. are the initials of someone's name, or if they are only signs reduced to letters. And why do we think of the first letter? It could also be a middle letter, since Clarice likes to study the middle. In any event, we do have a letter and not a name. The sign could be a little star. It is not the simple banality of anonymity. It is a nonderogatory reduction of a person to something weightless, to the point of having the least self possible designated by a letter.

It is difficult and dangerous to work at the very level of the thought of innocence. Let us suppose that I take another motif, that of grace. Grace refers to a world, which can be a superior world, where someone decides not on human but on divine grace. I want us to leave the ground but not so as to forget the reality principle, especially the principle of our quotidian reality. I would like to avoid the trap that consists in constituting innocence as an infantile state, where it becomes synonymous with irresponsibility. One could say that in paradise, the question of responsibility was kept silent or did not exist. But we are no longer in paradise. And since, at the same time, we have to think of paradise in order to be able to work on these complex notions, let us not forget hell. Clarice never forgets that there is no paradise without hell.

Innocence is always linked to risk, since by definition it is outside of a certain type of knowledge. It risks being misunderstood and leads to catastrophes. There is a dangerous innocence and a misleading innocence.

Innocence, with its mark on the side of a first, *primary* knowledge, which is bliss and on which I insisted elsewhere when I worked on the Biblical character of Eve, is something that in ordinary reality can lead to regression, of which one has to be aware.

For example, a writer like Knut Hamsun was fascinated by a primal, archaic libido, close to nature. During World War II, he threw himself into hell while mistaking it for paradise. He started to celebrate Nazism in all of its glory, interpreting it as the ideology of nature and of the primitive form. He did in Norway what Ezra Pound did in Italy. He started from a personal myth of resistance to bad culture and became a racist without noticing it. I insist that there is always, even if we are navigating in largely mythical spaces, a political side to our problem, and it is important never to lose sight of it.

With Clarice, we do not touch directly on a problem of politics but on a problem of political morals and of a very direct rapport with reality, with life, death, vengeance, crime, and so on.

"Michael Kohlhaas": Innocence Has No Father

The most political text I want to read is a true treatise of the relationship between grace and politics in general, entitled "Michael Kohlhaas." The story cuts across all aspects of Germany — political, juridical, cultural, religious — since, in the middle of the novel, we come upon Luther himself with whom Kohlhaas has an exchange. It questions also the value of individual and collective struggle, of war.

The text begins by telling, seemingly in the most innocent mode, the story of someone who, as Kleist says, is the most just of all men. Michael Kohlhaas is a just man who, in his negotiations with reality, reaches a point where he is being considered unjust. And between the two polarities, there is a continuity, a slippage from one to the other. We can raise the question of the nature of injustice. Everything is happening from the beginning in a scene that has the structure of a primal scene. Kohlhaas is a horse merchant. He is good, confident, and refined. As he does every year, he is going from town to town to sell his horses. "Michael Kohlhaas" could be read like a romantic novel, with its emphasis on details of which none is gratuitous. Everything is staged inside a tragic dilemma that can be clearly defined. Michael Kohlhaas arrives from the country:

"In a village that still bears his name, he owned a farm on which he quietly earned a living by his trade; the children with whom his wife presented him were brought up in the fear of God to be industrious and honest; there was not one of his neighbors who had not benefited from his benevolence or his fair-mindedness — the world, in short, would have had every reason to bless his memory, if he had not carried one virtue to excess. But his sense of justice turned him into a brigand and a murderer."[5]

Already, in this paragraph, a reinscription of a question found in the "Marionette Theater" can be heard. Is it possible to go beyond the limits of virtue? Kleist does not say that Kohlhaas is a brigand, but that he became one out of a sense of justice. Something positive leads to a negative. Kleist is on the side of Kohlhaas's virtue.

"He was riding out of his province one day with a string of young horses, all fat and glossy-coated, and was turning over in his mind how he would use the profit he hoped to make on them at the fairs — part of it, like the good manager that he was, to get new profits, but part, too, for present enjoyment — when he reached the Elbe, and near an imposing castle standing in Saxon territory he came upon a tall gate that he had never found on that road before" (39; translation modified).

We can note in the sentence the fat and glossy-coated horses and the fact of riding out of one's territory. We exceed the limits of his virtue *and* the limit of his territory. Like a good merchant, he is calculating his profit. But he is also on the side of pleasure and that is his feminine part.

"He came upon a tree *[Schlagbaum]* that barred the road he had always known to be open before" (translation modified).

We truly have a scene of the unconscious. Each detail has meaning. The open road is suddenly closed through a *Schlagbaum,* a tree, that is, something living, virgin and of the forest. Kohlhaas himself is going to recall the forest as well as its opposite, since the tree has been uprooted to make an obstacle, a barrier, literally to bar the road.

"He halted his horses just when a heavy shower of rain was coming down and shouted for the tollkeeper."

Nature intervenes in quasi-Shakespearean fashion in the affairs of men. There is a strong opposition between he who knows how to live, who knows how to make others live, who knows how to let pass and who is on the side of the living — and the others. Those who do not like horses will not understand what this is about. The love object in this story is the animal, made strong and beautiful by love and made miserable by the lack of love.

One of the horses had a broken leg, a detail that evokes the bear's paw and the boy's leg of the "Marionette Theater."

Kleist is the most inspired pre-Freudian poet in the world. From the beginning of the story — or from some kind of inauguration — a system of signs or of signifiers appears upon which Kleist does not comment. To comment would be to hold on to, to keep back, to frame. Kleist gallops freely and if we do not read all of his texts, we do not realize that everywhere there are horses with or without broken legs:

" 'Well what do I owe you? . . . If they had left the tree for that pole standing in the forest it would have been better for both of us.' And he gave him the money and started to ride on. He had hardly passed under the toll bar, however, when a new voice rang out from the tower behind him: 'Hold up there, horse dealer!' and he saw the castellan slam a window shut and come hurrying down to him. 'Now what?' wondered Kohlhaas and halted with his horses.' "

The minute he thinks he has passed, another closure and an arrest ensue.

"The castellan came up to him and, leaning into the wind, asked for his pass."

This scene follows the schema of Kafka's "Before the Law" except that Kohlhaas does go through the door. But as soon as he has passed through the first door, there is another halt.

" 'Pass?' said Kohlhaas, a little disconcerted."

Kohlhaas assures the keeper that he has always gone through without a pass and wants him to realize that he is mistaken. Kohlhaas respects the law.

"But the castellan answered that he was not going to slip through the eighteenth time, that the ordinance had recently been issued for just that reason, and that he must either get a permit for himself right now or go back to where he had come from. After a moment's reflection, the horse dealer, whom these illegal demands were beginning to exasperate, got down from his horse."

Kohlhaas begins to give up a little bit of his body. He puts himself somewhat in the position of Kafka's man from the country and loses, so to speak, some of his height:

"After a moment's reflection, the horse dealer, whom these illegal demands were beginning to exasperate, got down from his horse, handed the reins to a groom, and said that he would speak to the Junker von Tronka himself about the matter. He made straight for the castle too."

The scene reminds the reader of Kafka, but the young baron whom Kohlhaas reaches is not the law. The baron and his drunken companions are interested in the horses the way one could be interested in women. Like Kafka's man from the country, Kohlhaas loses in stature and size by going from one guardian to the next, from the tollkeeper to the castellan, from the steward to the Junker. It all takes place in less than an hour. He loses the flesh of his flesh—that is, the horses, which he has to leave in the castle after going through all the guardians, or an infinite series of policemen.

"Taken aback by such a shameless demand, Kohlhaas told the Junker, who was wrapping the skirts of his doublet about his shivering body, that what he wanted to do was sell the blacks."

There is a perfect double-bind. The object of the trip is to exchange the horses for more horses or more pleasure. And now Kohlhaas either goes back and will not sell his horses or in order to sell his horses and have more horses, he has to leave them behind.

"The horse dealer, seeing that he had no choice but to yield, decided to give in to the demand."

He stays on the side of respect for the law. In the first chapter, the drama is put in place. The reader will see how this just man will exceed the limits of virtue. What did he do to transgress but push virtue beyond its own limits? We have to recall the schema of the "Marionette Theater."

Kohlhaas is both masculine and feminine, capable of pleasure and of rules. He has a good rule that leads to harmonious, well-balanced pleasure. He imagines that the law is of the same order. For the first time in his life Kohlhaas meets the law, not that of the old Junker who loved the horses, but another law, which leads him to God since there is a mention of Luther.

We have to articulate the question of confidence, that of innocence and guilt between quotation marks.

Kohlhaas is someone who, from the moment he is threatened, resists castration in an absolute way. He is in a contradictory state. The situation is the same from one end to the other, and all he can do is retreat. But if he retreats, he castrates himself, and if he advances, he is going to be decapitated. He chooses to advance. Kleist asks the historical question of the possibility of a third solution. What force, Kleist asks, is capable of opposing the law victoriously? Kleist answers indirectly. He will answer Kohlhaas with Arminius. The horse dealer will not win against the law, the emperor, the state, and God even if he shakes up the establishment of the law. Why? At an analytical level, Kohlhaas is someone innocent who insists on having his innocence recognized. This is a quotidian dilemma. However, to have one's innocence recognized does not make sense, yet that is part of his innocence. It cannot be done. An innocence that wants to be recognized is mad, in a dangerous way. Innocence imposes itself and does not have to be recognized. It has no father. An innocence that wants a father is lost.

Arminius does not want his rights *(droit)* to be recognized. He *imposes* them. Kohlhaas is too feminine. He does not have a chance. From the moment the tree is not in the forest but bars the road, it is all over for him. Either he retreats or he goes into the forest and regresses. Or, if he decides to impose his right as merchant, he will arrive where he did. Kohlhaas is going to play with a reality that always is what it is, historically and politically. The question is one of recognition and of legitimation, raised in relation with and in contrast to innocence. For an innocence that has no father, we could recall Kleist's admirable story, "The Marquise of O_____."

All of Kleist's texts have the same stakes, but the outcome differs depending on whether it is the story of a man, a woman, a king, a man from the people; whether it takes place in a democratic regime or during a revolution. The strength of the

Marquise is to not have a father, because she is a woman and already has children. She can be pregnant and virgin at the same time.

The movement of Kleist's puppets describes a curve. In *Agua viva,* Clarice Lispector describes a similar curve related to the body and to breathing. The moment of the curve is full and perfect if one succeeds in maintaining the indifference of a geometric compass. In order to maintain this arch, one has to forget and follow one's own body without being distracted by the world. Clarice describes this living logic of a certain movement in relation to a rose. When the plenitude of possibilities is exhausted, one touches upon the impossible that puts an end to the possible. Thus, rather than being something leading to its opposite, it would be the natural term of something full. Afterward, one has to stop. Of course, one can always start up again the way Clarice does, but with something else. For her, after the rose, there will be a mirror, a closet, or a tiger. She starts up on another movement describing another curve.

When there is a calling, we answer or we do not. If we answer, we take a leap and there is grace. There *is*. Period. We are in an absolute that has to be articulated with a singular. There is grace, so will I have some? I as a singular being can find an articulation with all that is unlimited, absolute?

To talk about it, something painful has first to be accomplished. One has to go *out* of the circle, in order to speak of the circle. But when one leaves the circle, there is no more circle. There remains only one thing to do: that is to leap back into the circle. This is the metaphor Kafka uses to speak of the relation between self and work. For him, the world goes by like a luminous arch stretched out in front of us. The only way of becoming aware of it is by leaping into it.

What do Kleist and Lispector do? As acrobats of the soul, they have developed an extraordinary dexterity at the participation of the singular in the absolute. At the moment of intersection, in the briefest of moments — to recall the metaphor of the asymptote and its coordinates — something touches, brushes, and that is where and when one takes the leap.

Clarice and Kleist, who do have recourse to this kind of practice, are not so much giving an account of the outside as putting the circle into motion. They do it in such a way that a circle of light goes by and they can seize it. It could be called a practice of breathing.

Abraham's yes does not need to be pronounced. God says something and Abraham starts up his movement. His answer is immediate. There is not even the slightest place for a verbal articulation, it is all pure movement.

How does one communicate what is incommunicable? Certainly not through the word. The word mediates, separates. Movement is what is communicated best and least. Nothing is easier than to communicate movement to a puppet. But it is also difficult because we are inhibited, disquieted; and communication of movement is something physical, related to the body. It scares. It *is* to make love. But most people resist it. They go back into their selves and become rigid.

We need a passivity that is not weak or masochistic but supple. We need a capacity to accept, that is, a generosity. We need an active passivity capable of bearing transition and transference. Clarice calls it "a good distraction."

An ideal marionette would begin to move under the touch of something that would go through the body. It would be the impulse that music gives to the body.

The movement of the bear, like that of the puppet, describes a kind of perfect curve because of the leash that prevents him from unleashing himself. The bear, a kind of supreme puppet, is in relation with a certain human scene, that of the teddy bear, from the cradle on, so to speak. One goes from the puppet to the very extremity of the curve, that is, to the bear, after having gone through all the possible nuances, but always in extreme lightness.

I come back to the moments of equilibrium. The question is vital. A curve oscillates between two poles and goes through a central point. The metaphor of the scale will allow us to think about such situations in Kleist's text *Betrothal in Santo Domingo*. The real scale that weighs in the Egyptian Book of the Dead is related to the question of the number two. This number, inside a movement, appeals to the relation between body and soul. Movement is only possible *between* force and grace. The number two, of course, is also that of the couple. That is why, in Kleist, we have to study the value of engagement and of a graceful exchange. The question needs to be asked only when a *real* twosome exists. With a false twosome, there is always going to be imbalance, as in the case of the young man and his image. With a real twosome, grace and equilibrium are necessary givens.

In the "Marionette Theater," the scene with the young man referring to pure grace is already impure and increasingly so to the point of absolute impurity. The reader arrives on the scene at the moment of descent. The passage about purity takes place before the story actually begins. When reading the text closely, as scrupulously as a preservation of grace requires, we see from the beginning that grace is about to be lost. It is condemned from the very opening of the scene and is lost in the middle of the text in relation to the narrator's demoniacal character.

When figured by a scale, equilibrium carries in its semantic wake everything that pertains to ballet and dance.

We can take up once again the Mallarmean play on the dice. We are in the register of infinite balance with the German *Fall*, the English "fall" or "case." The German *Fall* is harsh. In French one could find something softer, derived from *casum* which leads to *cas* but also to *chute*. *Einfall*, "a "sudden idea," and *Zufall*, "chance," all lead us to engage the relation between event and accident. From one language to another, the value of the accident, or of the fall, is also displaced. We have to see what is fortuitous. In Kleist, we can work on different values of "fall": One can fall *into* or *from* grace.

I will continue to study in Kleist's texts the question of brushing, or rubbing, which is the opposite of fixation; it is something unlinked but necessary. In the

"Marionette Theater," the dancer tells the narrator that there is, in dance, a moment of non-dance. It is the very moment when the dancers have to rest and start up again. The puppets could economize this moment since they do not rest. They have no gravity. They only touch, brush against the surface while describing a curve. Brushing is necessary, but has no weight. It is a question of how to *se poser* — "to be posited," in respect to lightness and brushing, and in respect to the relation between a curved and a straight line. The asymptote brushes against the straight line — which has a physical as well as metaphysical and moral value; we will have to see where its necessity is.

We can put Kleist's text next to Clarice Lispector's short chronicle, "Because they were not distracted." Both texts take up the necessity of a certain degree of distraction.

Clarice Lispector's "Because they were not distracted": A Fall from Grace

I come back to a chronicle by Clarice Lispector, "Because they were not distracted," that could be called "a fall from grace." The story is a parabola, and as such it is part of Clarice's ruseful work on style. It begins in the middle of what seems to be a story. As in Kleist, whose stories are entirely in a dream, for Clarice, the dream is reality. It is an inner experience at whose end we have a lesson. The protagonists learned something. The lesson is:

"Unless one is distracted the telephone does not ring; that it is necessary to go out for the letter to arrive, and that when the telephone finally does ring, the wasteland of waiting has already disconnected the wires."

The two sentences contain the same textual violence. Something implacable tells us that it is not worth praying when we have already lost our distraction.

In "Because they were not distracted," the curved line is indirect and the straight line is direct. The direct line consists in going straight, it is the best of rights *(droits),* not the right of the law, but of what is *absolutely* right.

In the second paragraph, we have something indirect. We could introduce a lexical change and work on the mediate and the immediate. We could also displace it on the side of language and work on naming. Naming becomes the intermediary, it makes up trees in relation to a forest.

We can think of the sentence in *Agua viva* that says that an animal never replaces one thing with another. Animals have an imaginary but no unconscious. They have no superego, hence no ego. The question of calling and of answering is important. The bear does not repeat his movement. He improvises and invents incessantly while the fencer tries and calculates. And calculation is part of speculation.

The second to the last paragraph in the "Marionette Theater" will serve as a new point of departure:

" 'Therefore,' I said, somewhat distracted *[zerstreut]*, 'we would have to eat again from the Tree of Knowledge in order to return to the state of innocence?' " (translation modified).

We are back in the theme of innocence and of the fall. "Somewhat distracted" goes *toward* distraction, which is never an absolute but oscillates between being "distracted enough" or "not distracted enough." Distraction oscillates.

In the "Marionette Theater," the center of the story, the story of the young man, is framed by two symmetrical points. Similarly, in Clarice Lispector, we have a structure in two parts, but not in the same mode. In Clarice, the young man is linked to a descending movement, to a loss of grace. But Clarice inscribes a sudden loss and a brutal cut. In the white space between the two paragraphs, there is a violent reversal. In Kleist, loss comes about progressively.

The two paragraphs are of almost equal length. The first one starts with "there was," the second with "until." "Until" inscribes the moment of the fall, of rupture: "Until everything transformed itself into denial."

Denial bars everything. We are inside an ensemble of which "no" is the synonym. As much as there was presence in the first paragraph—a presence that could not even be measured—this much there are only limits in the second. The exclamation point that ends the first paragraph marks a limit for the second. Suddenly, we are into "until," which has the value of a "since," and everything has already been decided. "Until" introduces time where there was only present and presence. The sentence does not begin with an affirmation but with an apocopated conjunction, a disjointed reality.

From then on, we engage everything that pertains to the register of *no*. In other words, we are in hell. At the end comes the explanation of the transformation of presence into *no*.

I am going back up to the first paragraph. There is, in the first and second paragraphs, repetition, reappearance of words in different modes. The first paragraph is literally flooded with letters and phonemes. In the second paragraph comes the rhythmic insistence of the words *todo* (everything) and *não* (nothing). The first paragraph was taken in the word "together," which we also find at the end. "Together" marks the end of grace. We can see how, little by little, the loss of grace infiltrates the text:

"There was the gentlest ecstasy in walking out together, that happiness you experience upon feeling your throat rather dry and upon realizing that you are so astonished that your mouth is wide open: they were breathing in anticipation of the air ahead of them, and to have this thirst was their very own laughing; they conversed and laughed to give substance and weight to the most gentle of ecstasies which was the happiness of their thirst."

They are still on the side of joy, thirst, and exchange. The happy circuit reads "this thirst was their own water." The movement of the pendulum is in equilibrium. In the slight movement of loss, there occurs the moment of necessary touching or brushing. The protagonists are not angels, or else they would not exist. They wander about without wanting to. They do not choose their streets but are carried off: "They walked through street after street, conversing and laughing." As they are walking, they "sometimes touched." The Portuguese word *tocar*, "to touch," is also used for the ring of the telephone. They touch without doing it on purpose and, as it says in an enigmatic sentence between dashes, " — thirst is the grace — ." But, Clarice adds, "the waters are the beauty of darkness — as they touched there shone the brilliance of their water" (translation modified). In our reading, we must pay special attention to a series of displacements — for example, from singular to plural, or from "waters" to "water," a technique we already had in "Sunday, before falling asleep." We can work on dis-traction, di-vision, on separation and gaps and on personal pronouns:

"Then began the great dance of errors. The ceremonial of inopportune words. He searched and failed to see; she did not see that he had not seen, she who was there in the meanwhile."

In this rather symmetrical system, they are both going to be guilty. But the text inscribes "he" as the first one to be so. The whole drama of the couple is here. He did not see and she did not see that he did not see. She is secondary in relation to him. He begins by not seeing. She could have made up but she did not see his mistake.

The insertion between dashes " — thirst is the grace, but the waters are the beauty of darkness — " is a warning. Thirst, for Clarice, is the keeper of grace. In *The Passion according to G. H.*, metaphorically speaking, if one is hungry or thirsty, a need that one has is given. If one is hungry or thirsty one has. Thirst *is* water. The danger in the story goes through touching: "as they touched there shone the brilliance of their waters." This is the moment of reversal. In the statement, "the waters are the beauty of darkness," nothing is divided by a qualifier. Beauty takes its source in the special quality of these waters, which is to be obscure. Thirst is obscure. Waters are also thirst. The grace of waters is not to be dark, but obscure. The expression itself is obscure and escapes the reader's perception or appropriation.

It is a touch that brings about the catastrophic word — and let us recall that in *The Passion* the supreme value is what is without shine: "As they touched there shone the brilliance of their waters." Thirst is no longer sufficiently on the side of grace, "their throats becoming even more dry in astonishment." At the beginning, we read "that happiness you experience upon feeling your throat rather dry." A little bit more and it becomes too much. A point of fleeting equilibrium is always at stake, a thin line between the not enough and the too much. They are pushed toward each other by the cars. It is not their fault, but the fall takes place:

"How they marvelled at finding themselves together!"

It is all over. We are on the side of admiration admiring itself, seeing itself, referring to itself and limited by punctuation.

The shine is in rapport with the water that lost its quality of obscure transparence. It has become water that is arrested, fixed into a mirror. This shiny water cannot quench thirst. Instead of a quenching of thirst *(désaltération),* there is going to be violent alteration *(altération).*

"Until everything transformed itself into denial."

Clarice explains in the second paragraph why touching did not necessarily have to lead to a catastrophe but in fact did.

"All this because they wanted to name something; because they wanted to be they who were."

We are on the side of recognition, of loss through naming, of the danger of language that mirrors.

"They were about to learn that unless one is distracted the telephone does not ring."

We continue to be in metaphor. The telephone is also allegorical. If a calling is to be, someone has to hear it. The call is a surprise. For something to happen, there has to be agitation, movement. "It is necessary to go out for the letter to arrive." One has to go out of oneself and lose one's body for something to happen. If the telephone rings after we have asked for it, nothing happens since communication is already cut.

"The wasteland of waiting has already disconnected the wires."

We have to follow the trinkets of water and not the telephone wires.

Communication and Noncommunication

When we evoke a telephone connection, we think of two people connected to each other. If we speak of two rooms that adjoin *(communiquent)* we think of space and passage. The second metaphor lends itself better to what I am saying when I speak of sexual difference and of a sexed body in which the whole mystery of sexual difference takes place. Even the puppets and the angels, who seem to be sexless or of indeterminate gender, are always inscribed by Kleist on the side of sexual difference.

At the heart of his play, *Penthesilea,* in the course of the frenzied dance of two people who are attracted to each other in such a way that the world no longer exists, everything is reversed. At the very moment when Achilles is ready to embrace Penthesilea, she remains so strange to him that he needs to have her name repeated many times. Her strangeness for both is such — in a scene that takes place in the middle of the text, as in the "Marionette Theater" — that instead of a moment of grace, a general trembling occurs. The question treats of life and death. A symptom is, for example, the disappearance of the name. Is this a good or a bad sign? For Clarice Lispector, names screen something that has to be gone beyond.

In a silent instant, Achilles and Penthesilea, who until now have communicated only through arrows — in a "now-instant," as Clarice would say — communicate with each other. They exchange information on their genders. Achilles questions the mystery of Penthesilea and she tells him the story of the Amazons. Kleist chooses to give the Amazons a fictitious history that does not refer to a kind of primitive lesbianism, but to a rejection of men by women because of the injustices inflicted upon them. Kleist pleads for a women's movement. He develops the Amazons' history at length, up to the point when the women decide to mutilate themselves but not at all from *within* the order of a phallocratic pleasure. Kleist takes up the etymology of the Amazons' name, "without a breast." The name refers to a symbolic castration and goes through a poignant mode of realism rather than through the mode of the sublime. This castration has bodily effects, and one of the characters who publicly mutilates herself falls to the ground.

Kleist insists. Everywhere, oppositions cancel each other out. One Amazon cuts her right breast in order to be able to draw the bow. The sexual symbolism is very strong but at the same time what happens to the women's defending corps goes beyond what was intended. The Amazons put a crown on the forehead of the queen who, in spite of everything, is phallicized through this gesture.

"The Amazons, that is: the breastless ones!
This done, the crown was set upon her head."[6]

Achilles is amazed but disquieted and hopes that the Amazon's example was not followed. He is horrified by the potential meaning of the gesture.

"You women do not follow her, I hope,
In this example?" Penthesilea answers naïvely:
"Not? Indeed we do!
Maybe not quite so eagerly as she

[Man ging so lebhaft nicht zu Werk als sie]."

To Achilles, who is afraid that the "monstrous legend" may be true, and that there are no more tender and sweet feelings in the Amazons, Penthesilea replies:

"Fear not!
Here, in this left breast they have taken refuge
And are, by that much, nearer to my heart.
Not one shalt thou find lacking, friend, in me."

Penthesilea cancels the annulment — that is, the effect of castration, or of phallic-ization. All tender feelings are still there. They have been communicated from right to left. All that gives life to the body of this woman is reinvested, just like libido, toward the left, or the side of the heart. Not one of the tender feelings is missing. While proposing a median reaction — that of Achilles — expressing the ordinary, Kleist nevertheless dares to express the extraordinary.

A simulacrum of symbolic castration should lead to a kind of general phallic stage or phallocentrism. But what does Penthesilea do? She reduces this gesture to another that would be necessary historically and politically. She has to struggle though this does not turn the Amazons into men. Her body is marked by femininity *and* masculinity.

Communication through the Body

When we speak of communication, we not only speak of means but also of what confers value upon it, from the parasites in the long-distance call to mental parasites, from long to short distance. The systems of exchange — looks, touching, seeing, and speaking — all go through different levels of the body, and all that deals with brushing *(frôlement)*.

Bears and animals in general are important and have a symbolic value in Kleist. The magic bear is like a totem or a god. There are also the libidinal horses that carry all the pleasure and despair of Michael Kohlhaas.

The animal does not have more or less knowledge, but has knowledge of another kind. The localization of knowledge in the body determines what we could call a corporeal intelligence. That is how the bear becomes, as Kleist puts it, master of the master.

To respect the presence of the animality of the animal is a fabulous exercise that needs to be done with a technique that resists narcissistic capture of the savage body. Animals are always treated like blacks. And I am saying this on purpose because Kleist treated this question in his times not only politically, but symbolically, at the level of color. How do we treat animals? Do we not constantly try to colonize them and transform them into French Algeria?

In Kleist's text, the bear intervenes at the level of the look. The story of the bear unfolds on two registers. We are in a kind of harmony or musical accord. The first time, M. C., the dancer, speaks:

"At this juncture," said Mr. C. amiably, "I have to tell you another story, and you'll easily see how it fits in here.

"While on my way to Russia, I spent some time on the estate of a Livonian nobleman, Mr. von G., whose sons were just then passionately interested in fencing. The elder in particular, who had just come back from the university, was somewhat of a virtuoso. One morning, when I was in his room, he offered me a rapier."

The context involves the symbolization of the sword as part of a ritual of mastery at the university. Students spent their time in duels and the length of the intellectual phallus was measured by the penis. There was a constant doubling of the symbolic struggle in this way. Everything in this passage is overloaded with the phallus through various scenes of mastery. The discourse and praxis of the master tend to kill. In a Hegelian mode, the struggle ends in death.

The other system of interest is that of father and son. In this text, we are in a world where everything has to be questioned, especially symbolic kinship relations. Kleist writes:

"The elder in particular, who had just come back from the university, was somewhat of a virtuoso."

There is provocation. Of importance is the indication of the initiative that slides right away toward virtuosity.

"We parried, but it just so happened that I was better than he. His passion caused him to be confused."

This refers to the scene with the puppets who would be superior to humans because they are not affected, neither on one side nor on the other. They are not caught in the narcissism of representation, which would cause he who dances the part of Paris to wiggle toward a certain side. Passion confuses, alters:

"Almost every thrust I made found its mark, and finally his rapier flew into the corner of the room."

This catastrophe is followed by an intervention by Kleist:

"As he picked it up, he half-jokingly, half-irritatedly, said that he had met his master."

Half and half, not entirely, because he knew that in the relay of mastery, each finds his own. As he says:

"There was a master for everyone and he now intended to lead me to mine."

The law of mastery claims that there is always another more masterful than the self. But who will be the master's master?

"His brothers laughed loudly and called out, 'Go ahead, go down to the stall!'"

And we are again on a descending slope.

"Together they took me by the hand and led me out to a bear that their father, Mr. von G., was raising on the farm.

"Somewhat astounded, I walked up to the bear."

Astonishment and alteration are on the side of the human, not of the bear.

"The bear was standing on his hind legs, his back against the post to which he was chained."

The bear's point of attachment is similar to that of the puppet attached to its threads.

"He was standing on his hind legs . . . his right paw raised ready for battle. He looked me straight in the eye. That was his fighting posture."

The question of the bear's gaze is important, as he is not a blind animal. We write with our eyes closed and the more we close our eyes, the more we see. But the bear does not need to close his eyes. Only humans do, in order to see otherwise. For the animals the bear's immobile gaze would correspond to the insistence of the gaze at the beginning of *The Passion according to G. H.*, where Clarice says that she wants more than to see. To see prevents us from more-than-seeing. Clarice insists on a seeing that is more than seeing, on a vision of vision and not on a vision of spectacle. The bear's secret is that he sees straight but when we see, we project. We see what we have already seen, what we want to see. We see through a mirror. We see ourselves seeing but the bear does not:

"I wasn't sure if I was dreaming."

It is not a question of not knowing what to believe, since dream and reality intersect in Kleist.

There follows the dance of the bear with all its extraordinary economy of movement. On the one hand, the narrator, engaged in a mode of hysterical spending, is in a continual agitation. On the other, the bear makes a minimum of gestures, as if he described his own curve:

"I tried to mislead him by feinting thrusts."

But the bear is in a state of innocence, hence absolutely indifferent to being misled. A feinting thrust, it can be said, really marks a test of guilt. The bear is outside such a game. He is outside all the work on parade:

"He stood, his paw still raised for battle, his eye fixed on mine as if he could read my soul in it, and when my thrusts were not meant seriously, he didn't move."

In a certain way, the bear reads in the soul and if we humans were not so busy looking into our own eyes, we could see what is happening in the eyes of the other. But generally, we mirror ourselves in the eyes of the other.

Kleist studies questions of paws and legs that are related to dance. In our occidental ways of thinking, dance refers to legs. In the Orient, the accent might be more on equilibrium. We favor the lower part of the body that is half legs, half sex. Our dancing movements are on the side of phallicization of the body. The Orient takes up the hands, the upper body, that is, the arms and shoulders. Kleist constantly writes of legs.

In *The Passion according to G. H.*, Clarice Lispector had begun by saying, in a violent statement, that she lost her third leg. Both in Kleist and Clarice, the third leg refers to a primal scene and to the question of the Sphinx. To emphasize the leg always implies an accentuation of the question. Oedipus's answer to the Sphinx deals with man. It is the very question of the phallic part, of its necessity, perhaps even of its possibility. Both Kleist and Clarice seek the possibility and study the implication of doing without it.

The question of alteration can be read through a comparison of different modes of alteration. From one Kleist text to another, its value differs. Alteration carried out to an ultimate point leads to loss. In "Betrothal in Santo Domingo," Kleist writes how something of the order of union leads to disunion, to breaking and to a necessity of distancing. Loss may be slow, progressive — or abrupt and violent. When, as in *Penthesilea*, it is violent, it is manifested as a fall.

In "Betrothal in Santo Domingo," the different rhythms lead us quickly from white to black with yellow as a median time. Colors function as symbols. There is also a median time, that of yellow. When saying that we go from confidence to a loss of confidence, or vice versa, I have, in fact, to circle what I am saying. There is no possible passage from one to the other. Confidence and faith occur only once.

Confidence

In these texts, the value of confidence has to be questioned. This cannot be done without thinking through Kleist's schema of the absolute, that is, the passage to and from the absolute. There we need something not of the order of a concept, something light, of the order of a brushing *(frôlement)*. In the dance of the puppets, it happens when they brush against the floor, in that half-time without duration. The value of the betrothal, or of confidence, is questioned both in "Betrothal in Santo Domingo" and in *Penthesilea*. Distinction must be made between pure and impure confidence. A destiny must be invested in the terms because (and Kleist emphasizes this) pure confidence can be thought and lived. But human confidence is always at the mercy of the space in which it unfolds, like a dance. It is not only spatial, but is subjected to the laws of gravity and to sociocultural laws. Hence the recurring questions, in Kleist's texts, of paradise and hell. Paradise escapes historical memory, it is before history. After paradise, we enter into the beginning of memory. All of Kleist's characters are carriers of historical and cultural memory. Kleist works within the bodily struggle in history and continues to ask the question of the "liberation of confidence," while taking into account social and cultural pressures. In "Betrothal in Santo Domingo," we deal with colonialism and racism. In all of Kleist's texts thousands of such questions are being asked, always over a residue that is the battle of the sexes.

Kleist speaks of *la chance (Zufall)* both as luck and chance. Does chance or luck have to do with confidence? I will speak of the question of linking. I am not losing the thread of my discussion. In Kleist, a treasure of signifiers is found among links, attachments, detachments, and alliances.

At a banal level, we can talk of an amorous attachment. In all these texts, the theme of attachment and detachment prevails. We have to be careful not to oppose them absolutely, but stick to them to make them communicate. There is no opposition between the two terms. On the contrary, they need each other. One cannot be detached from detachment or from attachment. One term holds to the other. An amorous attachment holds only when tinted with detachment. What happens from one to the other is the color yellow or the point of brushing. All comes back to quantity or force.

Kleist begs the question of the paradise he had lost but wants back. In the "Marionette Theater," neither the place, nor the garden, but innocence itself is called "paradise":

"I told him that I was well aware of how consciousness could disturb the natural grace of man. Before my very eyes, one of my young acquaintances had lost his innocence, all because of a chance remark, and had never again, in spite of all conceivable efforts, been able to find his way back to its paradise. But what conclusions, I added, can you draw from that?'' (242).

The explanation of the nonreturn to paradise is given by a very imperfect narrator. But the equation between innocence and paradise has to be noted. Innocence is the German *Unschuld,* the nonfault. The young man could never again find the ensemble innocence-paradise. The narrator's statement is both learned and ignorant. Obviously, as soon as one makes an effort, paradise is no longer possible.

Of importance is the question of loss, and the desire to find something again. I said that there are two types of confidence: pure confidence and impure confidence. They are not opposed, but situated at different moments in experience. Unfortunately we always read everything in a second tenor, that is, afterward. The questions raised by Kleist and Clarice are secondary questions, *des questions secondes.* But all hope is not lost. A second innocence is not necessarily impure. It can be found again if, as Kleist says, following the loss of a first innocence, we go around the earth to arrive at the other side. The image of the passage to the infinite opens to the possibility of another, second innocence that cannot not be reached. This is stated as lightly as possible by Kleist in the ''Marionette Theater'':

'' 'Therefore,' I said somewhat distractedly, 'we would have to eat again from the Tree of Knowledge in order to return (*zurückzufallen*) to the state of innocence?' ''

'' 'Quite right,' he answered. 'And that's the last chapter in the history of the world' '' (translation modified).

First there is an accident. There is chance or a catastrophic event linked to the German *Fall* and the English ''fall.'' One falls from innocence into knowledge, which, contrary to what one might believe, is not progress. It is not regression either, but loss. It is the loss of the possibility of another, nonsymbolic, nonintellectual knowledge. This is all bad. We are led humanly to use this kind of knowledge that ''progress'' would make into a path leading around the world up to a point of its reversal into a second innocence. Kleist does not say that anyone has ever arrived there. He only says that we should do so and the answer is: ''It is the last chapter of the history of the world,'' which is not described since we are not there yet. If we arrived ''at the end of the history of the world,'' if we arrived at the end of the book we are writing, or if we could write its last chapter, then we would close the Book and we would find ourselves not before the book as Adam and Eve but after the Book, on the other side of history. But one has to have traversed both history and its narrative. We can no longer be innocent innocents, since we belong to the world of the afterward. Nor are we bears. We are human beings, speaking and being spoken. We cannot benefit from the bear's status of purity. We have left paradise or the space of the nonfault. We are now on the path between nonfault and the limit, rather than the effacement, of the fault.

When I say we are not bears, I touch upon history and memory. Knowledge goes with speech. That is why, in our world that is ''not distracted enough,'' the real "innocent" — and in our world we have to put quotation marks everywhere until we get to where we can drop them — would be the being who does not forget. Clarice Lispector goes on repeating this. False innocence is seeming innocence that pushes back the possibility of the fault. The most innocent innocence would not forget human guilt in general. I am not concerned with the dilemma of sin, of morality and religion, and that is why instead of the word "guilt," I use "fall." I prefer to think, with Kleist, that Penthesilea's *défaillance,* her failing, is a loss of balance. From the beginning of the pursuit, she is described as losing her physical balance. From the beginning of her pursuit of Achilles, she continuously falls down. She falls and so do her horse and Achilles. Penthesilea is someone who is truly imbalanced. Her madness and her aberration are sometimes said to be moral. In the field of the Amazons, a continual oscillation prevails because the old captains who lay down the law are on the verge of judging Penthesilea, whom they believe to be mad.

Nothing-to-lose

At the moment when knowledge appears they have all they want. In paradise, Adam and Eve did not know that they had something to lose. When one has nothing to lose how does one manage to lose? By falling into terrifying ruses, the very ruses of God.

In "Michael Kohlhaas," the horse merchant is in the habit of going through the territories freely. He arrives in front of a barrier that did not exist before. This is the first interdiction in his encounters with a series of emissaries of the law. The story never pronounces the word *laissez-passer* (safe conduct). It is *still* on the side of innocence. Under the pressure of the law's representatives, in a kind of step by step, Kohlhaas undergoes the apprenticeship of misfortune, that is, of the threat of the law, which little by little takes on a content, a meaning. Kohlhaas was innocent of the law, a little like Eve, but someone tells him something, and suddenly he starts to feel that he had something to lose. For example, he starts to feel that the bastards in the castle want his horses. He is so afraid that — since he still belongs to a good economy of loss — he is ready to lose them, but harmoniously so. Kohlhaas thinks that it is better for him to lose his horses in an exchange, rather than through violence. His intention is to win them while selling them well:

"Sir, I bought those blacks there six months ago for twenty-five gold gulden; give me thirty and they are yours" (41).

He keeps his balance in relation to a loss that he foresees. But because Kleist is a realist, he shows how the world is divided. Two knights thought that this was a good bargain, but since we are in a world of evil, evil wins. The Junker does not want to pay money for the bay and the deal is rejected. Kleist's realistic notation follows:

"Kohlhaas said that the next time he came that way with his animals they might perhaps strike a bargain, took leave of the Junker, and, gathering up the reins of his horse, started to ride off. But just then the castellan stepped out of the crowd and said it was his understanding that he could not travel without a pass. Kohlhaas turned and asked the Junker if there actually were such a requirement, which would seriously interfere with his whole trade. The Junker, as he walked away, replied with an embarrassed air, 'Yes, Kohlhaas, I'm afraid you must have a pass. Speak to the castellan about it and go on your way.'"

The law is improvised. It is all the more violent insofar as it does not know itself. The law is forever born from the law. Kohlhaas begins to fall under the *coup* of the law, in an imperceptible and inconsistent fashion:

"Kohlhaas assured him that he had not the least intention of evading whatever regulations there might be for the export of horses; promised that when he went through Dresden he would take out a permit at the privy chancellery; and asked to be allowed to go through just this once since he had known nothing at all about the requirement."

He pleads innocent in the world of the law, which is an aberration since one is guilty by definition there:

"The castellan, turning to the Junker, said that Kohlhaas at least would leave a pledge behind as security for his taking out the permit. The Junker stopped again inside the castle gate. Kohlhaas asked the amount of security, in money or in articles, that he would have to leave in pledge for the blacks. The steward muttered in his beard that he might just as well leave the blacks themselves."

Kohlhaas has entered the game of the law. He did take the step that condemned him for good. Nobody told him this detail, which becomes a decree: "for the black horses." Through his utterance, he suggests something to the other. At that moment Kohlhaas has a premonition. He knows before really knowing and starts on a slow fall. His knowledge of the law is insufficient for a social being. He has not understood yet that the law does not forgive. He still believes that law and justice go together and that one can ask the law, like the Father — since we are entering afterward in infinite relays of figures of the law, imperial, regal — for something that, in reality, it will never be able to give. One can ask something legitimate of it but not something just. That is going to be Kohlhaas's experience. This alteration takes place over thousands of steps.

Questions of Alteration

In *Penthesilea* the stakes are completely different. As in "Betrothal in Santo Domingo," alteration is swift and violent. From the moment one begins to have a premonition, the conscious is born from the unconscious. In Kleist, black and white function as colors of innocence and fault. They are not emblematic but refer to night and day, to something visible and invisible. Similarly, in *Betrothal in Santo Domingo,* the story in black and white is a story of colors. Oppositions do not exist; everything is forever transitional. The story questions the symbolic value of black and white. Kleist questions true whiteness and blackness. He is no leftist. He does not say that the true whites are the blacks, and vice versa. He does not proceed by oppositions but mixes black and white. Oppositions are not to be thought in the classical sense of hierarchies. An extraordinary, radiating light has to be borne on Kleist's questioning of the moment of alteration, of something that would be pure at first, be it man or woman, black or white.

Silence

It is not necessary to speak to let the other be. There is no need for silence or speech. But human beings do not tolerate silence and tend to speak excessively. I had spoken of distraction; I now want to speak of the value of silence, of a certain silence that runs through all of Kleist's texts. In Clarice Lispector's "A Sincere Friendship," it is obvious. Speech is not bad. All that is excessive is bad, for example, forced speech, speech that is *too much*. In "Betrothal in Santo Domingo," Gustav makes the question of confidence appear around speech and silence:

"We had exchanged no vows."[7]

The story is about a young native woman, Toni, who sacrifices herself to save her white lover, Gustav. Toni is someone who does not ask for words. She thought that she had been capable of reading in Gustav the story of his first fiancée. Toni does not speak. She recognizes Gustav in a certain silence — through a certain story, but in silence. One can follow the trace of speech and silence in "Betrothal in Santo Domingo" to see how the drama is played out between the word and giving one's word, between a spoken promise that could also be on the side of nonconfidence. If I say "I promise," I have no more confidence, in myself or in the other. Pure promise would be a silence without use, assured by the confidence in the confidence of the other. With the "confidence of the other," we are touching on the stakes of betrothal. Toni makes a gesture to save Gustav in a scene of silence that is one of both threat and innocence. She makes all the gestures without a word. She hears the Negro Congo Hoango's gang return unexpectedly, and with it a death threat for Gustav who, in the meantime, has become her lover. Gustav continues to be referred to as "the stranger." A stranger in relation to whom and what? At the heart of the story, the stranger remains strange:

"And without saying another word [Congo Hoango] began to ascend the stairs accompanied by all his Negroes and headed for the stranger's bedroom.

"Toni, before whose eyes, in the course of a few minutes, this whole scene had taken place, stood there, paralyzed in every limb, as though struck by lightning. She thought for a moment of wakening the stranger."

Then comes the moment in the story where I want to ask my question:

"But on the one hand, she saw that, because of the men in the courtyard, it was impossible for him to flee, and on the other hand she knew that he would reach for his sword and, given the numerical superiority of the blacks, would be felled immediately. Indeed, the terrible realization to which she was forced to come was this: that the unfortunate man himself, if he were to find her in these circumstances beside his bed, would think her a traitress, and, instead of heeding her advice, in a mad, unthinking rage would senselessly run into the arms of the Negro Hoango."

In her unspeakable anguish, she suddenly sees a cord:

"Heaven knows by what chance, [it] was hanging on a peg on the wall. God himself, she thought taking it down, had put it there for her friend's salvation. With it she tied the young man by the hands and feet, making many knots, and, paying no attention to his struggles, pulled the ends together and fastened him to the bedstead, then, rejoicing at having mastered the situation, she pressed a kiss on his lips and hurried to meet the Negro Hoango, who was already stamping up the stairs."

The story is totally incomprehensible outside of a Kleistian space. It does not say that Gustav was awake. We only think he is because we are told that he struggles. From the fact that he is awake, we could think that he did not receive the gift. The scene is reminiscent of Samson and Delilah. The latter ties the former seven times in such a way that he never wakes up. Once he is tied up, she tells him to wake up quickly because the Philistines are coming. Nothing allows us to read that Gustav did, indeed, receive the kiss, which does not change the interpretation of the following moment. When he is well awake, he concludes:

"The Negro, returning his sword to its scabbard, stepped up to the bed and asked the stranger: who he was? where he came from and where he was going? But since the latter, struggling and twisting to free himself, did not answer except to moan pitifully and painfully: 'O Toni! O Toni!' — the mother intervened and explained that he was a Swiss by the name of Gustav von der Ried and that he came, with a whole family of European dogs who at this moment were hiding in the caves near Gull Pond, from the coastal settlement Fort Dauphin."

Kleist takes the precaution to tell us that Toni thought about waking Gustav but did not have time. It is an unfortunate accident. One can ask why she did not try. Kleist provides an explanation by saying that Gustav "in a mad, unthinking rage would senselessly run into the arms of the Negro Hoango." I have not decided about the destiny of this singular remark. We can construct an epilogue by bringing all our unhappy memories to this scene. At the level of the story, there are no oppositions. Yet here there is one favored by Toni though she is not morally superior. She is afraid she would not be able to speak to Gustav. Speech is outside of the circuit. Gustav would throw himself into Hoango's arms less out of love than out of terror, enacting thus the scene of the first fiancée, that is, Terror.

Toni does not have confidence in her very confidence. The scene is completely without explanation. Each protagonist is related to the silence of the other. Everyone's destiny, and especially Gustav's, is decided by something that was not said.

When evaluating capacities of confidence, we know that Toni leans toward confidence whereas Gustav — and this leads through a question of color — is on the side of nonconfidence. To find the thread of the analysis, we have to see how Gustav's rage is triggered by something specific, that is, the cord with all its knots, which has to be understood as pertaining to structures of attachment and detachment, of tying and untying. Toni does not expect the danger where it surges. The ties make Gustav completely mad, blind, incapable of thinking and of guessing the situation.

Toni's fear can be equated with the impossibility for a man — for example Samson — of ridding himself of a phantasm of castration. A lack of confidence, a suspicion, transmitted as a form of cultural heritage, precedes Kleist's story. Would this still be the case today? Is fear of castration reserved for men? I think that women too can have a symbolic and imaginary fear of castration; Penthesilea, for example, seems to have this fear.

In "Betrothal," Gustav refuses to be dispossessed of his phallic position. The minor episodes in the story, including the way he and Toni make love, are unbearable for women. We can see the difference between Gustav's relation with Toni and Peter von Strahl's with Kätchen von Heilbronn: the difference is based on respect. Gustav does what he does because he is not on the side of respect. He may be on the side of love but the latter is not pure.

Kleist's text, a hymn to Toni, is most subtle. Gustav is the least ugly of the Swiss. If he were totally unworthy of Toni's love, there would be nothing left. The mise en scène at the beginning of *Betrothal* — that is, the passage about the massacre — is there to give Gustav a true excuse for his lack of confidence. But afterward, with Toni, the reader discovers simultaneously with her the story of the first fiancée. Toni gives as much as Gustav calculates. In order to be sure of her, Gustav subjects Toni to a bodily test. It is only from the moment when she gives herself to him that he lets go of his lack of confidence, of his reserve. Since he is the least evil person, he gives back something. "Betrothal" is made up of a series of tests, including that of the first fiancée, who has already given up her life for Gustav. The latter would be a jerk if the first fiancée had given her life for him. Kleist inscribes how — and that is why it is necessary to take up attachment and detachment — Mariane, the first fiancée, has the strength to separate herself symbolically from Gustav in order to save him. She lives her death alone and by doing so, she gives him a life. She pronounces the sentence that Gustav retells without analyzing it. Seeing that his fiancée had been caught instead of him, Gustav tries to denounce himself. The following scene works on an alternation of speech and silence.

"But she, who was already standing beside the guillotine, when questioned by some judges to whom I was unfortunately a stranger, answered, as she turned away from me with a look that is indelibly imprinted in my soul: 'I do not know this man!' Whereupon, a few minutes later amidst drumming and shouting instigated by these wolves impatient for blood, the knife fell and severed her head from her body. — How I was saved, I do not know; a quarter of an hour later I found myself in the home of a friend, where I fell into one swoon after another and, half out of my senses, was loaded toward evening on a wagon and brought across the Rhine."

"How I was saved, I do not know" belongs not to the first but to the second moment of the story. Toni thinks that Gustav has understood and that she can give herself to him. But the reader, remembering the first sacrifice, knows otherwise. He who lived the first scene will surely live the second. It is a structure. Because Gustav talked, the young woman was caught in his stead. He was wanted because he had made his counterrevolutionary opinions known publicly. Of importance is that the girl is capable of saying that she did not know Gustav. This moment of absolute renunciation and risk in order to save him comes back to extreme recognition. To say "I do not know this man" of someone by whom one is known in the Biblical sense of the term is, for a woman, the height of the gift, but also of sacrifice. Kleist does not ignore this frightening paradox. Gustav is always being saved while being completely unaware of it. But to be saved without knowing it will catch up with us.

Silence is the atmosphere, the climate of confidence. In a true confidence, communication takes place in all kinds of ways, without words, because words always go back to the bad end, to the force of the law, the force of the word or the word in force. Communication through silence is eminently readable in Clarice's chronicle "A Sincere Friendship." Or communication can go through the gaze, as in the episode with the bear in the "Marionette Theater." The bear can never accede to speech since, by definition, he is one who communicates through the body. That is the essence of the animal, not of humans. The test for human beings comes from the fact that there *is* speech and that we need to use it well. If there were no speech, it would not matter. But since there is, it all has to do with a question of choice and a decision. When two human beings do not speak is communication cut? That is the very question of our anguish. Not to speak, to be with the other in silence, is the mark of supreme confidence. We can ask the question about a refined mode of an amorous attachment. To say "I love you" is the worst aberration. True love could do without saying it, though not without *doing* it. Speech can even cut communication. All these texts raise the question of when communication is cut and when alteration reaches a moment when it becomes negative. When is the communication made between Penthesilea and Achilles? First, there is understanding. Through an utterly untranslatable language of arrows, Achilles and Penthesilea hear and understand each other. In the brief moment they are together, there is a kind of beautiful duo. Then communication is cut, not magically and all at once, because Kleist has a very strong rapport with the real. The cut is determined in a thousand ways. There is an ephemeral moment of equilibrium that could be called the moment of grace. It is followed by disequilibrium and loss that do not have one and only one cause. One can say — and that is where the question of the other is vital — that Achilles did take the necessary leap. One can show confidence only once and all at once in a kind of coup de grâce.

Achilles is ready to go over to Penthesilea. He says to himself that since she absolutely insists on taking him with her, he is ready to go, and he agrees to all her conditions, even to that of being captured by her. It is only on condition of capturing the man she loves that Penthesilea can raise him up again and love him. Achilles, having understood Penthesilea's historically phantasmatic necessity, is ready to rid himself of his own desires, phantasms, and arms, to go over to the other side. At least that is what he thinks. He thinks he can do it by pretending to be vanquished by her. His analysis comes from the most noble of loves. He uses a ruse of love. In order for Penthesilea to believe that he is going to be vanquished, he goes on to invent the conditions of the struggle. That is where Achilles' limits begin to show. He is not the other. He is ready to go as far as he can but he remains Achilles. He cannot in the historical context — and besides, nobody can — put himself in Penthesilea's place. The apprenticeship of the other that he is capable of making lacks a tiny something. And in any event, Penthesilea did not travel the same distance as Achilles. Each would have had to travel half the distance so they could have met in the middle, in the very place and at the moment of grace. To guess Penthesilea, Achilles would have had to be divinely intelligent. Penthesilea was unable to cover the distance, both for historical and circumstantial reasons. Since she is wounded, she is physically quite diminished. She is completely amnesic and incapable of interpreting Achilles' will. Does he want her to guess his ruse? No, he wants her to think that he is going to attack. The ruse is going to turn back on Penthesilea herself. Achilles forgets that she has been altered and is no longer where she was at the beginning. She can no longer be identified with her warrior model and has lost some of her phallic traits. The Amazons behave as men only temporarily. As soon as they have killed their men, they become women again. Penthesilea cannot come back to that provisional masculine position and Achilles is not quick enough to perceive it. Nobody can hold it against him. He cannot identify absolutely with Penthesilea. As a warrior, Penthesilea has lost against Achilles in advance, and as a man, she can no longer affront him. There remains the other side. She retraces the curve, as described by Kleist in the "Marionette Theater," from the other side. She goes over not to the side of femininity but of animality. There remain wolves, dogs, and elephants. I am giving a subterranean interpretation of some of the stakes in the text. Fatality is inevitable. It is determined by historical conditions that precede the encounter between Achilles and Penthesilea. That is why it is a tragedy. What could they have done to avoid it? Given their model of departure, they were destined to death. One of them should have been able to take a leap out of this scene where all the winning values are masculine, martial values. But they do not think about it. They cannot imagine another space, or an elsewhere. Given the very primitive atmosphere of war and confrontation, they do not have enough ingenious suppleness nor enough strength to become other in order to save each other. In this scene between Achilles and Penthesilea, an absolute double-bind is put in place by history.

Communication is not always cut in Kleist. For example, in *Kätchen von Heilbronn,* a play of great subtleties, an important episode deals with going out of the window. The character of Kätchen herself is not very appealing because she is too much of a saint. But there is a comic element in the love scenes between her and the Count, the equivalent of the scenes between Penthesilea and Achilles. At the very moment of grace, Kätchen says to the Count: "Verliebt ja, wie ein Käfer bist du mir."[8] This great find in the history of literature can be put side by side with Clarice Lispector's cockroach. When Kätchen says this to the Count, she speaks from the depth of her sleep. The question of silence and of communication is treated in the mode of white magic and Kätchen's secret is to have been able to do what women generally cannot do without dying. She is able to keep silent so that the other hears what is being said silently or what cannot be said with words. She does not speak too soon. Kleist tells us that it is because God is with her. She knows how to stay in harmony. She has the strength not to speak and realizes the danger she and her lover face as long as the moment of grace has not come. And who decides? God and the angels. She is of the most absolute faith. Kleist did not go to church, so God and the angels appear as for someone who does not believe, that is, in a dream. It is in the space of the dream, of the unconscious, that the two lovers in *Kätchen von Heilbronn* find each other long before meeting.

If there is an opposition between characters such as Kohlhaas and the Junker, Kätchen and Kunegunde, there is none between Penthesilea and Achilles but movement from trust to distrust. Here, alteration takes place within a continuity. Elsewhere there are violent oppositions between the world of the law and that of life and death. These oppositions can be found in all of society. To say that there are no oppositions is to say that there are no values completely cut off from their opposites. One is more or less guilty. There is alteration but always in a space that is not completely that of the enemy. I did not speak of the totally black characters, and there are some in "Betrothal in Santo Domingo." But these are only limit cases.

In *Kätchen von Heilbronn,* the young girl is named "das Kätchen." She is neutralized — by the neuter article, *das* — in a space that is not situated within a parental or social code. Rather, it is a question of class. Nothing would separate Kätchen from the Count, if it were not for a class difference. The question of class in relation to a capitalistic and phallocentric world goes from the Judges, who are not nobles, to the Emperor. Kätchen is admitted into that space. She leaves the neutral status of her nonexistence when she is being legitimized. Hers is not a pure, detached love, and Kleist does not support it. A twist in the story indicates his ideological position. We learn mysteriously and confidentially that she is actually the Emperor's daughter. There is a real and a false father. The false father, Theobald, makes claims for his daughter. Kleist treats him in ambivalent terms, both as an idiot and as someone who inspires pity. Nobody knows the truth, except for the mother who no longer exists. One night the Emperor whispers something about a dance and about something that happened. It is as if Kleist himself had wanted to pardon the ensemble of Kätchen, the two fathers, and the mother. The only thing that remains from the accident is the mark. But the Emperor does not want to demoralize anyone. He does not recognize his daughter but adopts her instead. The emperor also satisfies the dream predicting that the Count would marry a noble girl. We may wonder about Kleist's project. If Kätchen, who is just a bit too white, did not say to the Count "You June bug," the story would be unbearable.

What does Kätchen do when she throws herself out the window? It may perhaps be read as a double gesture of both giving birth to and humiliating herself, or as Freud would say, of *niederkommen*. The child who comes out is Kätchen herself. When she throws herself out the window, she distances herself from her father. She wanted perhaps to follow her Prince but the opposite takes place. She breaks her legs and is immobilized. Her leap is a kind of *niederkommen*. She plays at being the child but she also makes a child. Who is the Father? The Count? Again, gaze and vision determine all these violent gestures. To break a leg prevents one from walking for a while. It comes back to a loss of knowledge, like a propitious fainting. It is a way of absenting oneself. This is to be found in multiple traces in Kleist; it touches on the question of standing or holding up, but also, in a way, that of not making sense.

Similarly, after a certain point, Penthesilea can no longer stand up. She says that her legs are broken or that they give under her. For this to happen she would need to get rid of her third, orthopedic, phallic leg that helps her stand upright, be logical and reasonable. All these women have this in common: they can no longer stand upright. They have decided to go over to the other side, through the window if necessary, to the side that could be called madness. It could also be an outside of the father, of the law. It is a test of castration, neither physical nor imaginary, of a woman for a man. It is probable that for a woman the passage of the rejection of crutches, of the decision no longer to hold on to an upright position, is maddening, but less maddening than for a man who is supposed to carry himself upright. These kinds of epopeias, the goal of which is to reach a state of innocence or grace, always begin with a loss of the upright position or of one's equilibrium.

After Kätchen has jumped out the window, she tells the episode, and is accused of being a puppet by Peter von Strahl. The comment is enunciated in a derogatory way. For the reader, this signals that everything happened as if she were at Peter von Strahl's mercy, and as if, henceforth, her movements, those of a divine puppet, could only be determined through him. She cannot answer the slightest solicitation that does not come directly from him. It would be awful if the Count were not also a dreamer. When she jumps out the window, one can say that she escapes the ordinary laws of gravity as well as those of kinship and alliance.

We will have to come back to the legs, the paws, either, as Freud says, limping or walking on all fours, or else to the theme of the fall that precedes redemption. In order to come back in through the door of the castle, we have to fall out the window.

I want to work on the temptation of being the other. First, I would like to insist that one can think loss other than in the negative, other than as punishment, in a movement that goes up to the very extinction of loss, to the loss of loss that would be the most human path to grace. With the danger of the fall, I go back into the space of Biblical reference. If there is temptation, it is on the side of having, of being the other. In the world of thought, this is related to understanding. All is happening between understanding and not understanding. To understand is to have, to take, to appropriate the other, and once that is understood, boredom sets in.

Freud gives his libido a viscous consistency, a kind of resisting fluidity. One can imagine a moment when this fluidity becomes crystallized. Some economies do not flow well. They jell and thicken in the sense of marmalade. Usually, a contentment sets in that either suffices or does not. From this contentment, there is a new drive toward a new desire, a new mystery. I insist on the value of movement, of mobility, and of a good viscosity. I also repeat that grace can only be in movement. One never *has* grace, it is always given. Grace is life itself. In other words, it is an incessant need, but even if it is given, like life itself, this does not mean that it will be received. To have received grace does not mean to *have* it, once and for all. Adam and Eve were the only people who "had" it but without knowing. And they were in Paradise at a time when there was no having. We mortals have the *chance,* the luck of being on the passage of grace. In the "Marionette Theater," there was a tiny, very subtle detail that consisted in marking the moment of brushing *(frôlement)* in the puppet's movement. The brushing makes the difference between an innocent innocence that we do not know — like that of Adam and Eve before they were expelled from Paradise — and another, for which we have to look, as Kleist reminds us, at the other end of the world. In Clarice's terms, we would find it after having gone through knowledge so as to arrive at the other end of knowledge, and there again to begin not to know any longer. That is when we arrive at the second innocence that, contrary to the first, does not not know itself. This second innocence is precisely the grace one gives to oneself. I would say, one does without *(on se fait grâce de)* knowledge. To be capable of it, one has to know that one knows. But at the same time, one has to be disenfranchised of knowledge. This can be done in a very delicate movement of detachment. For example, we know something but we do not hold on to it. We all know how much we hold on to what we know or what we think we know. One has to know how not to possess what one knows. I tend to criticize the prejudice for truth, which consists in knowing that one has knowledge and in giving it a mortal, limited, subjective, or even a universal value. To have only the value of knowledge is not to have the value of life, or love. It is only a *moment* in a process of reasoning, a step on a certain methodical path, a moment or a means, something of a useful or necessary passage but limited to a certain usage. It is not an end in itself and is without final value. It can be abandoned, lost, or given up. This kind of lightness in the gesture of appropriation is something that is not cramped, but supple *(délié)*. These qualities can be found with what I call the other or the second innocence. To repeat, I am not speaking of an innocence that does not know or of one whose mark is to be constantly threatened by the demon of knowledge. But it is threatened in any case and has to be so. It must run the risk of losing itself; it can never be a state. If it is not constantly threatened, we are not susceptible of either having it all at once, or of losing it. That is what I mean by "brushing." In the dance of innocence, there occurs an imperceptible moment of brushing, a risk of interruption. This risk is the mark of the human being, who otherwise would be on the side of the divine. Humans are always at the door of paradise, on the point of losing it and not inside.

I come back to the word "confidence," which functions in the same way. Innocent innocence is not of interest to us. The notion applies either to the village idiot or to the newly born child. What can be called innocence, in the course of human life, is the most acute stage of awareness of the possibility of human guilt. One can be innocent only if one is absolutely guilty. At the end of an infinite guilt, one can become innocent.

Grace and innocence have no meaning outside of being in relation. The Biblical Paradise *is* without other. Grace and innocence have no meaning outside of a relation of temptation with their other. We can read such temptations in texts like Kleist's, where it is always a question of linking and unlinking, of binding and unbinding, of attaching and detaching, in love or in friendship.

Attachment-Detachment

"Goodbye" implies "God be with you." In the French *adieu,* the connotation is more lugubrious, since it implies "I will not see you again." In English, there is an implication of benediction, of blessing. What does this mean in a series of substitutions? God comes in my place, accompanies you. I do not go without you, God be with you. Hence me as God, or me-God. The negotiation of detachment is quite subtle. I detach myself from you on condition that God replace me. It is always a question of one with or without the other.

We could work on *au revoir,* an incredible word, a kind of erased denial. The moment of departure is effaced and we are already in a recall. (I make these remarks at a semantic level.) How does one separate from someone in circumstances that are coded, or in circumstances that are not? Most coded formulas are screens of politeness implying that one will not see the other person again. On the other hand, in a relation of continuity, the formula becomes something brutal and means: I do not want to see you any more. Why? Because we never resolve or finish thinking through our relations with separation.

Of importance in working on attachment-detachment is the question of the link; this recurs often in Kleist. The link may be manifest, that is, attached, and not only linked by a trait such as the *trait-d'union* (hyphen). Here, we can recall what Heidegger said on the trait, the *Zug*, on what attracts, unites and separates, on what joins and disjoins. We can insist on what links, on the ring or the circle, as found, for example, in Shakespeare's *Merchant of Venice*. The shape itself, its geometry, is of importance. It joins Kleist's pronouncements on the two straight lines that cross in infinity and that, in fact, are curved lines. But for Kleist, straight lines are interrupted. The ring is not interrupted and raises questions of alliance. In Kleist, an important symbolic as well as dramatic function is given to the good and the bad link, to the good and the bad attachment, to the cords that, contrary to the hyphen, are braided and textured. The cord is already attached to itself. The ring, whatever its metal, is a sincere (that is, a pure) metal. That is why rings are made of gold. We want our alliances to be without alloy. We want metal that is symbolically pure. But the attachment is of one trait, even when there are two rings.

In *Penthesilea,* stories of linkings proliferate everywhere. In "Betrothal in Santo Domingo," the moment of reversal also goes through stories of linking. It does not function in the same way as in *Penthesilea,* and the link is not pure. Instead of a ring, it is a bound link, a bound linking *(du lien lié, du liant lié).*

I have always been fascinated by what can be detached from the body, by what is detachable and "linkable," such as hair. We can think of the story of Delilah, who could not be happy until she cut Samson's hair. No link was strong enough for her as long as he held on to his hair by his own strength. Freud had located the origin of writing in the braiding of pubic hair by women. Weaving would be the first sign of writing. Freud's hypothesis is rather funny. It implies that there would be an origin on the side of the body but also not of the body since it would already be detached. At the same time such braiding negates the possibility of detachment since the hair is being attached. This is precisely the movement of writing.

Can there be an end? The question is of importance. Do I exhaust everything by speaking? When we say to the other, "I understand you," is this true or false? Neither one nor the other. "I understand you" is more of an approval of the other than a feeling of hearing what the other is saying. "I understand you" makes sense only when we put the body on stage. Communication takes place at the level of the body. We receive, or hear, with the body. A certain force, which would belong to women, consists in knowing that true communication does not go through television or the newspapers. It does not mean that such communication is mute. But it is related to the body. This raises the question of the value of speech, of its development, of what it carries *(fait passer)* or does not carry.

We constantly move in paradoxical spaces. When I say to the other, "I understand you," I can replace the expression by "yes" or even by "I do not understand you." The most precise statement is to accept not to understand. To say this is to divide the relation with the other into positive and negative. One can say it in a negative way, disapprovingly, or, to the contrary, in the mode of acceptance. The approving kind tends to be uttered silently or even murmured.

The question is not, Is it necessary to say everything? To say *everything* does not mean anything. One can only say, one can never say everything. In common speech, to say "I want to say everything" is a substitute for something else. Can I say what I am afraid to say? But the question here can be asked thus: Is it *necessary* to say everything? When is it possible *not* to say something, without having to keep silent or hide, being in a *certain* silence?

I am trying to work on the link between a first and a second innocence. The "second innocence" should be our goal, our ambition. This innocence has to be earned, whereas the first one needs to be lost. At the same time, a system develops between the two until we reach the second innocence, which, contrary to the first, is not innocent of itself. I put this in relation with what can be thought of as an exchange between self and other, something that can be heard as: self-same and other, self and other, or self-same-and-other. I do not want to make an opposition between self and other. I want to make conjunctions, an exchange, in such a way that the other remains other. Is this possible? I relate these questions, which bear upon sexual difference, and I relate them to the question of the other, that is, to alteration, positive or negative, or to innocence. I am moving in a space of respect, *but* I start from the first innocence that lost its innocence in an encounter with the other. Yet, despite not being innocent, the second innocence is not guilty either. It must remain strange to itself. It salvages what is strange. When I am saying this, I look toward Kleist's "Betrothal in Santo Domingo," and think of the astonishing moment when the first fiancée, Mariane, who is about to be beheaded, utters this simple sentence concerning someone whom we may perhaps no longer even call her fiancé: "I do not know this man." This is the most beautiful declaration of love. She says it in the mode of recognition and not reproach, the way we can read it, for example, in Racine, where it can mean "I am the only one who is still close to understanding you." Mariane saved the man to whom Kleist continues to refer as "the stranger." Contrary to to what holds in a classical space, "stranger" is valorized. But the stranger is also threatened by the fact that strangeness can be abolished.

I keep on wandering around in this space, and I will say that one has to read *all* of Kleist. My favorite text, "The Earthquake in Chile," crosses my own text in multiple ways, phantasmatic, unconscious — and South American, since that is my phantasmatic place, probably for reasons of trembling and displacement.

Some losses happen all at once, as in the Judeo-Christian world; others happen more slowly, during a passage to the infinite, as in the "Marionette Theater." A *coup de dent*, a snap, marks nevertheless the moment of rupture. Then something is going to be altered more or less quickly (or slowly) until the moment of complete decomposition. The moment of loss of innocence — or grace — can be positive or negative. If we take the system of the puppets, with their ideal and graceful dance that is movement alone — and grace can only be in movement — breathing, living, there is, however, a movement of nonmovement and of nondance. That moment does not exist, it is not there any more than a *now* or a *present,* already past. It is not even a moment of arrest, it is what Kleist describes as brushing. This vital brushing starts the process again and is not what interrupts, as in the case of the clumsy dancer. It is the transparency of an *in-betweenness* of two human beings, moving back and forth from one to the other. There has to be a moment of brushing, because without it there would be continuity and not even a self. If we use the metaphor of the puppets, it is easy. In real life, it is much more difficult. We belong to our species; that is, we are not angelical, and we behave like heavy robot dancers. To fray a passage toward the other is a humanly difficult art.

In Kleist, "The Earthquake in Chile" occupies a space related to a possible time of loss of grace. In *Penthesilea* or in "Betrothal," we do not take sides. In *Penthesilea,* we can continue to ask ourselves about the origin of loss of grace. Is Adam or Eve the cause? Is it Achilles or Penthesilea? To decide is to make a mistake. It is impossible, just as in the Bible, to assign a cause. In fact, one should make a trial of the trial. A decision in favor of one or the other must go through a noninvested analysis. For or against is the same thing. What happens in Penthesilea or Achilles is the tragedy of history. In the space in which they move, the air is not pure; Achilles and Penthesilea are not puppets, they are humans. They cannot escape the gravitational pull of history. All kinds of maledictions of the sexual image weigh on both of them, be it the virile image or that of the Amazon. Each felt strong enough to be torn away in a leap from this scene. But the scene is too enormous, too overcrowded.

Kleist works admirably. He stages two camps, each being rather divided. Neither camp, the Greeks' or the Amazons', is presented according to an ideal image. The camp functions as a superego, but poorly. Each camp trembles at this demand. The two protagonists give themselves to a dangerous operation that will eventually fail, though it had its moment of success. But as always in Kleist, this moment cannot last. Failure arrives when Penthesilea loses her memory after experiencing a real shock. She lets herself be carried off by love, all the while taking into account a sexual opposition in which she does not believe. At that moment, there is a return of the repressed, that is, of the battle of the sexes. It is triggered by a minute event, which at the same time is important, since it is war itself. It is the heritage, the memory of a compulsory battle. Everything happens at the sublime level but these questions do arise in ordinary life. There, one does not stay faithful to war for having sworn to be faithful to one's ancestors. A misunderstanding arises between Achilles and Penthesilea, revolving around a question of hearing well or poorly something that has never been uttered. To hear well is to hear what is never said, what has to be kept silent beyond the message. In the relation of Achilles and Penthesilea violence comes back, because, as Kleist says in despair, one cannot erase relations of power in a world still enclosed in the walls of history.

The kind of montage that surrounds the scene with Penthesilea is impossible to overcome.

One cannot erase relations of power, and that deals with questions of absolute confidence, in the Kleistian sense. What is "absolute" is *absous,* that is, cut, isolated from the social. A confidence beyond calculation is the same thing. Penthesilea, from Achilles' bad calculation in his state of noncalculation, accedes to a bad memory. In a lightning flash, she accedes to an inverse belief. Everything that in a leap toward absolute confidence she had stopped believing — that is, that sexual war is the fate of humans — she believes again in the same instant way, in the mode of faith. She does not receive it rationally, but she receives it in the mode of faith. Rationally, she cannot believe it. She is not someone who carries hatred or vengeance in her. Her belief in war is hers through obedience. For her, war is an apprenticeship. She is going to believe in it all the more as she does not believe it. It is obvious that the most absolute confidence is situated at the most ultimate moment between life and death, at the moment of greatest distrust; for example, that of Mariane or Toni in *Betrothal.* It is at the moment of life or death that the question of confidence or nonconfidence is decided. These are two sides of the same gesture, of the same movement. I can invert the proposition by saying that the greatest lack of confidence is situated at the moment of confidence. There is no greater lack of confidence than that which is most unlikely. For example, what kills Tristan and Isolde is the moment when what is inseparable begins to think the moment of separation. The quotidian defiance is nothing, and against that we have great defenses. We have no defense against supreme defiance. That is also the story — easier to analyze because it is so overdetermined — of Othello and Desdemona. There is no reason for defiance, so when defiance appears, it is complete. It is always played out in a paradoxical mode. If one cannot have confidence in the being in whom one has absolute confidence, one goes mad. That is what happens to Achilles and Penthesilea. We hope that they are capable of making, or of giving, grace, that they have learned a lesson of happiness. Not at all. They are hardly up again, when they precipitate themselves not toward grace but, as usual, in the direction of hatred. They will never again know grace. Their error is political. (Though not in the sense of political parties, because with them grace does not exist. With them, only calculation exists.) People who have a revolutionary ideal can work from such a necessary error, saying that there must be grace and with it one can transform the world. They think that an upheaval can displace all of human mentality, and that happiness is desirable. This *is* an illusion. The protagonists in *Earthquake in Chile* believe in it and are made to pay for their belief right away.

However, I want to insist on the *necessity of an illusion.* The illusion consists in believing that people who have been hostages, from time immemorial, of the world of calculation and the world of the law are capable of leaving it. Here, I am not sending a pessimistic message. I think that nothing can destroy in us the part made for happiness and love, happiness or love. But I also think that nothing can transform the part that is not made for it. A politically just procedure would be to look for and regroup forces capable of the same happiness and to not let oneself be altered by the bad, other, part.

1982–83

Notes

1. Heinrich von Kleist, *Werke und Briefe* (Berlin and Weimar: Aufbau Verlag, 1978), 483–84.

2. Heinrich von Kleist, "On the Marionette Theater," trans. Christian-Albrecht Gollub, in *German Romantic Criticism,* ed. A. Leslie Willson (New York: Continuum, 1982), 241.

3. See Hélène Cixous, *Reading with Clarice Lispector,* ed. and trans. Verena Andermatt Conley (Minneapolis: University of Minneasota Press, 1990).

4. Clarice Lispector, "Because they were not distracted," in *The Foreign Legion,* trans. Giovanni Pontiero (New York: Carcanet, 1986), 108–9.

5. Heinrich von Kleist, "Michael Kohlhaas," trans. Martin Greenberg, in *German Romantic Novellas* (New York: Continuum, 1985), 39–121.

6. Heinrich von Kleist, *Penthesilea,* trans. Humphry Trevelyan, in *Plays* (New York: Continuum, 1982), 231.

7. Heinrich von Kleist, "Betrothal in Santo Domingo," in *German Romantic Novellas,* 164.

8. Heinrich von Kleist, *Kätchen von Heilbronn,* in *Werke and Briefe* (Berlin and Weimar: Aufbau, 1989), 208. [You love me like a Junebug, that is, up to your ears. _____ Trans.]

Chapter 3

Apprenticeship and Alienation Clarice Lispector and Maurice Blanchot

"The Foreign Legion": A Text of Strangeness

In reading "The Foreign Legion," I once again experienced the density of Clarice Lispector's writing. The arrival of a chick in the house around Christmas time reminds Clarice of a former neighbor's daughter, Ofélia, and of her encounter with a little chick at Easter time. A first surface is openly narrative, whence we could work on various types of narration. But little by little, a vast network of philosophical significations imposes itself. Clarice develops a philosophy of the world, with its laws and its economy, in her short texts but not in her long texts such as *The Apple in the Dark*. "The Foreign Legion" begins in an atmosphere of strangeness, first with the title, the meaning of which escapes the reader forever, and then with the following sentence:

"And if I were to be asked about Ofélia and her parents, I would reply with decorous honesty: I scarcely know them" (translation modified).[1]

The tone is one of familiarity. We know that Clarice is talking though we are not always supposed to know it. The voice that narrates — and here we could appeal to the well-known distinction between *voix narratrice* and *voix narrative* — is presented as being known, yet it remains strange. There are some strange people who are named: Ofélia and her parents. We are caught in a familiarity that is doubly strange and where everything concerns what is "hardly known."

There is more than one story and there is the story of a story, presented according to techniques of narration that are not entirely known to us. The first paragraph blurs everything. Clarice seems to say: If you ask questions, I will tell you that I do not know. She is on the side of not-knowing, on the side of what she calls *real* knowledge or real love.

The intervention of a tribunal at the beginning of the narration is violent. The tribunal will not completely disappear. A fictitious tribunal, a fictitious jury are going to be there in movement from one scene to the next throughout the entire text. There is always some kind of a look, some kind of judgment. From one end to the other, Clarice is being accused, but of innocence. In this struggle between Clarice and Ofélia, guilt and innocence are in continuous exchange. Yet guilty or innocent of what, since it is the same thing? Perhaps, one could say, of knowing or not knowing.

This reminds the reader of Maurice Blanchot's tribunals — as, for example, in *La Folie du jour (The Madness of the Day).*[2] The interpellation of a tribunal is a metaphor of a certain human state, I do not want to say a human condition. The metaphor, found in Kafka, is taken up again by Blanchot in *The Madness of the Day.* It is the theorem, the algebra of the relation to a masculine law. It can be read with "The Foreign Legion," yet it is on the other side. In *The Madness of the Day,* the narrator, whose identity we do not know, is trying to tell a story that he will not be able to tell. The question of narration is constantly raised. The question of what can be told is also raised by Clarice in "Felicidade clandestina" ("Secret Happiness"), where she says at some point that she will no longer be able to tell the story because part of the experience escapes the laws that are the very condition of narration.[3] In *The Madness of the Day,* Blanchot declares at the very beginning that the story cannot be told. He tells us: no narrative, no more pure narrative. He tells us something rather bizarre with engimatic events that are, at the same time, in the text. He tells us perfidious banalities such as: It was at that moment that something happened. Everything leads to the fact that the narrator who is at the origin of the narration is apparently considered to be mad. The doctors tell him: You are an intellectual, so you are capable of telling us what happened. The doctors, representing the look of the law, are saying: You have to give an account of who you are and of what happened. We are in the Kafkaesque impasse of "I do not know myself, I do not know you and you do not know me." How does one tell a story if, in the place of truth, there is no law that decides: Here truth begins. The question is how to answer between truth and lie. By constrast, we can read how Clarice answers the question in "The Foreign Legion" when she says at the beginning:

"Before the same jury I should testify: I scarcely know myself — and to each member of the jury I should say with the same innocent look of someone who has hypnotized herself into obedience: I scarcely know you. But sometimes I wake from a long sleep and turn submissively toward the delicate abyss of disorder" (87).

Clarice is docile, rather than obedient; she is closer to apprenticeship than alienation. With her, we are in a process of apprenticeship and go toward a revelation. We go toward the abyss of disorder, far from the decorous honesty which is, however, not completely and violently opposed, but simply differentiated with subtlety. Clarice is "going to try to speak" in this delicate space. Everything is in the delicacy of the attempt, approximation and trembling. The analytical mechanism of this paradoxical enterprise is close to Blanchot's. Clarice's expression "without traces" is picked up later by "sentiments are like sudden water" (87). Yet in water there can be no trace. Clarice's text, focusing continuously on the question of loss and reserve, is pushed forward by a movement of appearance and disappearance. It began with "disappeared," which is then relayed by "appeared":

"My sudden acquiescence in knowing was provoked today when a little chick appeared in the house."

Something was not going to stay on the side of grace. The chicken arrives, and Ofélia arrives. There is no systematic search and no capture. Clarice is in a position of receptivity and so is the text, which lets itself be invaded by an ensemble of signs. The text gathers without linking, it trembles and is always about to disappear. It is situated in a space that is hard to narrate, where signs are not verbal, but signs of silence and of looks. We continue to hear a silence and experience its lightness, its imperceptibility.

Clarice describes Ofélia's family which is a bit savage though socialized through a project. Everything happens in hallways or in elevators where the space is extremely violent since intimacy and distance are the most strongly marked. With Ofélia, the textual play focuses on the child but it also introduces the story of the Hindu and of English colonialism. There is the story of birth and of a whole semantic or symbolic network of childhood, of kinship structures, never expressed in a classical mode. In fact, the child himself may be the parent. There are all kinds of variations on the child, especially around the story of the chick, with the accent on sexual difference. The first part of the story is masculine, the second part feminine. The scene of adoption of the little chick is important:

"Do you want to be its mummy?" (89).

This is the question the little boys ask the narrator-Clarice in the first paragraph. The text is full of compact paragraphs. From time to time, a short sentence appears all by itself, marking a turning point each time. The first one is that of the adoption of the chick. It constitutes an Oedipal scene in which the youngest boy specifically asks his mother to be the chick's mother. The other break takes place in relation to the hand:

"So I stretched out my hand and held the chick" (90).

To hold out one's hand is a highly symbolized gesture. It is a materialization at the level of the body of the deepest communication and almost defies explanation.

The second part of the story deals with how Ofélia was almost never a child because she never had to deal with desire. One of the aspects of the text deals with desire. We could give the text a different title. The event is a belated birth, but not any kind of birth. Ofélia gives birth to herself because Clarice-as-mother allows her to bring herself into the world. In this text, everyone ends up belonging to

"The Foreign Legion." Yet one could bring about the play of a letter and replace the *g* with an *s*: the text works on "lesion." And we could not work on "lesion" without its being foreign.

The dialogue between Clarice and Ofélia is one of extreme violence. The antagonists have very different levels of consciousness. Because of the difference in maturity, Clarice precedes the girl in the analysis of the scene. By preceding her, she has a loving position in relation to the protagonist and does everything to guide her. She has to go through complex operations that can be expressed only through speech and silence. But to the reader, everything is told. An enormous struggle between Ofélia and Clarice takes place. The text is organized around very marked oppositions, such as immobility and movement, silence and a breaking of silence. When Ofélia's locks are immobilized, the realistic notation is symbolically charged. Ofélia plays a lot off her hoops and locks. She begins in a strong phase, the first one of the struggle. Absentmindedly, Clarice types on her machine.

"'What's that?' [Ofélia] asked" (95).

Clarice's first sentence is one of denegation and resistance. There is going to be a skirmish over naming and the designation "chick" reveals the chick's presence. Ofélia resists with all her might. She does not want to admit:

"The chick?" (95).

From the moment she says "chick," she is moving into the direction of what she still opposes, that is, the desire of the other. She knows it is a chick but she must call it "it." Under the "it," the chick is represssed. Ofélia silently summons Clarice to do the work of naming for her. It is a behavior that would resemble that of obsessional neurosis. It is taboo. The importance of the chick is measured in Ofélia's silence. It is enormous and fabulous, but she is not yet at the stage where she could say: "Ah, a little chick." She has to follow the whole trajectory of initiation into language as repression, symbolization, and mastery opposed to pleasure. Clarice knows this and from the moment she hears that young Ofélia is on the path leading toward the chick, she helps her along with all the intelligence in the world. She no longer precedes, but accompanies her little by little and lends herself to this kind of slow practice, to this almost ritualistic repetition. In order to help her approach the chicken and recognize "oh, it is a chick," as every little child would say, she has to cross all the deserts, all the zones of petrifaction of the body until Ofélia's second birth. At the same time, there is an immense power struggle. It is Hegelian, at the same time beautiful and dramatic. If Clarice had given the chick too soon, Ofélia would not have been in a state of receiving it. Clarice would have deprived her of the ability to receive. In order to be able to give her the little chick, she must first stage the scene in which the little girl will go of her own accord to see the chick, to desire and take it. Clarice undoes repression. It is almost an instant cure. Repetition of the "it" marks the stubborn refusal of the little girl who does not know how to receive.

"'That!' she said unbending."

"We might have remained there forever in the vicious circle of 'that?' and 'what!', were it not for the extraordinary resolution of that child who, without saying a word, but with an expression of intransigent authority, forced me to hear what she herself was hearing" (95).

We are still in mastery. Ofélia would like Clarice to give in to desire before she does. For the moment, the two rhythms are not completely harmonized. When Clarice says:

"It's the chick" (95),

she hurts the girl. She engages familiarity and does not accompany the girl into strangeness. The chick is known. The mechanism of the little one consists in resistance and make-believe covering up what she knows from the very beginning. She gives in slowly, not to Clarice, but to her own desire. Clarice helps her accede to her own desire. Clarice is aware that the girl is entering into a struggle of love. When she says:

"I bought a chick,"

she knows the explanation is useless but decides to play the game of Ofélia's liberation. We leave from point zero, from the market place. The echo of the inscription of the chick will lead toward the real chick. The scene that is being produced is that of the possession of the child through the chick.

"Before my fascinated eyes, like some emanation, she was being transformed into a child" (96).

We learn that, reproducing her own mother, she had incarnated the figure of the repressive mother. She was so much of an anal mother that she laid down the law. She was a little law-woman up to the moment when, through Clarice's intercession, traversing the rite, she is being transformed into what she always should have been. After a painful scene, she arrives at "yes," but through a long labor, similar to the bodily labor of a woman.

"Shall I risk it? shall I give way to feeling? she asked herself. Yes, she replied to herself, through me:

And my first yes enraptured me" (97).

There are many yeses on this page until the admirable sentence:

"Until then, I had never seen courage" (97).

Ofélia puts down her arms. She speaks for the first time in a tone accompanied by shame:

"Is it a chick?" (97).

Is it a boy? a girl? She speaks of herself too. There is agreement between her and Clarice but the struggle continues. Ofélia is only halfway there:

"Ah, a little chick, she said pensively" (97).

The "ah" puts something into language, into grammar from the register of breathing. It is an exclamation of surprise and of arrival.

Clarice is guiding her at the right pace. She takes her slowly to the next stage, helps her overcome her resistance. Ofélia's speech is so much of the Lacanian *je sais bien mais quand-même,* that she has to advance by retreating. She pretends not to understand what she understands because she is so fragile. Clarice plays the part of midwife who sometimes tells the woman to push, at other times to hold back.

"In the kitchen, I repeated, sounding authoritarian for the first time, and without adding anything further" (98).

She sees that the child regresses, so she pushes. At some point, Clarice's maneuver almost aborts:

"Why don't you go into the kitchen and play with the little chick?" (98).

She goes too fast and Ofélia takes advantage. So Clarice adds:

"Only if you want to."

A person who loves has to face Clarice's problem of what it is to give to the other all the benefit of desire.

"Did I have the right? But I had no choice" (98).

It is the same "if you want" as in "Felicidade clandestina" ("Secret Happiness").

"Go and see the little chick only if you want to, I then repeated with the extreme harshness of someone who is saving another" (98).

She has to get there. Clarice measured all the impasses, difficulties, knots in the scenes of confrontation between desire, law, and permission. Permission is related to prohibition. As soon as one allows, one prohibits. Clarice takes on the most difficult position, that of giving the desire to the other. This cannot be done except in the mode of charity and disinterest. That is why Ofélia is finally enraged:

"Well, I'm off to see the chick in the kitchen" (99).

It is a moment of defeat for both. The angry child goes into the kitchen not as child, but with a rounded back. The two have not succeeded in finding harmony in the happiness of pleasure. One has the impression of being at a negotiating table. Clarice accompanies her the best she can:

"Yes, off you go, I said slowly" (99).

But the miracle takes place when Ofélia is in the kitchen alone, without the combative face-to-face encounter. At last, the meeting between the two chicks can take place.

"It's a little chick, she said" (99).

There is a moment of recognition followed by the strange and marvelous episode of laughter, where the tension is at last resolved for a moment.

The simplicity of dialogue is in relation with the situation of scenes of this kind. Those are extreme scenes, situated in the space of birth, situated at the level of the primal scream. The scene is written in detail, in a rarefied way. Clarice's texts are written there where the first words emerge from a silence that may be a silence beyond or below.

Tragically, for such a dialogue to keep its extraordinary lightness and power, its ability to reach our understanding, given our generalized deafness, our heaviness and precipitation, we have to resign ourselves to do what Clarice does and accompany it with a substructure, with a kind of immense commentary from which the birds can take their flight. All the intelligence of one's body should go into certain words. An immense commentary on mute scenes surrounds the dialogue. Writing saturates the whole space, which, in fact, is mute.

"I also knew that only a mother determines birth" (89).

For Clarice, the mother is the good mother. I would say only one thing in order to render Clarice's text unassailable. While she takes every possible precaution in respect to idealism, refining and dividing her text incessantly especially on the subject of love — Clarice is not duped by words — there *are* places where she no longer divides. When she says "mother," the connotation is always that of the good mother. In "Felicidade clandestina" ("Secret Happiness"), she named her "the good mother," while here she is an absolute "mother." This kind of confidence can be questioned.

"I, a little presumptuously, felt happy" (87).

There are distinctions, differentiations between three types of attitudes: the husband's, the boys', and hers. It is only in the *après-coup,* in the aftereffect, that we realize that she is the only one who dared to be happy. The others have different types of behavior and other affects. One also realizes that to be happy is something audacious. All is happening between the eyes and the mouth, except at certain moments when we find Clarice's hand. The text focuses on relations to desire, on its absence, its presence, its evolution. It goes through a look that speaks in a mute text. It is also a text on reading, since Clarice is in a position of reading. She deciphers others incessantly. The text works especially on the opposition between general silence and words and between silence and chirping. Something violent happens libidinally: the apparition, the birth, and the event "chick" strike the ear. The moment of affect is marked by chirping. Often in Clarice we had visual scenes but here the event is audible. Philosophically, this can go very far.

For me, her allusion to Christ is saved by the fact that everyone is Christ. Everyone pays and represents the experience of Christ. The little girl is at the same time chicken and egg. Clarice pushes everything to a sublime degree where to love is not to love oneself. She herself retreats at the end in order not to let Ofélia feel the weight of love. Her incredible tact comes through in the sentence:

"I also knew that only a mother determines birth, and ours was the love of those who take pleasure in loving" (89).

The good mother is the one who does not take herself for a mother and succeeds in absenting herself. She does not precede, she follows. She has to let the child *make* her into a mother. She has to be the locus and not the master of birth. She has to let happen the ultimate scene of encounter between the little girl and the chick — in other words, the scene between the little girl and herself. Here, the text can be taken as exemplifying another mirror stage. It could be put in place of Lacan's text. It is another analysis of the child's coming upon herself, of the process of individuation and of difference. It is not analyzed theoretically but told, written. To resolve birth, the mother has to accept dissolution. There is a comical side in Clarice that lets her be tortured by the little girl out of charity and maturity, and to mark that she is neither solicitor nor complacent. She tells us that the little girl is not likable for, if the girl were not this way, Clarice would be of a virginal and sugary maternity. Ofélia fights for life and not against the other. The only moment when what is happening between the two could be called love is the moment of approval and inspiration, when she speaks of the "tortuous love" (99). After she has accompanied Ofélia to her birth, she says that love can take place only on condition that the mother be dead. And she writes it:

"This also meant my freedom at last and without any quarrel; farewell, and I smiled with nostalgia" (100).

The separation is marked strongly, and then she says:

"Oh, do not be so frightened! Sometimes people kill for love" (101).

She says this in the absence of the girl, knowing that scenes of good faith are often accompanied by violence that can lead to death. "The Foreign Legion" is the story of a passion.

The little girl plays an inverted game of *fort-da* with the mother. It is she who comes and goes. The mother tolerates it, but makes her understand that she suffers:

". . . there's no need to hurry back" (93).

Yet the little girl only has the mastery of a little girl. She has two levels, that of categorical affirmation and that of denegation. Clarice has infinitely multiple levels. She accepts being Ofélia's playground, and thus the question of goodness is eliminated.

In the first part, the little boys are so small that they believe in parental power. There are two moments in this story, that is to say, one narrative follows another. Some threads cross both parts but there are also interruptions. First there are little boys, then a little girl. The stakes are no longer the same. In the first part it is a question of goodness and of "bad" goodness. There is something the parents have not told their children. As adults we grow out of this opposition. The boys accuse the parents of not doing something for the chick or humanity. The parents have not told their children that one cannot do anything for humans except help them give themselves birth.

Then, there is the exercise of love. There is a difference between the child and the chick. One can love the chick without psychology. Love for the chick comes back to oneself. It is easy, one loves it and loves oneself. To the child one can give, but only on condition of tearing oneself away from a scene in which one gives something to a smaller one that chirps louder.

The height of love is shown when it is a question of hatred. It requires true abnegation of the one who wants to bring about birth. It requires withstanding what, narcissistically, is hard to take. Clarice lets things happen in order to let the girl act. She does not love the little girl. She is exasperated, but she tolerates

Ofélia in order to give her access to her path, even if she is exasperated. All this takes place against a true background of love that, after Ofélia has left, can be expressed in grandeur and abundance, since it no longer risks threatening the girl.

By contrast, in Blanchot's *The Madness of the Day,* I can mix some cocktails around the law of gender and the madness of the day, on the madness of gender and the law of the day. The text deals with essential values — such as madness — that we also find in Clarice Lispector. But in Blanchot, madness is given over to the police and to medicine. He has a rather leftist point of view with all the implicit violence that goes with it. In Clarice, madness leads more toward revelation, to extreme delicacy, to everything that can be read about the agents in her story entitled "The Egg and the Chicken."[4] Similar zones are in question. Blanchot's short text, *The Madness of the Day,* begins with this well-known sentence:

"Je ne suis ni savant ni ignorant (19). [I am not learned; I am not ignorant (5).]"

This is completely inscribed in Blanchot's economy: I was born neither nor. Everything happens in the space of a certain type of negative that could be, but is not, the sublime negative we find in Clarice Lispector. In Blanchot, it is really always a retreat and an incessant evasion. The other focus of meaning in *The Madness of the Day* is the metaphor brought about between the day as date and as something that escapes quickly in the text. At a given point, it is a question of seven days:

"Yes, seven days at once, the seven deadly lights, become the spark of a single moment, were calling me to account" (11).

The reader can remain in the simple illusion that it is about seven days making the day, giving light, but Blanchot plays on the masculine gender of the day *(le jour):* the seven capital sins. There is a constant play of mirroring and reversal that wants to subvert the distinction of gender. Insistence is placed on masculine and feminine, on a kind of aborted reflection on the difference of gender. At the same time, the text deals with a literary genre, the *récit,* story, and the last sentence reads:

"A story? No. No stories, never again" (18).

In Blanchot, it is a question of a story that accompanies what is without story, that answers the demand for a story carried by the text. The text continues to ask the subject to tell what happened to him. The text tells what will never be told. These are important and troubling stakes. The themes that are more or less treated in Blanchot, where it is always a matter of avoidance, *are* dealt with by Clarice Lispector. In Blanchot we find models of tactics of avoidance, of inverse recognition of the vital importance of certain questions or positions. In Clarice Lispector, the positions are always in movement. The most striking example is in *The Passion according to G. H.,* where she advances from what could be called an acute note of contradiction to the next acute note of the next contradiction, up to a moment of ecstasy and revelation.

The question of the story *(récit)* is also useful for reading "The Foreign Legion." To begin, I decided to camp inside the text, to use one of Kafka's expressions, between the city and the desert, because it is around campfires that the essential part of this text is situated. But we have to pay attention to the technique of storytelling as well. Though we stay in its heart, we must remember that the whole story deals with the recall of a memory, with an amnesia of such subtlety that we cannot even say that the story belongs to the order of memory. "The Foreign Legion" deals simultaneously with the return and the nonreturn of Ofélia.

What is the issue? In order to deal with questions of gifts and presents, some passages of Jacques Derrida's *Glas* might be helpful. We also have to deal with the signifier I proposed: "lesion," as suffering. How is one to evaluate, interpret, this suffering? There is something absolutely tragic in this text that Clarice gives, or rather dedicates, to the little girl — she can precisely not give it to her — that is a lesson of life, a complete and difficult lesson of having to face the value of a certain type of suffering. But when Clarice finally succeeds in formulating it, the little girl is no longer there.

In Clarice, happiness is always secret. Perhaps at a certain level the beautiful, which belongs to aesthetics, is replaced by truth. The beautiful is annulled in a kind of neutralization of the beautiful and the ugly. At the limit, instead of the too beautiful, we have what is too much alive, even mortally alive. Something is so much alive that one can die of it, or it can die. This is the message that is being sent out in "The Foreign Legion." The chick, like the child, trembles at the limit of its own disappearance. Most people have difficulty living side by side with life *and* death. If one says that life is mortal, there follows a psychological and affective state of trembling and emotion, of passion, a moral state of what, very coarsely, can be called love, that is a need to go on breathing on the fire. It is tiring and terrifying. In Clarice's story, there is an element that is deep and mysterious, on the side of night:

"But if a woman were to appear to me in the night holding a child in her lap" (89). This, in Clarice's paradoxical logic, is situated on the side of a literal brilliance.

When assuming the maternal function, Clarice dares to be harsh. Her harshness is not negative. The other has to be given a chance to be born without being helped prematurely. The mother has to be able to let the other suffer until maturation. We can distinguish between primal scenes and scenes of birth, scenes where everything that had been repressed explodes, that is, generally, the alterity of the other. In *The Passion according to G. H.*, Clarice had the revelation of a rapport between her self and the mortal, immortal flesh of the cockroach. Such a continuity can only exist in a rapid suspension of the self, though the latter always comes back right away. It is a sacrificial process. In "The Foreign Legion," another version of the same experience takes place. Here, motherhood is written as a witnessing, as assistance.

"What is it?"

But whatever it was, it was no longer there. Through writing, Clarice suggests the brevity of the moment. She is going to insist on the rapid, imperceptible aspect of birth. Since she has been a witness, she can tell us afterward what she saw. If it had happened to her, she would have had to rewrite *The Passion*.

To keep it going is the positive torture of the one who plays the (good) mother, not of the one who is going to give birth, but of the one who lets people be born. The child has to do the labor herself and can only be born if the mother makes her go to the end of her own birth process. Clarice describes how to transform while accompanying, for example, in silence. This does not mean that there is no answer, but that the mother will not give an answer because the child herself must produce it. Her silence, as she says, is saying yes:

"Yes, my silence replied to her, yes."

Everything is happening in an affirmative silence that is not a silence. Her first "yes" provoked the birth of the girl. At that moment, the girl's heart starts to beat. In the first phase of the story, Clarice was her playground — then she became the ground of the formulation of desire, of the constitution of a subject, torn by the other. Clarice is the territorial silence from which the child can ask questions while answering them in the very act of being born. Child mortality comes from *being*, rather than from *having* born. Clarice promotes birth as an activity. If one is born without having made an act of birth, one is dead.

According to philosophers such as Jacques Derrida, there is no pure gift. One could say, though, that if a gift is to take place, it would be in these scenes of a very heavily symbolized maternity that goes much beyond an anatomic maternity and consists in letting oneself be taken by the other. It is the most difficult thing in the world. What needs to be given is a gift to take, not a gift of something that is already there. The possibility, the violent right to take something that has been accorded has to be given.

A dead I, closed off from its vital cut, arrives at a living I through the test of desire. The dead I deprived itself of the other who opens and induces suffering. It is only left as a question mark that is not followed by its construction. This is accompanied with her sentence:

" 'I must go home now' " (100).

that is to say, back to her prison, with its hoops, locks, and cake decorations.

" 'If you don't mind' " (100).

Ofélia returns to the law and permission. The drama, as in a Greek tragedy, ends badly, after a moment of absolute happiness which has been the moment of birth, the moment when Ofélia has desired everything, including pain, everything that includes being for nothing.

We could be mistaken about such a story and think that the death of the chick was related to sadism in a children's story. Not at all. Ofélia killed herself and the desiring being in her. She was involved in a story of love that was beyond her strength. Yet it was closer to love and *not* just desire. Of the two families in the story, one can say that one is fluid and the other is dry. Fluids in Clarice are generally marked positively, with a discreet materiality she does not exploit. For her, this is all quite symptomatic.

Ofélia's quest goes through the ear. The chick is present in the first part, but in the second everything happens in its absence, in relation to the gift.

The turning point of the text occurs around the question: "But if a woman were to appear to me in the night . . ." (89). In the first part of "The Foreign Legion," Clarice raises questions of love, desire, wisdom. The text is strong but light. There are little boys whose number increases to include the father. Everyone turns into a son making demands on the mother. The second episode deals with Clarice's courage in accepting not to know, of living in not-knowing *(non-savoir)*. The second part, introduced by "if," is not situated in reality. We are suddenly in a mystical and symbolic space, in a scene that can only take place "if." It can only happen among women. In answer to the son's request, Clarice tells her powerlessness. In the scene between the mother and the sons, she tells her solitude in front of her sons' demand that she have power. But there is another kind of innocent power, or rather, an innocence of power, this time at the request of a woman. This occurs specifically "at night."

What follows is almost comical. The other family are tanned and well dressed. Clarice retreats to give them space. The movement, dictated to her by the situation, is close to Clarice's theoretical position: to give space to, to leave space for. The whole story turns around the staging of desire: Do I accept myself as a desiring being, in an open and painful relation with the other? Ofélia's mother goes as far as she can. In the scene on the park bench she confides to Clarice that she would have liked to learn how to decorate cakes. The reader sees at the same time the limit of her desire. Her libido is arrested at the stage of decoration. But her confidence is a desire to expose something of her insides. When Clarice understands what has been given to her in spite of herself, she tries to give it back, because her generosity is faultless. It is accompanied by a tiny little notation at the beginning: Clarice is alone because she who accompanies feels terribly alone. It is even the definition of the greatest solitude. A true solitude is not unbearable since it allows for otherness.

The two families are different, but not completely opposed. In Ofélia's family, a kind of closure is seen in the fact that her mother constantly comes to take her back, while Clarice constitutes herself in a space to be crossed. We can read in fine detail the story of Solomon's judgment — that is, the story of the two mothers in which the true mother gives up her child rather than letting him be cut into pieces. Similarly, Clarice drops Ofélia; she tries to get rid of her but never without a form of love. Toward the end, when Ofélia leaves, Clarice does not want to exert a desire to keep her but she had taken pleasure in presence. The text is full of little scenes of mourning.

The problem for Clarice is how to undo the prohibition that weighs down on Ofélia, or how to give her the chick. Precisely *without* giving it to her. How is she going to make her go to the kitchen? By not allowing her to go. By letting her take the chick with an extraordinary art of total nonreserve, since she lets the other take it and do with it what she wants. But desire submerges Ofélia in such a way that she takes only in order to lose. Clarice sees the maneuver of Ofélia's desire and closes her eyes. Clarice lets her do what she wants to the point of total abdication, something she can only achieve by working on her typewriter. She is conscious of the drama that takes place but lets Ofélia have the supreme experience. The question of breathing is of importance:

"Why — I wondered — why am I trying to breathe my life into her purple mouth?" (98).

Through this we hear that she is dead, is purple like someone who lacks air. Clarice often speaks of this mouth-to-mouth respiration, which is not that of a prompter on stage. She wants to give respiration, not inspiration. Freedom has to be given its chance, including the chance to lose itself. She says:

"I know I should have ordered her to go rather than expose her to the humiliation of such intense desire."

This is the height of contradiction and the hardest thing to do. The greatest position of kindness would be to relieve Ofélia's desire and say: I order you to take it. But that would be humiliating. It is a kind of double bind. Clarice says:

"I know that I should not have given her any choice and then she could say that she had been forced to obey."

I feel toward this text the way Ofélia feels toward the chick. Something tiny contains the secret of life and death.

"On the floor lay the dead chick."

Clarice does not mourn the chick but cries over Ofélia's fate. She would have liked the story to end well, or would have liked to be able to talk to Ofélia some more. Ofélia went back to her place, to the law, with a feeling of having done something wrong. After a moment of freedom she went back to a classical scene of judgment. Something happens that escapes Clarice at all levels.

Clarice mourns for Ofélia, and her ultimate message about killing out of love is addressed to other Ofélias. The story keeps haunting her at Christmas time, because she is in pain. Something did not happen — that is, the moment when Ofélia could have realized that she need not be afraid. Ofélia could not face the death of the chick, she was afraid, and Clarice did not succeed in ridding her of this fear.

In a certain way, Clarice likes Ofélia:

"It is Ofélia who did not return: she grew up. She went away to become the Indian princess whose tribe awaited her in the desert."

She goes over into another imaginary civilization. But the Hindu princess is someone dressed with veils and decorations. She is not the naked child Clarice invited her to be. Clarice does not speak of elevation but of ground and dust. Ofélia could not help going toward a destiny that Clarice does not consider to be the strongest or the truest.

When I spoke of "lesion," I referred to the moment when the wound is inflicted through the appearance of the chick — in other words, something strange in Ofélia's life. It is the sudden irruption of a truth, that of a self limited by the other. It is also Clarice's lesion expressed by something painful at the end. She does not have the impression that she is going to master all of Ofélia's affects. She expresses something of a lesion in the mode of fatigue:
"I was very tired."
I refer to the Hegelian dilemma in *The Phenomenology of Mind,* where being comes into consciousness through a first wound, through something that is the other. That is the lesson of culture and of civilization. When one is conscious and gives oneself to be desired, one gets hurt. The cultured position consists in being capable of elaborating this wound, in negating it in order to transform it into something positive, and to arrive at a feeling that the other is necessary as other and that the other as other is always painful and disquieting to the self.

Clarice does not embody banal charity. She knows that love is made of a part of hatred and that the moments of greatest intensity, those one could call love, are filled with hatred. Here, hostility links the protagonists. That is how we could speak of "lesion." To live one has to let oneself be hurt. Ofélia eliminates the cause of her lesion. This can happen in childhood. When we cannot take the violence of love, we suppress the object. Clarice's ultimate lesson is that one should not be afraid of loving, neither of letting the chick live, nor of not being able to refrain from killing it. The equivalent to "This is the way things are," which Clarice told the little boys in the first part, is:
"But I swear that this is breathing."
It is the very definition of the human and the living. And when we breathe, it hurts.

"The Foreign Legion" is a sublimely beautiful and tender text. The reader receives a real lesson on development, growth, and transformation that goes to the very end of its responsibility. An abandonment of responsibility is always tragic. The story is also a lesson in the inevitability of pain. As a tragedy of vital transformation, it is the story of passion but is much more painful than *The Passion according to G. H.* It is a demanding and comforting text and the reader has to share the courage of this text.

I must return to insist on what could be called the "last word" in a scene that takes place between Clarice and Ofélia, starting with a dilemma that goes through "therefore" and *fort-da.* We can work on what links the two feminine beings, questions of contact and noncontact, on attachment and detachment, on separation, on questions that for me are the most living, the most pressing, because they go through the body of a woman. The first part of "The Foreign Legion" goes through the masculine, the second through the feminine.

The story makes us see the extremely violent relationship of Ofélia, veiled and purple *(violet)*, with Clarice. Their rapport is fixed and rigid. Ofélia goes through a whole ritual of settling in each time she arrives at Clarice's apartment and before she opens her mouth. Her behavior as obsessional neurotic locks her up — it is continuously a question of her locks — and shuts her mouth. In this system of repetition, the *lock* is semantically charged. Everything is held together, locked together by her verbal "therefore." Ofélia tries to repress her formidable anguish, which is finally going to burst in relation to the chick. From the beginning, the bodies are deeply affected by what is going to happen. True birth will take place through Clarice as matrix, because with the real mother Ofélia is locked or walled in. The space of Clarice's silence is needed for something to happen. There is the surface scene, the dialogue described by "therefore." Ofélia seems to arrive at the locus of her desire while repressing it. She arrives where she needs to be so that something may happen, but she really does not want it to happen. In all these exchanges, these dialogues, the narration tells us that something of a true desire is not expressed. The narration does not do without a staging of the bodies: the two protagonists are face to face, each behind her machine. Ofélia's mechanical repetition can be perceived in her hoops and her rituals of settling in, but also in her way of saying "therefore." The little girl is mummified, in a position described as "with her hands folded on her lap." She gathers and closes herself, makes "therefore" to herself in these false exchanges and immobile movements that take place during the first phase. The break happens with the appearance of the chick. The little girl clutches herself in a way that produces closure and is destined to exclude any event or birth. But in a strange way, she also clutches Clarice. What keeps bringing her back is a kind of counter-therefore, expressed in the word "strange." "Therefore" and "strange" go together in inverse fashion. What she comes to look for — and Clarice guesses it — is something strange. She says to Clarice, "You are a strange woman."

Ofélia clutches Clarice in a tragic way that indicates the need she has of the other. What is negated by discourse and by the position of the body is undone by Clarice's gesture. The rigid shell cracks and something of a real body can appear. When Ofélia makes the gesture of reaching for the chick, her hand appears where there were but rigidly crossed fingers. The physical reaching out is also the moment when Ofélia goes out of herself:

"It's a little chick."

Ofélia, whose strategy had been to foresee everything, is moved by her own observation. At that point, she enters into a space of "more than seeing," similar to that of *The Passion according to G. H.* When there is no more prevision, there can be vision. The vision replaces the *coups* of "therefore" with *coups* of the chick:

" 'It's a little chick!' she said."
She looked at the chick in her outstretched hand, then looked at me, then looked once more at her hand" (99).

The look circulates in this scene. It is no longer a fixed trait between two people, but that of a moving revelation. At the same time, separation takes place. Ofélia's hand is still separated from her body. Then something begins to happen:

" 'Poor little thing, he's mine': and when she held the chick, it was with a hand deformed by delicacy. — Yes, it was love, tortuous love" (99).
At the moment when, at last, something passes from one body to the next, at the moment when she lets herself be moved, crossed by another life, she laughs and is torn in every direction. But right away, the imminence of the "therefore" is felt again:

" 'He is very tiny, therefore he needs a lot of attention' " (99).
The little girl does not know how *not* to know. A moment ensues when she no longer knows and that is where the essential astonishment occurs, where living things can happen. Throughout the entire story Clarice insists on the importance of not knowing:

"But if a woman were to appear to me in the night holding a child in her lap. And if she were to say: Take care of my child. I would reply: How can I? She would repeat: Take care of my child. I would reply: I cannot. She would insist: Take care of my child. Then — then, because I cannot remember anything and because it is night — then I would stretch out my hand and save a child. Because it is night, because I am alone in another person's night, because this silence is much too great for me, for I have two hands in order to sacrifice the better of the two, and because I have no choice" (89–90).

In all this, Clarice holds out the hand to heal, a condition of love without mastery.

Jacques Derrida, *Margins of Philosophy*: The Philosophical Text and Its Other

I want to digress and, after reading how the limit and otherness are inscribed in the poetic text of Clarice Lispector, I propose to read it in a philosophical text, that is to say in the first section of Jacques Derrida's *Margins of Philosophy,* entitled "To tympanize — philosophy," put alongside a text by Leiris. We read:

Philosophy has always insisted on this: thinking its other. Its other:
that which limits it and from which it derives its essence, its definition,
its production. To think its other: does this amount solely to *relever*
(aufheben) that from which it derives, to head the procession of its
method only by passing the limit? Or indeed does the limit, obliquely, by
surprise, always reserve one more blow for philosophical knowledge?
Limit/passage.[5]

Philosophy has always wanted to think its other, to interiorize, incorporate it. From the moment it thinks its other, the other is no longer other but becomes the same. It enters into the space of what can be thought, it loses its strangeness. In the same paragraph, Derrida, in order to strike another blow to philosophical knowledge, raises the question of whether the other would be able to escape this maneuver of incorporation at the limit or by surprise. Next to this passage, the quotations from Leiris underline philosophy's need to hold on, to grasp:

> The acanthus leaf copied in school when, for better or for worse, one learns to use the fusain, the stem of a morning glory or other climbing plant, the helix inscribed on the shell of a snail.

The real question is: Can there be otherness? Does philosophy accept otherness or does it reduce it to the Hegelian space that does nothing but dialecticize, annul, cancel, or incorporate it:

> This already enervated repercussion, of a kind that has not yet sounded, this timbered time between writing and speech, call for/ themselves a *coup de donc*.
> As soon as it perforates, one is dying to replace it by some glorious cadaver. It suffices, in sum, barely to wait (xxviii–ixxx).

> [Cette répercussion vannée déjà d'un type qui n'a pas encore sonné, ce temps timbré entre l'écriture et la parole (s') appellent un *coup de donc*.
> Dès qu'il perfore, on meurt d'envie d'y substituer quelque cadavre glorieux. Il suffit en somme, à peine, d'attendre (xxv).]

This is Derrida's problem. He never says anything simple and his utterances constantly divide themselves. The reader finds the contrary of what is being inscribed right before or right afterward. Derrida's thought is mobile and it is true that it remains undecidable. The two paragraphs are completely encrypted. The most contradictory meanings go through these four lines. There is a development on *vanner,* on *van,* which alludes to Artaud's Tarahumaras. Derrida alludes to a system of drums, a system of *van.* If one reads *répercussion vannée,* "an enervated repercussion," one also hears *vanné,* "tired." "D'un type qui n'a pas encore sonné [a kind that has not yet sounded]," is going to be *le type,* "a kind of," but also in colloquial French "a guy." "Le temps timbré entre l'écriture et la parole [this timbered time between writing and speech]," refers to the tympanum, the eardrum of repercussion, of dissemination, to the whole Derridean dilemma, but one also hears *timbré* in the sense of crazy or mad.

Everything that happens in the paragraph is something in the order of madness, of the oblique, of something that escapes reason. As soon as we read "perforating," we also hear *père fort,* the Hegelian father, the paternal figure, of which one knows that he is going to efface himself to leave a space. The good father in the

Hegelian model and moral is always the dead father. The *père fort* must be between Hegel and Oedipus; he must be displaced and transformed into a corpse. As soon as there is a *père fort,* one longs to substitute him with a glorious corpse. The *père fort* — Lacan took this up also — *perfore*. And for Derrida, this becomes an exchange between masculinity and femininity.

"One is dying to replace it by some glorious cadaver." The law would have to be eliminated so that the son who would no longer be subjected to the father can rise. But one dies nevertheless, of envy, or from killing.

"It suffices, in sum, barely, to wait." To wait for what? For a system of substitutions, of deaths, that is supposed to produce effects of life. We "wait" for three pages and arrive at the essay entitled "Différance," which begins with the following sentence:

"I will speak, therefore, of a letter."

And there follows the important article on *différance,* about the fact that writing and inscription are primary. There is no first and *then* an afterwards, the text has already begun, hence the first sentence which begins with *donc,* "therefore." Derrida underlines that, for him, a new relation to difference must be found because it has always already begun. But it is also true that difference in an undecidable system can only be annulled, and this is a woman reader's ongoing problem with Derridean texts. If one says to Derrida that his text ends with a corpse, he will say, but not at all, the corpse is not there. He will say that he only talks about it. One wants it to be there, but at the same time it is not true. Yet while reading it, we receive the effect of a corpse. We are in a very complex space. On the one hand, there is a discourse produced in extreme mobility, an undecidable practice where nothing is ever closed, but on the other hand, and at the same time, we continue to receive effects of death.

The *coup* of writing — and of the text — is to be capable of dismissing what reality could not stand. We touch upon a real bottom of reality, though philosophers would say that this is not true, that it is but an illusion. At a given moment, something has been decided, but it has been so by the body. Philosopy cannot say anything about it.

Since we are taken in a constituted ensemble of text, philosophy, and body, the discussion can be interminable. We can always accuse the other of illusion, phantasm, or projection. We cannot prove anything, we can only affirm or decide. Derrida is going to *decide* on the undecidable, the way he is going to *decide* on the side of an impossibility of deciding sexual difference. But in the same way, we can also decide on the side of a decidable that is not taken in any type of philosophical discourse — on the side of Clarice Lispector, for example, where knowledge no longer lays down the law, where not-knowing *(non-savoir)* takes over, not an ignorant nonknowing but an open knowing, which lets things happen.

If one stays in the space of the *coup de donc* (therefore) one accepts the proposition Derrida demonstrated that everything has already begun. It intersects with

Heidegger's statement: There is, being, that is, something that is affirmed. In Clarice, it would be on the side of the gift. For her, there *is* gift, there *is* having. But what she says cannot be demonstrated: it can only be experienced, lived, or rejected. Of course, some worlds, like Ofélia's, are ordered by the law of the *donc,* of "therefore." One wonders how Ofélia was born and whether she came into the world with her locks. But Clarice lets us see that there can be interruption, an opening of the lock and, by surprise, birth.

The problem of this kind of discussion which, so far, has the same stake as philosophy, is — and that is what Derrida keeps on saying — the incorporation of the limit. Can we imagine that the incorporation of the limit reserves always another turn to philosophical knowledge that, even if the limit would take a leap, would still be in a hurry to catch up with it? The problem with philosophical discourse is that it can be developed rapidly in an abstract way, in spirals. But there is no space for living chicks. The latter can be found only in poetic texts. There are tulips in philosophical texts on aesthetics. But tulips have no legs, they are planted, inscribed, subjected to the look. Philosophers have treated immobile objects. Heidegger wrote on the pitcher but not on the chick. To work on what escapes can only be done poetically.

Kierkegaard declares that, as philosopher, he cannot say anything about Abraham. He can only follow him. But Clarice can *be* Abraham. Kierkegaard speaks the truth of the philosopher, after which he must become mad. We may wonder whether, at that moment, he is still a philosopher. Perhaps yes. By association, I remember a remark by Philippe Sollers, a kind of publicity slogan opening a book of his: "Women are death." And he adds that he does not understand why women are not happy with this statement, because, after all, death is life. He could take any passage from Freud's *Beyond the Pleasure Principle* that shows how life is the path to death and analytically, theoretically, he would be correct. But we read: women are death. This is precisely the example of what, in fact, emerges from the textual space. When we read Sollers's sentence — and even if we argue afterward — we have read an effect of death. When we read a text, we should be able to make a musical, tonal evaluation. What effects does the text produce on the reader? An effect of life or death? Is what remains going to be suffering or pleasure? In Clarice's texts, whatever the suffering and the passage through loss, what remains, perhaps, is *never* death, or the corpse. In "The Foreign Legion," the corpse of the chick implicated in the text will not remain.

Love and passion are inscribed in two different spaces, though at one point they flow into each other. In love, there is labor with the other, of the other, through the other. It is a question of presence or absence of the other and concerns the impact and the power of the other on the self. The most difficult thing is to be loved, to receive the love from, to be taken in the love of, the other. Here, I say things that Blanchot could recuperate. The love the other bears you is not a bad thing. But the responsibility of love, of being loved is the most difficult thing in the world. An exemplary trajectory — it can be a solitude — touches in an acute way on the movement of love. What happens is silence, the absolute, Abraham. Something cannot be said but only lived. Is passion without other? Not necessarily. Passion is the moment when two people, in a miraculous way and in a time that cannot last, are absolutely at the same height, as if the vibrations of one being were produced in the cadence and rhythm of the other. It is always of the order of a summit. But love, to speak in Kleistian terms, is the curve, the path, to the limit. It is as if the movement of passion consumed, burnt all the elements of the other that make up the labor of love. Yet love itself, a complex composition, is full of nonlove.

"The Foreign Legion" is composed of a succession of moments of surging. The structure of the text, as well as the structure of the protagonists, is constituted by instants of appearance, like that of Ofélia, of a surging of being, of affect and of emotions. It is accompanied and followed by astonishments and I take "astonishments" in a strong sense of the word, as a suspense and a brief moment of immobilization. Something happens in this moment of immobility — for example, the petrifaction of Ofélia into the locks of Medusa. Yet the story is taken through a double process of mutation, that of Ofélia's transformation from a false woman into a true child, and that of the bursting in the psychic, imaginary body of something that had been repressed — for example, Ofélia's desire. A revolution of the whole person produces signs that had never been made, as if one accepted *coups* of life. These *coups* are always lived as tearing, as hurting. Here we are close to *The Madness of the Day* and other texts. In the universe of mystical bursting, the event itself is always lived as a tearing of the thick flesh of resistance, as a happy wound but as a wound nevertheless.

The moment of laughter is particularly important. Another kind of writing could have erased the trace of this event. But Clarice makes it appear as an event. In Blanchot's *Madness of the Day* we also find a foregrounding of certain events without which writing would disappear. We can think of the famous passage giving the narrator's vision of an event in the street in which Blanchot restores the scene for the reader through writing.

To assist me in reading the stakes of a game of *fort-da* in "The Foreign Legion," I want to recall another text by Derrida, "Le legs de Freud" ("Freud's Legacy") in *The Post Card*.[6] What happens to Ofélia could be compared to what happens to Freud's grandson with his spool. Ofélia is someone who wants to keep the mastery of all arrivals. She makes things come and go, she masters what could happen, to begin with herself.

Freud's little boy is someone who works on separation. His story is complementary. What Freud puts forth in the story of the little boy — and what Derrida takes up — is the decomposition and the direction of the movement. Freud names two times: *verschwinden,* "to disappear" and *wiederkommen,* "to return," — as the sum of interest for the little boy. For him, the return constitutes the moment of pleasure. For Ofélia, it is less the moment of return than the abandonment of mastery and the possibility of an appearance. Freud noted that there was a division at work in the scene that was happening in the little boy's room. In the hidden psychic scene, the little boy does not feel like being at the mercy of his mother's appearances and disappearances. He wants to get rid of his passivity. How can he do so, given his position? By inventing a game that reproduces the comings and goings of his mother, except that this time the child orders the movements of the mother substitute—that is, his spool. The child keeps the first phase, or the part of the game consisting in sending objects far away from him. The text raises questions of economy: Is throwing toys away a game or work? That is the question Freud raises for Derrida. No one knows. How do we separate play from work? The child is supposed to play at distancing. Freud says that the game consists in rendering the toys useful for something else than play. The game is a mutation of the *function* of the object, a reduction to a simple "go away" and a keeping at a distance.

The other, more complex phase is that of the spool. The spool is attached to a thread and the child is at the same time the one who sends it away and the one who brings it back. He is *both* the child and the parent. He disperses and gathers, he gives and takes back, all by himself. He is everybody at once. He both plays and works. He is part of this moving ensemble but eventually, everything comes back to him, the way everything always comes back anyhow. And here, I would like to say something that commits me on a theoretical level: The story of the little boy is a masculine story. Freud interprets it along the lines of "everything must come back to the little boy who is everybody at the same time." The object that is moving around is the penis, with which he can do his exercises of castration and resistance to castration. He plays with distance and separation. One could take a differential *point d'appui* (basis). After all, Clarice's story is marked by differences. On the one hand, there are the little boys, and on the other, there is the little girl. The little girl precisely does not bring everything back to herself and this becomes a problem. First, she has something in common with the little boy. She needs to master the movements. Ofélia comes and goes and Clarice is in a position of passivity. Everything comes together in this structure, which for the little girl is the closed, anguished structure that does not let anything happen. Ofélia comes to see Clarice, in order to repeat indefinitely so that nothing can happen. Then there is a real break, the bursting of a kind of closed and stifling structure. The event *has* to happen, the chick has to come. Ofélia has no mastery over it. And Clarice understood that. This is the only part of the story that happens on Clarice's side. She does everything so that the chick arrives at Ofélia, by surprise. If not, she, Clarice, would keep some of the chick for herself. Hence she does not *name* what chirps, or she would prevent it from happening. She has to let the chick strike Ofélia. In order for something to happen, something must escape the mortal mechanism of language. What happens precedes language and there are no words to express it. The work is similar to that in *The Apple in the Dark*. Ofélia is a real machine. Then, miraculously, something unforeseen happens that is beyond her strength. As long as the spool, the object of the *fort-da,* was there, she left and remembered. With the chick, she tries a *fort-da,* to feel all the torments of love, but at the same time, something fatal happens and infiltrates love, that is, the immediate virtuality of death. In love, she thinks of death. To love is to struggle so that births do take place and to continue to win against death. Ofélia lost her autonomy only once. She succeeded in losing only once, but to gain a life, of course.

In the Lacanian elaboration, the surging of the subject, constituted at the price of a division, is considered as necessary and positive. Lacan's displacement of the "cogito ergo sum" is the by now classical critique of Cartesian naïveté, its categorical affirmation of the "I think therefore I am," and of the limit of doubt. Psychoanalysis by definition subverts the logical, undivided I. To re-mark the division, one can write Descartes's sentence while cutting it: I think: therefore I am. All I do is think, and that is subject to uncertainties. Lacan's displacement consists of a formula or a word play. We do not have the same values in Clarice Lispector. We find an "it," but for her the "I" is bad. It is a loss. The only moment when there could be a subject occurs when Ofélia says:

"Well, I am going to see the chick in the kitchen."

From the moment she gives in, she gives up a little mastery. When she says: "I am going to see the chick in the kitchen," she announces that she is finally going to follow her desire, whereas before she preceded and closed it. But the tragedy with the chick occurs. Her final "So, I am going," is not at all the same as the "I am going into the kitchen." It rather moves in the direction of loss. The only moment of true happiness is that of laughter; then, again, we are on a descending slope.

Maurice Blanchot, *The Madness of the Day*: A Text of Evasion

The Madness of the Day is a book that hardly drives the reader mad. Though it speaks about it, and admirably so, the text fights madly against madness:

"But I was scorched from head to foot; at night I would run through the streets and howl; during the day I would work calmly" (6).

The narrator behaves like a madman at night, but at that moment we have to hear "day," because it is to see the day that is true madness. As a text that bites its tail and begins the way it ends, it has to be read over. We cannot get out of the text, though it constantly is a question of getting out of doing so. *The Madness of the Day* is also a piece of writing that does not succeed in beginning, and that, at the same time, does not finish to begin *not* to begin, or *not* to begin to begin. All the classical oppositions that would give form — and this is also Clarice's question: How to give form to something that would be continuous — are reshuffled in a system of paradoxes where inside and outside flow into each other, where beginning and end are continuous. In Blanchot's text, night and day can be exchanged, enclosures do not look like enclosures, and madness reigns as reason supreme.

Blanchot completely masters his text. Not the slightest trace of an effect of meaning escapes him. His text reinscribes incessantly. A sum of elements work like mad from one end to the other. That is why the reading is so difficult. There is not a word that does not come back ten times, displaced, transformed, or repeated. It is the least gratuitous text in the world. It is a real trap for the unconscious and is totally dissimulated. The text is not really lying, but Blanchot refuses access to the reader. The text jealously keeps its secret, so that when we finish reading we have not read anything. But at the same time, Blanchot makes allusions to what he reserves (keeps), because *The Madness of the Day* is a text of retention, of translation. The text reads as if Blanchot had walled in something that had happened. His wall is made of mosaics, composed of specific words, not just any kind of words. One is tempted to do a subversive reading, to lift certain veils to get a glimpse of things, of a certain force of reading and living, despite the prohibition on seeing.

We end up not reading the text if we begin to read it seriously. We end up being referred back to this kind of wall so that, what the text never talks about, what we never talk about because the text is constructed so that we never do, is precisely what it is about: that is, madness. The text does not want to give itself to be read. That is what it is written for and that is Blanchot's strength. His text is a *coup de forme*. The project of this text is a dissimulation that functions as a screen. Blanchot's text is written without mercy, without grace, because it is about madness — and I am critical of such a project — considered by the narrator as the greatest treasure, which he will not give up. The treasure of madness exists but is completely inaccessible. For Blanchot, the path is outside, one stays outside, and the text sends as its message: You will not enter; I do not want you to enter; I will not give you my madness. I will talk to you about it, but I will not give it to you. The text produces its own outside. It is completely enclosed and saturated. The reader wanders along the text's closure. Blanchot wants us to stray along the closure so that there is a total absence of chronology, since inside madness there is no time, only the day, eternal or ephemeral, it matters little.

The text is written in the imperfect, the tense of narration. We read the text, led on by the imperfect that makes us believe that it is past, but at no point does the text make us believe that something *is* past. In this mad text, there is not outside and the past is still here.

The Madness of the Day may be a text on God, on madness become God. It is as if Blanchot said: What if I took myself for God? But for what God? God for us, in our mythologies and religions? At the limit, one could say that the narrator is impotent as an all-powerful God, and that the text is about impotence as well as power. It is evident that God is infinitely powerful, but that does not mean anything for us. As humans, we can say that God is impotent, since he can act only as God, and so his value or his qualification does not have currency in a human world.

The much quoted first sentence: "*Je ne suis ni savant ni ignorant* [I am not learned; I am not ignorant]," is rightly taken in its banality of a double negation, which sends us into a world of impotence and castration. It gives us the tone of the text. But it is also the definition of God, who is neither knowledgeable nor ignorant. All the definitions of God cannot be produced except in a space of negative theology. God is not visible, he is neither this nor that, he is naked. God is not the one who speaks. Rather, the text is the confession of a man elevated to God's state of neither/nor. The divine situation is outside of the world, outside of the *je/u,* of the I and of play, outside of time, of an event, of creation. God creates, but he is not created. In the book of Genesis, the creation of God is not seen and for good reason. In Blanchot, we see the history of a man who, through accidents, finds himself catapulted to the trans/final place of human experience, signified in the fact that he sees the day, since he said it himself in the text:

"I see this day and outside it there is nothing" (6).

The light of the day allows us to see. We see and do not see the day. We see the day only in the linguistic expression "to see the day." Inside the day, thanks to the day, we are able to see. The narrator sees what it is impossible to see, that is, the very condition of vision. To say that we see the day is a metaphor. The text plays on birth. One day the narrator sees the day, though he is already born. He takes a *coup de lumière,* a stroke of light, a figure to say what is said otherwise in a less prohibiting manner in both Lispector and Kafka. In the final text of *Hochzeits-vorbereitungen auf dem Lande*[7] Kafka states that to have been on the other side of death is tantamount to having seen God. One cannot see God face to face. But it so happens that Moses *almost* saw him. Those are *limit experiences.* Clarice continuously talks about them, but she does not play, like Blanchot. She never says "I have seen the day" yet the whole process of *The Passion according to G. H.* consists in letting the reader understand that there is a super-vision, capable of seeing our quotidian organization, the world, appearances, reality in general, everything that the economy of ordinary life prevents us from seeing. It has to be noted too that he who sees what we cannot see without totally changing our economy becomes strange. He who sees what Clarice gives us to see — because Clarice *gives* us to see, while Blanchot *prohibits* us from seeing — he who sees that the egg is white, who says "the white of the egg," exhausts something. Blanchot incessantly alludes to this unique experience of the surprise of the world. In *The Madness of the Day,* the narrator has surprised the truth of the world. He saw what history, news, and daily life organize in such a way that we never perceive it and continue to act like well-behaved citizens: that is, the secret of life and death. These are essential questions, touching on the strangeness of the mortality of human life, which is also capable of going momentarily beyond mortality, of glimpses of eternity, of what we never think about, because we are constantly running, taking the subway, getting up from chairs, and imagining that our fate would be replaced by television, by newspapers, a fate decided by a very general, median desire — that is, a desire for power. But the desire to see the desire of those who are not like others — hence, who are mad — is not a desire for power, but a desire to see things as they are. The worst catastrophes happen to those who see the beauty of a blade of grass: They do not pass exams and do not vote.

How then does one become mad? Some people like Clarice Lispector seem to have been born with a talent for strangeness. Already when Clarice was little, she did not tell stories but registered little sensations of trembling. She was considered mad. Others become mad more or less accidentally. One goes to school to be cured of madness. But there are accidents in life: One sometimes loses the necessary blindness required for the ordinary vision of the socialized, professionalized self. There are a variety of accidents, real or spiritual, and to each his own. We do not know what happened to Blanchot. But he did have an accident. Some people are sent in the direction of strangeness by a car accident, by something that makes them see the world otherwise. In the hospital we have a vision of the world that differs from the one in which one acts as if human beings were not mortal. Life is difficult to live if one thinks of death not as a threat, but as another relation to life. Blanchot explains clearly, if one wants to listen, that everything deals with a capacity to accept death, without fear, considering it as a moment of life:

"Men want to escape from death, strange beings that they are. And some of them cry out 'Die, die' because they want to escape from life. 'What a life. I'll kill myself. I'll give in.' This is lamentable and strange; it is a mistake" (7). Though this seems paradoxical, Blanchot says that to want to escape death is to want to escape life. That is what we are constantly doing. Blanchot notes that most people are so afraid of the danger of living that they prefer to die alive, rather than to live alive. But his homage to women is explosive: "Yet I have met people who have never said to life, 'Quiet!,' who have never said to death, 'Go away!' Almost always women, beautiful creatures" (7).

The statement opens but does not close exclusively on women. We go over to "creatures." The majority of creatures capable of not saying "Go away!" are women.

There is another incident:

"I am not timid, I've been knocked around. Someone (a man at his wit's end) took my hand and drove his knife into it. Blood everywhere. Afterward he was trembling. He held out his hand to me so that I could nail it to the table or against a door. Because he had gashed me like that, the man, a lunatic, thought he was now my friend; he pushed his wife into my arms; he followed me through the streets crying, 'I am damned, I am the plaything of an immoral delirium, I confess, I confess.' A strange sort of lunatic. Meanwhile the blood was dripping on my only suit" (8).

This story may have real roots. Blanchot may have lived the anecdote that we find transposed here. It may also be a figurative anecdote connoting a kind of aborted crime. Someone made a gesture and there is passage to action: "The man, a lunatic, thought he was now my friend." The lunatic is not someone who *dares* to be mad, like in Dostoyevsky, but someone who has missed his madness.

Elsewhere, there is an allusion to war:
"Shortly afterward, the madness of the world broke out. I was made to stand against the wall like many others. Why? For no reason. The guns did not go off. I said to myself, God, what are you doing? At that point I stopped being insane. The world hesitated, then regained its equilibrium" (6).

"The guns did not go off" can be read as a metaphor; at the same time, the sentence draws in the theme of war. Is it a madness become too mad or is it true madness in this paragraph? There are several passages to the limit. The scene is the same as in Dostoyevsky's *Idiot*. He is going to die and lives his death: "Why? For no reason." Otherwise we would be back in the space of guilt. Here it is gratuitous. It is pure death, hence pure life. Is there grace? He had his moment of illumination. "I said to myself, God." He has become God and admirably so. At the same time, God has become a kind of communal invocation. But in this vocative, it is Blanchot who has become God. God speaks to himself. What can God say to himself if not "I am not learned; I am not ignorant"? But the question must also be heard at the most banal level. Banality is always here to remind us that it suffices to become sufficiently blind in order to see what is hidden and visible behind the banal. The banal sentence tells us: the madness of banality or madness behind banality. And, of course, when he says to himself: "God, what are you doing?" he stops being insane.

From then on, he makes sense, he becomes really mad, mightily and marvelously mad. He is no longer insane and stupid.

Blanchot's terrifying but admirable art, toward which one can be very ambivalent, lies in the capacity of writing with repetitive words, ready-made expressions, clichés, what, in fact, is a formidable search, that, when he wrote the text, must have been pretty much completed. This is Bataille's art too. The more it is clichéd, the stranger it becomes. But it is also prohibitive, and as little poetic as possible. The story is double, and in its form it remains fixed, as horribly grammatically French as if Blanchot were a simple descendant of Descartes, while everything else is shaken from the inside. That is what he tries to get across as a message of illusion. In order to speak of clarity he says:
"I had to hold my own against the light of seven days — a fine conflagration! Yes, seven days at once, the seven deadly lights, become the spark of a single moment, were calling me to account" (11).

One of the twisted threads of signification in this text is the work on masculine, feminine, or the exchange of gender. Our attention is first fixed on the title, then there are allegories, there is misery, there is the story of the *tact* which begins to stray, but the tact does not become a person. What pertains to allegory happens to be, in French, accidentally or not, words of feminine gender. One follows grammar, and the grammatical gender brings about an allegorical gender. The personification of the law has a knee, a *genou*, a *je-nous*, an "I-we" as articulation. From the beginning, gender is emphasized. A privilege is given to women capable of saying yes to life and death. There are ruses of the text and the way water rises, the feminine rises in the masculine. From the beginning, we think of the day as masculine *(le jour)*, but little by little it is being feminized through phonic effects:

"I had to hold my own against the light of seven days *[sept jours]*" (11). I can hear "seven days," *sept jours*, as *cette jour*, "this day," in the feminine. Similarly, the phonic confusion of *sept-cette*, "seven" and "this," brings about *sept clartés capitales*, "seven deadly lights," and we are completely in the feminine. Seven masculines lead to a feminine that becomes "the spark of a single moment *[la vivacité d'un seul instant]*," that is, the femininity of an instant. The insistence on phonic effects produces a kind of musical narrative that slips into the illusion of the "story-no-story" of the greater narrative. This is Blanchot's way of telling readers what he lets them guess if they are mad enough to hear it. And if they are not mad enough, at least he will not have surrendered his secret to fools.

Blanchot's love of madness is admirable. But we cannot appreciate his reserve. That is where we see the difference with Clarice's text. Clarice tries to make us see the day that she has seen, as she says in *The Passion according to G. H.* Her whole process consists in working like a madwoman so that a certain path can be frayed toward the point of blinding; while Blanchot completely capitalizes on his madness, Clarice does not feel like keeping the treasure of madness to herself. In both writers the same place is in question, but Clarice wants to communicate her experience. Blanchot, as we can read in *Writing of Disaster,* believes this experience of revelation to be incommunicable. Nothing moves him, except a desire to keep his treasure. In order for his treasure not to disappear entirely — because whether he writes to God, to himself, or to a madman, he nevertheless writes — he hid it in the brief scene of *Writing of Disaster,* in the primal scene of the child who saw but will not tell. Blanchot writes: I will not tell you. He draws something the way he would write in sand. For those who understand the sign, it is good, and otherwise it is of no importance. Blanchot's short text resembles an alchemical formula. He hides from doctors and rational institutions that are truly enemies of the writer. One can say, perhaps, that he builds a wall against common sense. But there is also the fact that his is a masculine libido and that he lacks a capacity for pleasure to such a point that he cannot get out of his wall.

I take up the scene with the baby carriage, which is a gigantic event and at the same time the most infinitesimal sign. The event, framed with motifs of immobility, is written as a simple juxtaposition, without links, deductions or logical connections. Its very force resides in its madness. The reader makes the connections, but as in a primal scene of the imaginary, as in the Apocalypse, it is ciphered and suscitates myriad interpretations. The preparation of the scene — with a woman, a baby carriage, a door — and what happens afterward take on enormous importance. As when one rubs a musical cord, it produces a certain visual sound that affects us, but what we are going to say about it is subject to caution:

"Outdoors, I had a brief vision: a few steps away from me, just at the corner of the street I was about to leave, a woman with a baby carriage had stopped. I could not see her very well, she was maneuvering the carriage to get it through the outer door. At that moment a man whom I had not seen approaching went in through that door. He had already stepped across the sill when he moved backward and came out again. While he stood next to the door, the baby carriage, passing in front of him, lifted slightly to cross the sill, and the young woman, after raising her head to look at him, also disappeared inside" (10).

There is an accumulation of elements of reality. In phenomenological terms, we organize everything because our vision is one of habit. We organize, hierarchize, and introduce an order.

"I had a brief vision."

We have all the elements of the vision but what differs is that they are not in the order of importance in which a story would normally be told, that is, "I saw a woman who, etc. . . ." In Blanchot, all the elements of this scene are decomposed, rendered equivalent, arrested without being linked. They are not organized toward a goal or an end. The reader does not know what the people want to do and it is of no importance. All the links of cause and effect are cut off. The organizing mental instance is suppressed. If the narrator were not mad, he would have told us another story. He registers like a machine, or a camera. Certain movements that seem contradictory are put side by side. His vision is flat, without second thoughts, and the reader cannot understand it very well.

It begins with "outdoors," but in the preceding paragraph, we were "inside," "in the misery." There is an inside of misery, a strange world. "Slowly, it was tracing circles around me." But: "Outdoors, I had a brief vision." This vision — because in spite of everything we have a drive to give meaning — provokes in the reader a feeling that there is a hidden meaning. A moment later, she is said to maneuver the carriage. There are thousands of such tiny elements that make up an obstacle to the dramatic plot we would like to have. We have all the elements of a primal scene but it is not at all organized.

The meanings in this text are situated in such a way as to send intelligence into madness. The text is the very intelligence of madness, while in "The Foreign Legion" it is a question of intelligence only.

In Blanchot, everything is displaced: outside and inside. But inside is "in the misery," and outside is outside of him. Everything is full of cunning and happens at the level of the signifier. For example:

"The baby carriage, passing in front of him, lifted slightly to cross the sill." And right afterward:

"This brief scene lifted me to the point of delirium" (translation modified).

The links are made in a mad way. As with texts by Clarice Lispector, as readers we have to let go of what we have held onto all our lives — that is, interpretation.

Grammatically, the passage provides no difficulty. One does not understand the emotion that crosses the text and that functions as a way to read through it. After having been traced, most signs have been erased. There are about a hundred paragraphs in the text, and we can read them as if they were a hundred separate pieces. There are hardly any links between the paragraphs, which can be read almost paratactically. The white spaces give the reader the impression that the order can be inverted, something that, in fact, is not true. The entire causal line has been erased, which induces error in us. There *is* a connection between the previous paragraph and the one beginning with "Outdoors, I had a brief vision . . ." though not at a first reading. The previous paragraph about the library determines the present one, absolutely.

"I was beginning to sink into poverty" (9) is the example of an imperceptible subversion. Everybody understands the statement. But there is a modification: "I was beginning." How does one "begin" to sink into poverty? It is difficult to fall into misery slowly. Poverty *(la misère)* is acting, is the person who finds herself bringing something about. If we take the themes of beginning, we notice that they are falsified. There is no life without death, and a beginning must begin something. There must be a continuation and an end. But beginnings without continuation or end are not beginnings, and that is where we are at an impasse. The narrator began but then poverty acted:

"Slowly it *[elle]* was drawing circles around me; the first seemed to leave me everything, the last would leave me only myself. One day, I found myself confined in the city" (9).

These short, oneiric sentences almost constitute a chapter in two lines: "travelling was no longer more than a fantasy."

We read that the enclosure never ceased but it is only on "one day." Then there follows the description of the fable of the voyage.

"My clothes were wearing out. I was suffering from the cold; springtime, quick" (9).

The text contains a quantity of erased exclamations. Every time the narrator says "quick," the exclamation point is erased and falsification gives the impression of reading about a calling out. But the calling itself has been erased: "springtime, quick." And the following sentence tells us that spring perhaps does not arrive, but that libraries make the spring and provide heat.

"I went to libraries. I had become friends with someone who worked in one, and he took me down to the overheated basement" (9).

The sentence could figure in any novelistic text but since we are alerted by the ruse of metaphors, we cannot not see the link with his employer:

"In order to be useful to [my employer], I blissfully galloped along tiny gangways and brought him books which he then sent on to the gloomy spirit of reading" (9).

In the libraries, that is all he does. The question of reading is always pushed to a *dé-lire,* a delirious unreading "in the gloomy spirit of reading"; the mind becomes allegory:

"but that spirit hurled against me words that were not very kind" (9).

There is an apparent contradiction:

"I shrank before its eyes,"

He is subjected to the effects of a magic look just as if he were under the eyes of the doctors. The look of the other is all-powerful. The insistence bears on the magic effect because transfigurations and transformations are taking place:

"I shrank,"

and an unheard-of thing:

"It saw me for what I was, an insect, a creature with mandibles who had come up from the dark regions of poverty" (9–10).

This is obviously an allusion to Kafka. But right afterward, we read:

"Who was I?"

Was he Samsa, the insect of Kafka's *Metamorphosis*? No, precisely not, he is the way he is seen and this is the definition: He is an insect seen and he cannot negate it because the look of the other has its power. But who is he for himself? When a look focuses on us, we become what this look sees, but Blanchot's narrator is what this look sees *and* also:

"Who was I?" (10)

To a fabulous question, a fabulous answer:

"It would have thrown me into great perplexity to answer that question" (10).

The answer is suspended, hidden. It is outside:

"Outdoors, I had a brief vision" (10).

This paragraph answers the question, "Who was I?" but only once the path has been erased.

Let us take the paragraph at the letter. The text keeps us outside. It describes a closure. "Outdoors" *(dehors)* can be taken as an outside in relation to the library but that is not what is being told us. The narrator's vision is truly of an absolute outside. What does he see?

"a few steps away from me" (10)

The scene accumulates determinations and troubles the reader who does not know why:

"Just at the corner of the street I was about to leave" (10)

gives supplementary information, but at the same time it insists on "leaving." "To see" also reappears. The child returns in the paragraph but as a signifier, not as child. If we analyzed:

"I could not see her very well [Je ne l'apercevais qu'assez mal]."

What did he see poorly? The carriage, the ensemble?

"a woman with a baby carriage"
between commas, and in addition, he sees poorly. Usually, he sees everything or
nothing. Here, he has a kind of medium, insufficient vision.

The story of the man follows. One cannot fail to think that it is an equivalent of
a sexual scene:

"At that moment a man I had not seen approaching"
He had not seen the man approaching but the latter "had already stepped across
the sill." In French, the reflexive verb form has to be noted, the fact that the
carriage "lifted itself," *se souleva,* and the young woman disappears. The following paragraph skids on "excited," *me souleva:*

"This brief scene excited me *[me souleva]* to the point of delirium."

One cannot not read the substitution of the narrator for the baby carriage. Of
course, it is inexplicable. He says:

"I was undoubtedly not able to explain it to myself fully and yet I was sure of it,
that I had seized the moment when the day, having stumbled against a real event,
would begin hurrying to its end. Here it comes, I said to myself, the end is coming:
something is happening, the end is beginning. I was seized by joy" (10).

The scene can be read at many different levels. At a realistic level, it can remain
completely hermetic. At a symbolic level, we have all of Dante's modes of interpretation: the anagogic, literal, analogic, and the allegorical. Given what we have
already heard on the stories of the day, we may think that in a certain manner we
have here a kind of *butée* (limit) of reading. But it is also a displaced birth scene.
At this point, he becomes completely mad. The birth scene is seen from the inside
but it cannot be told any other way. The child attends his own genesis and birth.
He would see himself being born, or see himself see the day. At the limit, we
could say that the day itself is the child. But no one ever sees the day, except God
who is outside of the day. Maybe night can see the day. The day is the luminous
envelope. The narrator is in the situation of someone who has seized a mystery
that is equivalent to "I saw the day." He tells us an impossible scene, that is why
he says it in such a strange way. I am so much "outside" that I see the day, that I
see myself seeing the day. He sees his birth in the paragraph beginning with the
brief vision and this gives him extraordinary joy. At the same time, the story can
only be told as a pseudonarrative:

"I had seized the moment when the day, having stumbled against a real event,
would begin hurrying to its end. Here it comes, I said to myself, the end is coming."

It sounds a bit delirious but it is not. It is the instant whence the day is going to
hurry toward an end and toward a birth. From birth, we hurry toward our end. And
this goes back to what the narrator had said about living and dying: to see birth is
also already to see death, yet it is joy.

"The end is coming: something is happening, the end is beginning."

The insistence is on *la fin,* "the end," and on "she," on the feminine. In
French, we can open an immense feminine field in which we find "end" *(fin),*

"light" *(lumière)*, "clarity" *(clarté)*, "joy" *(joie)*, but all that is nevertheless bathing in something positive:

"the end is coming,"

for the good reason that life begins. Something happens that produces an obstacle, a limit. But as soon as something begins, the end also begins:

"I was seized by joy."

An absolute lure, it is one of the most atrocious sentences of the text. In Clarice Lispector, one would imagine a whole scale *(gamme)* of sentences that would give pleasure in happiness. But in Blanchot, we have one sentence and it is all over. Happiness passes like everything else. For him, there is a kind of short-circuiting between life and death so that what begins also ends.

"Now my life is surprisingly secure; even fatal diseases find me tough. I'm sorry, but I must bury a few others before I bury myself" (9).

He is already dead and immortal from being so. One can easily mark the difference with the story of survival in Clarice Lispector's *Apple in the Dark*. Martim's survival is going to be immense and of infinite wealth. Blanchot's survival is simply: "I was seized by joy." Period. This is a strategy of survival. We can even say that the end begins incessantly and that he does not cease dying. However, for the narrator to die is not to die. He has found the secret, though the instants of his life are really instants of continuous dying. His happiness lasted for four words.

"I went to the house, but did not enter" is of the order of not entering. Then the wall is here again:

"Through the opening, I saw the black edge of a courtyard. I leaned against the outer wall; I was really very cold. As the cold wrapped around me from head to foot, I slowly felt my great height" (10).

And for good reason, since he has become God.

"Take on the dimensions of this boundless cold; it grew with tranquillity, according to the laws of its true nature, and I lingered in the joy and perfection of this happiness for one moment, my head as high as the stone of the sky and my feet on the pavement" (10–11).

He discovered the "stone of the sky." He is forever happy with his stature and the stone of the sky. He is in a tomb. From the moment of birth, from the moment that he was able to live, there is an opening onto a tomblike eternity. Then there is a ploy:

"All that was real, take note."

This beautiful sentence recalls the imaginary without being a way of rejecting reality. All of a sudden we are interpellated once more with the request, "take note." We are in a position of scribe, maybe even of secretary to a doctor.

Afterward, there is the story of God. Without liking to do this kind of a reading, I will create a kind of outside, so we can see better what the strange sentences mean.

"I had no enemies. No one bothered me."

The narrator has the status of God.

"Sometimes a vast solitude opened in my head and the entire world disappeared inside it, but came out again intact, without a scratch, with nothing missing" (11).

Comes the story of the eyesight:

"I nearly lost my sight, because someone crushed glass in my eyes. That blow unnerved me, I must admit" (11).

Rereading the story, it would seem that it is on page 11 that the episode in which he almost lost his eyesight took place. "I nearly lost my sight." There too, it has to be taken at the letter, and at the same time we should ask ourselves what kind of sight he almost lost. In banal terms, we think that he had an accident. But there is no link between the two sentences. He does not need to tell us that the accident troubled him. It is the symbolic *coup* that shook him.

"I had the feeling I was going back into the wall" (11).

Given what we know about enclosure in Blanchot, this is very strong. All is happening as if the view from the outside, this slightly distant view of God, had become an extremely close-up view, something quite unthinkable. The narrator went back into the day. Now he is less God, less mad.

"The worst thing was the sudden, shocking cruelty of the day. I could not look but I could not help looking" (11).

He no longer has mastery over his vision. He is given over to the day and cannot stop seeing. I translate it into terms of madness. He has reached such a degree of madness that he can no longer take pleasure in his madness: he can no longer go back and forth between revelation, blinding, and resting in darkness. By contrast, Clarice Lispector also sees the day, but there is also the night during which she can try to reconstitute something; then there is day again. She has a system of instants. But Blanchot's narrator does not stop seeing. He has become painfully, not happily mad:

"I had to hold my own, against the light of seven days — a fine conflagration!"

There is no more night, only the day of days. And once this has been experienced, it is translated as:

"At times, I said to myself: 'This is death'" (11).

Why death and not life? Because there is here a blinding, unbearable continuity and there is no more outside. From then on, there are no more difficulties in the reading:

"But often, I lay dying without saying anything. In the end, I grew convinced that I was face to face with the madness of the day" (11).

This is exactly what he is describing. The last word of this paragraph reads:

"This discovery bit straight through my life" (12).

Until now, his madness was rational. Here, it has become permanent, hence irrational; it has no more end. The fact that he fell into this interminable day is of course a *coup de dent,* an inner breakage, in his life, since he was first outside and now he is inside. When he is cured — and here is the element of strangeness in the story — he dies of a need for madness.

"I wanted to see something in full daylight; I was sated with the pleasure and comfort of the half light; I had the same desire for the daylight as for water and air. And if seeing was fire, I required the plenitude of fire, and if seeing would infect me with madness, I madly wanted that madness" (12).
His desire *is* a desire for madness.

This is where we begin to enter into the second part of the text. The narrator went to the very end of his experience of madness and of its censorship. The first part is the story of his going mad, the second part is the story of someone who lives with the secret of madness and deals with the enemies of madness. In the second part, there is a love story with the law *(la loi)* (14–16). The law is woman, is feminine and his relation with her is told us right away:
"Behind their backs, I saw the silhouette of the law" (14).
The story of the law is fabulous and beautiful. With her he talks enormously, of course. He and the law are inseparable, since, as with the woman and the child, he is *with* the law. The law is part of him:
"The truth is that we can never be separated again. I will follow you everywhere. I will live under your roof *[toit]*; we will share the same sleep" (15).
If "I will live under your roof," is heard well, the *t,* in *toit,* "roof," can be removed: under the *moi* and the *toi,* we will have the same sleep.
"She got strangely worked up" (16).
The law exalts him. The law is a she-He, or a he-She.
On the next page we read:
"This was one of her games." [Voici un de ses jeux].
Un de ses je(u), "myself, I," of course.
In the second part, the question, What is the law? Who is the law? How? Why? What is its function and what comes at the end? A story, a *récit.* The law intervenes in a mode that is sometimes that of reproach, but of the order of a reproach-approach. There are several days, several laws, and several stories.
Some of the terrifying word plays have to be underlined. Blanchot, like Genet, works on phonic signifiers:
"Is my life better than other people's lives? Perhaps. I have a roof over my head and many do not" (6).
This "roof," *toit,* is also a "you," *toi.*
"I do not have leprosy, I am not blind, I see the world — what extraordinary happiness!" (6).
This sentence is part of a passage to the limit, to the infinite. He describes how his life is better than other people's. How? "Perhaps. I have a roof *[toit, toi]*." His properties are on the side of the negative. He situates himself in relation with a "you" in order to be able to go over to the other side.

We can add that throughout the entire text it is a question of a complaint, or the deposition of a legal suit. What would I complain or sue about? I have a roof *(toi,t)*, I have madness, I am happy:

"What extraordinary happiness!"

He situates himself on the border of unhappiness, far from the traditional definition of happiness:

"I see the day, extraordinary happiness."

All those who are not blind should be mad with happiness, since they see the world, but it so happens that nobody sees the world.

"I see this day, and outside it there is nothing" (6).

There are negations *(ne . . . pas)* everywhere, even in extraordi*na*ire. Of course, he is nothing outside the day, and nothing exists outside the day. When he says:

"Who could take that away from me?"

he begins telling us that in a certain way he is God. Nothing in the world can be taken away from him who sees the day. He can say that he is happy because he has something that is not threatened with loss, that nobody can take away from him.

"And when this day fades, I will fade along with it — a thought, a certainty, that enraptures me" (6).

This is the corollary of his divine position. He will not die, he will only be erased with the day. That is what we read under all kinds of ways of living and dying. The meaning is clear: there is no loss. He likes the day. He cannot lose the day, because if he loses it, he loses himself. And afterward, there is a distinction between this situation of non loss and classical loss.

"I have loved people, I have lost them. I went mad when that blow struck me, because it is hell" (6).

This is Blanchot's nastiness, because the madness of which he speaks in this paragraph is not a mad madness, it is madness to a certain degree, but never a supreme madness.

1982–83

Notes

1. Clarice Lispector, "A Legião Estrangeira," in *A Legião Estrangeira* (Rio de Janeiro: Editôra do Autor, 1964). Trans. Giovanni Pontiero, *The Foreign Legion* (New York: Carcanet, 1986).

2. Maurice Blanchot, *La Folie du jour,* (Paris: Fata Morgana, 1973). Trans. Lydia Davis, *The Madness of the Day* (Barrytown, NY: Station Hill Press, 1981).

3. See "Felicidade clandestina," in Hélène Cixous, *Reading with Clarice Lispector,* ed. and trans. Verena Andermatt Conley (Minneapolis: University of Minnesota Press, 1990).

4. Hélène Cixous, *Reading with Clarice Lispector.*

5. Jacques Derrida, "Tympaniser," in *Marges de la philosophie* (Paris: Minuit, 1972), i–xxv. Trans. Alan Bass, *Margins of Philosophy* (Chicago: University of Chicago Press, 1989), ix–xxix.

6. Jacques Derrida, "Legs de Freud," in *La carte postale de Socrate à Freud* (Paris: Aubier-Flammarion, 1982). Trans. Alan Bass, "Freud's Legacy," in *The Postcard* (Chicago: University of Chicago Press, 1987), 292–337.

7. Franz Kafka, *Dearest Father: Stories and Other Writings (Hochzeitsvorbereitungen auf dem Lande),* trans. Ernst Kaiser and Eithne Wilkens (New York: Schocken, 1954).

Chapter 4
Poetry, Passion, and History
Marina Tsvetayeva

The Inscription of Passion in Writing

I want to work on passion as path and on the encounter, perhaps the struggle, between passion and history. All this, for me, goes through the inscription of passion in writing. In the ensemble of texts one can choose from, a certain number burn either positively or negatively, with love or regret. At the intersection of passion, history, and writing, the texts of some Russian women poets are the most compelling. Marina Tsvetayeva and Anna Akhmatova write toward the individual but also toward what I will not call the masses, since the word is synonymous with death — and if I use it, it is because these women function in a Soviet space — but perhaps toward what one could call a crowd, or a society. The two women are turned toward each person and each individual but also toward what can become a totality, and a mortal one at that.

I am interested in the intersection between poetry and history. How does history make its path in a poetic work? We rarely see history in a literary text since it is so hard to deal with. Perhaps poetry does not know how to say or utter history. I only suggest this as a possibility. Or is poetry something stronger, something even more dangerous? History simply smothers and squashes. Yet some books show that one can remain poetic in the very midst of history.

My remarks could be entitled, with an expression borrowed from the Russian poet Osip Mandelstam, "The Noise of Time." Mandelstam died in exile, in a camp. He simply disappeared, as if he had reached a time when one also loses one's death, something that one generally keeps. When Akhmatova says, in one of her poems written in 1921,

> Everything is plundered, betrayed, sold
> Death's great black wing scrapes the air,
> Misery gnaws to the bone.
> Why then do we not despair?

And she answers by saying:

> And the miraculous comes so close
> to the ruined, dirty houses
> something not known to anyone at all
> But wild in our breast for centuries.[1]

I think of these generations, whose desire was a nostalgia of the unknown, of what no longer exists, or of what now only exists in books. Those who are born after the loss of paradise must have an extraordinary sense of life and of the *miraculous*. We can read Akhmatova's lines in the shimmer of a light that comes from origins we can never know. It comes from the heart, but we may wonder at times how the heart keeps on beating.

From path to path, I also want to work on journeys. Any journey is a metaphor of all journeys at all times. Our tourist era continuously sets out on journeys. Each time, if we worked on the journey we are undertaking, we would find in it thousands of different journeys. It is always a flight of some kind, a flight toward another life. It *is* another life, a death, an oblivion, a recalling, and a search. We know that when we change countries we also change hearts. In the nineteenth century, Flaubert, Nerval, and others left for the end of the world, then they came back to write in French. A journey may be one of affinity. We go to the countries we carry deep down in our hearts. Often we arrive at ourselves far from ourselves. Inversely, we can travel away from ourselves. I would like to work, step by step, on texts that travel through infinite inner spaces even if they cross a limited physical space.

Many poets develop a sense of positive loss, like Clarice Lispector, or Anna Akhmatova, in whose poetry we read of something never lost at the very bottom of loss, or Marina Tsvetayeva, in whose texts the stakes are something that she never had. Theirs are all texts of despair, that is, of hope. Elsewhere I have shown how the same happened in a much more novelistic way, fleshed out in the work of someone such as Karen Blixen.

If I insist on the point, it is because it can be said that human beings are not always good. Let us call the world around us "noise machines," in opposition to Mandelstam's "noise of time." We listen to the radio, watch television; we read the newspaper and we can say that the noise of machines is invading everywhere. Even an organization like Greenpeace is just another noise machine from which one cannot imagine that justice or truth will appear. The noise machines are more and more sonorous. The air in which we breathe life is given over to values that are the death of humankind, that are low-level, oriented by speculation, money, and profit. In the milieu of the media, people are entirely governed by the obligation to create scandals. Scandal is what sells. In place of the word, reflection, or thought, we need noise. The public has to be satisfied. The public is not stupid, the institutional powers are. But the media spirit has even infiltrated the halls of the university.

Therefore I want to plant some paths, some slowness, some trees, some thought and silence. The texts that accompany me on this journey work on this inside of an outside, on an inside-outside. Marina Tsvetayeva does both at once. Underneath a worldly surface, we can find in her oeuvre a woman full of wealth, an extraordinary tapestry, a writing gathering thousands of signs.

I am bothered by the word "journey," despite its occurrence everywhere in the texts I gathered, where it means much more a journey into the self. These texts make us travel so that from an apparently immobile contemplation we are led to infinite discoveries.

Many texts inscribe very strongly something of a path in writing, or a writing that advances like a path. All the texts speak of a need, a desire, or, to borrow one of Rilke's terms, a quest for direction. They all speak with insistence of a going toward, or of an active orientation. It is this movement toward something or somebody that opens what I would call "being in the direction of chance." Life can happen to us only in an instant, like in a flash of lightning, and only on condition that we be open to it and move toward it. It is felt as *more* than life, as an excessive overflow of life, as life unlimiting itself, leaping, opening toward (to quote Akhmatova) "the miraculous . . . not known to anyone at all." It may be death itself, not a sad death, but the passage toward more than the self, toward another than the self, toward the other.

If you follow me perhaps you will lose yourself, but if you do, you *are* following me. To find one has to lose, one finds only by losing. For Clarice Lispector, the other is the unknown, the nonself. To find is also to lose the self. While advancing, I am playing to find while losing. A thousand poets promise that if we lose ourselves — and we must — there always remains the path. That's what Heidegger told us in his *Holzwege,* his paths that lead nowhere. We have to let the path work.

The philosophical text (though it may be close to the poetic text, contrary to what one could say) does not let go, does not want to lose. The philosopher takes back what he has lost and gathers it in a noun. He has to capture, to plant. This gesture leads to proper names that are quite abstract and that capture the path.

In Heidegger's *Holzwege,* a long text on Rilke is titled with a quotation from Hölderlin's poem "Bread and Wine": "What are poets for?"[2] "What are poets for in a destitute time?" becomes a kind of theorem in the text. Heidegger produces a semantic gathering (103–4) around *Weg* (way), *Wagen* (wagon), *wagen* (to risk), *Wagnis* (risk), *wägen, wegen* (to make a way), *bewägen* (to bring into motion). *Wage* (balance) implied danger, since any movement was associated with danger. What weighs is also taken in this ensemble, since it sets into movement.

The most beautiful of them all is the notion of *wagen* (risk). Risk is the other word for life. Following Heidegger, we can say that being is without shelter *(sans abri),* without protection, but salvation is precisely in risk.

What saves us, Heidegger tells us, is to be without shelter. This sounds like a paradox. Yet risk keeps possibility in our lives open. Some of the best and strongest texts are those that have been written without shelter — for example, that of Etty Hillesum, who wrote her diary in the camps. Because she was confronted with death, she discovered in the very short space between 1941 and 1943 the secret of living. She writes: ''I have already suffered a thousand deaths in a thousand concentration camps. I know everything and nothing anguishes me anymore. One way or another, I know it all. And, however, I find this life beautiful and rich with meaning. At every instant.'' Or else: ''One day when there is no more barbed wire left in the world, you must come and see my room. It is so beautiful and peaceful. I spend half my night at my desk reading and writing by the light of my small lamp. I have about 1500 pages of a diary from last year, and one of these days I shall read it through. What a rich life leaps out at me from every page. To think that it was my life — and still is.''[3] I would change the quotation slightly into ''It is because I find this life beautiful and rich with meaning.''

When one has reached regions of such tragedy, one truly learns about the wealth of life and living, because poverty, literal nakedness, anguish, and loss make one discover it. There is an almost necessary conjunction or encounter between those who have the gift of writing and thinking and the violence of history. Is it possible to write a poem in a concentration camp? Perhaps I am wrong in asking the question. It is rather the poem that allows one to stand the concentration camp. At least, that is what Etty Hillesum tells us, and nothing could be more moving than to read this from such places of repulsion and agony. While she was sitting on trash cans, people marched by on their way to death. Etty was reading Rilke and she thanked him. Rilke owes an immense amount to Etty Hillesum, since she gives him a life. An exchange of life exists between the two and, admirably, the chain is not broken. That is how strong the continuity between poetry and the soul can be.

This is why I decided to look for texts that take up the most difficult moments of our existence, texts we find mainly in Russia, from the Revolution to the labor camps, and in Nazi Germany. There, we can see how fear, anguish, and death are made of life. Poets of that era were bound together by a strong love and gave homage to one another: Tsvetayeva and Akhmatova, Pasternak and Mandelstam — each continued to pronounce the name of the other while celebrating it. In the face of the devouring dragon, the narcissistic war waged among people stops. Everyone gathered to save poetry.

Akhmatova has a ''feminine'' resistance, and she lived a long time in extreme suffering. Tsvetayeva has a harsher destiny. In 1941 she commits suicide by hanging herself. She writes texts of such frightful intelligence that we can almost say that she dies of it. What she writes is so strong and powerful that it must have created a true glacier around her. She suffers all the mishaps of the others and even more. She is separated from her husband, Sergei Efron, whom she believes to be dead and whom she found again, a little by chance. She flees to France where she hopes to find a Russian community that will listen to her poetry, but she is completely rejected. She spends fourteen years in France in the most absolute solitude and the worst poverty. In Paris, she tries to publish her poetry and is refused. She even translated some of her own texts into French. In 1939, she and her son go back to Russia to join her husband and daughter. The daughter is sent to a gulag and the husband is arrested and shot. In 1940, Tsvetayeva herself is exiled to a small provincial town where there is no one to offer alms to her and she hangs herself. In her poems no words are spent on hunger; there is only work on poetry, and on an astounding force of life.

I want to read her dazzling and shattering *Neuf lettres avec une dixième retenue et une onzième reçue (Nine Letters with a Tenth Kept Back and an Eleventh Received)*. These love letters were written in Russian and sent to a man (the editor Volodny) with whom she was in love after she had fled to Berlin. Later, she translated them into French for publication. Tsvetayeva was incredibly diabolical and powerful. In these letters we can see that she declared her love to the people she met the way one declares war, or life. In a few moments, these "chosen" people were reduced to ashes. The nine letters are addressed to a man with a great deal of humor. At no time does she accept the slightest form of convention or code. We open the book, or the door, and we are right away in the depths of the human soul. There is an extraordinary unleashing of verbal force. One can imagine what the poor man to whom these letters were addressed must have felt. Perhaps he thought that she was crazy and that he had to take leave as quickly as possible. It was impossible to stay with her, unless one was really gifted — and some great poets were gifted enough to answer her. Her husband, whom she loved a great deal — even if she had many other passions — said that she was of fire, and that very quickly there were only ashes left. In a wink, she devoured the other, except for some rare equals, such as, for example, other poets.

Her letters are a marvel of passion, of a love that literally penetrates the other and caresses him from the inside. They are very violent, but also sad and funny.

In some of her short stories such as "The Devil" or "Mother and Music," Tsvetayeva writes about her childhood, especially — in a brilliant and a pre-Freudian way — about her relation with her mother.

Her "Lettre à l'Amazone" ("Letter to the Amazon") is published as a small volume under the title *Mon frère féminin (My Feminine Brother)*. The letter, written in French to Natalie Barney, seems to be a reading of the latter's *Pensées d'une Amazone (Thoughts of an Amazon*, 1918), a text about female homosexuality.

In October 1932, Tsvetayeva writes forty-five brilliant pages about all the openings and the impasses of female homosexuality. She is not antihomosexual, quite the contrary. This text of great strength was published posthumously in 1979, once again at a time when it could not be heard. The text bears the mark of the thirties and their modernity and power, and has to be seen in that context. We can see in it that intelligence is timeless. Now, in 1985, we can be in 1966 or in 1970. Some people are always in the present tense of life. One would have to invent a time of truth that, situated at the heart of the chance of life, makes fun of social conditions. That is the very question raised by Tsvetayeva in this letter. What chance do you have, she asks Natalie Barney, living with a woman, loving a woman, loving the most tender and the most lovable, what chance do you have for survival, or put in another way, what about the child?

> This lacuna, what is left in white
> this black hole — is the child.

> [Cette lacune, ce laissé en blanc, ce
> trou noir — c'est l'Enfant.][4]

There is a certain coincidence of dates. Tsvetayeva died in 1941, Etty Hillesum in 1943. Their writings cover the same years. All these writers had had to measure up to the worst by facing it. Now we have only oblique relations with war, destruction, racism. Then, it was direct. There is a kinship among all these texts that come from the same source. Each writer asks what she or he can do so that life be blessed. Why a poet in destitute times? And how to go about it so that the most tender words can say some of the cruelest, the most destructive things?

In *The Passion according to G. H.* by Clarice Lispector, the protagonist traces a revelatory experience she just had:

"Going to sleep is very much like the way that I now have of going to my freedom. Giving myself over to something I don't understand is placing myself on the brink of nothingness. It is going just by going, like a blind woman lost in a field."[5]

That is what we need to do. We need to abandon our old ways of looking so as to find again a space that would be the realm of the possible. As Clarice would say, life has to surge to be super-natural. Generally, life is natural. In order to go on this journey, we have to find the super-natural.

Some go on voluntary journeys; others, like Etty Hillesum, go on involuntary journeys. At that moment unwillingness has to be transformed into desire. Etty Hillesum turned her journey into hell into one to paradise. Some travel in thought, like G. H. in Clarice Lispector's text. But the journey is always the same. It consists in unburying, unforgetting life and in finding its secrets. Super-natural life changes its name depending on the poets, on their language, and on sexual difference. It can be a house, as for example in Novalis and Hesse; or it can be an animal as in Lispector and Tsvetayeva.

I propose to lend our ears to the scream, to the animal voice of Marina Tsvetayeva, and to begin our quest through her texts.

The History of a Letter

With Tsvetayeva's letters, we are back in the eternal problem of what a letter is, with all its paradoxes. I do not speak of those letters we exchange in extreme haste, those little arrows of friendship we address without calculating them and which are ephemeral, like written telephone calls. Tsvetayeva's letters are situated in another time when letters were imposed by space, distance, and real separation. Some of her letters are the very fruit of separation. They do not try to separate, but re-mark, underline, and accept the very impossibility of gathering. They were born of the belief that they will never arrive at their destinations. They were letters in the mode of a letter-object, a little tomb, or an urn that one sends in an envelope.

In Russia, at a certain period, there existed a tragic rapport with the letter. The letter was a cry for help, a way of making fun of death while knowing that one was condemned. Russia was already the country of deportation and exile. Tsvetayeva's letters were always true letters of separation. Yet all the great poets of this time were in correspondence with one another. When we read Mandelstam, a friend of Tsvetayeva's, we feel his deportation, his fear of persecutions and the death threats against him. Mandelstam had been arrested, kept without food for two weeks, put in a straitjacket, and then sent away from prison but refused a place to live. During his last days, he walked through the outskirts of Moscow without being allowed to stop. For him, instead of an earth, there is only a moving desert, exile and abandonment, laced with messages. In those times, people continued to call each other and listen to each other with their hearts in an extraordinary way.

Mandelstam, Akhmatova, Pasternak, and Tsvetayeva did not abandon each other beyond the abyss and the desert. They memorized each other's poems, gave breath to each other, made each other's heart beat. They lent each other an ear, gave each other their own blood. Others listened to them, twenty, thirty years later, especially Paul Celan who wrote a poem called "Und mit dem Buch aus Tarussa" ("And with the book from Tarussa") in *Die Niemandsrose (Nobody's Rose)*. The poem begins with an epigraph, a sentence from Tsvetayeva's *Poem of the End:*

All poets   are Jews.[6]

Tsvetayeva had pronounced this sentence in relation to Mandelstam. She herself was not Jewish but considered herself a poet. She uses the two words synonymously to indicate that Jews and poets are citizens of exile and inhabitants of the word. Mandelstam worked on memory, on wealth derived from poverty that would be the very resource of a certain kind of memory. One could imagine — though this is also a phantasm — that the Jews would be the keepers of a certain memory in which they would live since there is no other place for them in the world.

The tenets of Tsvetayeva's statement can be found in Celan's "Und mit dem Buch aus Tarussa," a poem about poetry and about childhood as a source of wandering. Celan's autobiography is like a tragic repetition, in another country of misfortune, of the Russian poets' tragedy. Due to the concentration camps and Nazi Germany, his nomadism ended in his suicide in 1970. As a poet, he received all the other poets' messages of love and distress. He received and transformed them. Yet his work does not bear a formal mark of the other poets' work. It only bears that of their heart. All these poets wrote to "sew themselves together," a somewhat vulgar expression for such an act. They wanted to be in accord with God and with the world. Etty Hillesum wrote to put herself, as she says mockingly, in accord with the suffering of mankind, and so did Clarice Lispector, in a different cultural and historical context.

With the exception of Etty Hillesum, they all felt abandoned, and nobody can measure their abandonment. I am startled when I read the chronicles Clarice Lispector contributed to a Brazilian newspaper, *Jornal do Brasil,* where she writes to five hundred thousand people: I am alone. And all these readers close their ears and abandon her. Who abandons whom? We cannot know. Similarly, Tsvetayeva's abandonment precedes everything, though at the same time she does not accept it. Perhaps her abandonment is so great that there is no consolation. Why did these women feel especially abandoned? I do not want to speak of Rimbaud who was a child but of these women who were mothers. And they were good mothers who did not abandon their children.

To Be Born Carried Away

I changed my mind about Tsvetayeva between my reading of her correspondence with Rainer Maria Rilke and Boris Pasternak in *Letters, Summer 1926* where she is superb but unpleasant, and that of other texts like *Nine Letters with a Tenth Held Back and an Eleventh Received,* "The Devil," "Mother and Music," and her poems. In those writings we are no longer aware of her *coups de griffe,* of her scratches and blows. We begin to hear her and we begin to feel tenderness toward her.

In *Nine Letters,* the letters have a pretext, that is, the man to whom they are addressed. At a first reading and without having a more elaborate relation to Tsvetayeva's work, the man produces resistance in the reader. Tsvetayeva is always in an active position. She seems to hold her puppet, agitate it, hit it all over and then, all of a sudden, drop it. The man seems completely passive, even though the real story may have been quite different. There is correspondence only from one side and noncorrespondence from the other. But Tsvetayeva uses force, a word recurring frequently in her letters, which are real *coups de force.* She never harmed the gentleman since nothing happened or, to paraphrase Mallarmé, since nothing will have taken place but the place. Toward the end of her letters, a trace of the addressee appears. I do not speak here of the extraordinary "posthumous" scene in which Tsvetayeva, some time after the love affair has ended, does not recognize the man she had loved when she meets him at a social gathering, but of the man's letter reproduced by Tsvetayeva. Two or three details in the letter signal such vulgarity that the whole "correspondence" becomes hard to believe. The reader quickly wants to dispose of this pseudorelation. Just before the "Story of their Last Encounter," Tsvetayeva published a letter she received from him and that she entitles "Eleventh Letter Received."[7] Tsvetayeva omits the year, 1922, and keeps the day, October 29. The man's letter is reprinted with Tsvetayeva's annotations:

"You understand, my dear friend, how difficult it is for me to write you, I feel so guilty toward you, especially because of a lack of education, inner as well as general, which you like so much" (11: 47).

The man would not admit guilt, if he did not feel it:

"Everything left me indifferent, and no power in the world could have forced me to do what I knew had to be mandatory. . . . Those who sleep do not go to the post office" (11: 47–48).

And Marina annotates the passage with the comment: "But they do go to the restaurant."

"I am returning your letters. . . .

"I decided to keep the little tan book in which you entered the final copy of the poems dedicated to me. Not as a document or as a souvenir, but simply as a piece of life bound in leather" (11: 48).

Tsvetayeva reacted violently to this expression, as we can read in her notes. The man adds:

"If I do not have the right to do so . . . let me know, I will send it back to you!

"I implore you, please send me back at once the book by B . . . with the dedication that I forgot to ask you to return before you left. You know how much I like autographs! Send it by certified mail, registered, please! As long as I do not have it, I will not be able to sleep soundly" (11: 49).

What vulgarity! We have to point out the person who was opposite her, who let her write letters to him and who was willing to have this kind of relation with her. In Tsvetayeva's letters, we see a constant element of cruelty. She writes to the man — since she tells him everything — that now he has her poems, he no longer needs anything. And she was right. The man was a simple collector of autographs, someone terribly ordinary. Did she know it when she had a love affair with him? It can be said that she both does and does not have a love affair with him. There are some elements of reality, but there is *especially* her fiction, emerging from something insurmountable that she calls the cipher of her fate. And this is her continuous assertion that she was born "carried away." While constantly asking someone to take her away, she cannot, by definition, be taken away since she was *born* carried away. And that is her tragedy.

On the one hand there are the letters, unbearable because of their grief, that are literary masterpieces. On the other, there is an insignificant partner who accepted playing a certain part because he wanted autographs from her. We may wonder about such people. Tsvetayeva writes in the end of this eleventh letter:

"They all kept my poetry. They all gave me back my soul (gave me back to my soul)" (11: 50).

The story of the last encounter, or the final scene, is both comical and cruel. If we read it closely, it becomes a scene in which Tsvetayeva works on something she calls in the last part, "Postface or a posthumous face of things" (55–56). Tsvetayeva deals with the quality of forgetfulness. In this last encounter at a New Year's ball, long after her love for the gentleman had ended, she fails even to recognize him. The scene reads like a comedy. Symptomatically, Tsvetayeva herself says that she did not recognize him. She explains:

"My total forgetfulness and my absolute failure to recognize you today are but your absolute presence and my total absorption of yesterday. As much as you were — as much you are no longer. The absolute presence in reverse. Such a presence cannot but become such an absence. Everything yesterday, nothing today" (Postface: 55).

Tsvetayeva moves along this paradoxical line.

"What is it to forget a human being?–It is to forget what one suffered through him. . . .

"My forgetting you is nothing but another title of nobility. A certificate of your past value" (Postface: 56).

The end brings us back to a reality and to a way of negotiating with its social scenes. The *Nine Letters* are literature. The letters were prompted by and lean on the gentleman, but they do *not* hope to arrive at their destination. Yet they call out with such force, desire, and nostalgia, that they cannot but move the reader. They are hardly triumphant and have to be read on several levels. The reader may be bothered by Tsvetayeva's position, which can best be seen in her all-pervasive work on the signifier. The unconscious is at work, but so is the poet. A great multiplicity of signs, always very organized, prevails. She might be close to Genet's writings. In Tsvetayeva, there is so much work on language that it has the effect of a screen. Behind the screen, a passionate drama appears, formulated in an anecdote, in a kind of quotidian scene of abandonment that we read in her ninth letter:

"My friend, you did not come tonight because you had to write (to your kin)" (9: 44), of whom she does not feel a part and from whom she feels excluded.

"Such things do not hurt me any longer, you accustomed me to them, you and everyone else, because you too are eternal: innumerable (like the other self, on the ground and in the sky" (9: 44). She alludes to a scene where she had waited for the man while lying on her balcony at night. This ninth letter is one of the most beautiful scenes of desire in despair or of amorous desolation. "It is always the same me that does not come toward the same self that is waiting for it, always"

(9: 45). In one leap, Tsvetayeva goes over to the absolute, the infinite, and the universal. She begins with a singular story with grotesque overtones, but through writing she arrives at an archetypal level. For her, it is the same eternal you, the same eternal self, the same tragedy between man and woman that can be refuted, rejected, but that she works through in a mode of desolation. At the beginning of the ninth letter she says: "From attention (tension), I was suddenly and violently overcome with sleep. I was listening for your footsteps, I did not want to have to reproach myself one day for having missed you" (9: 42). She encounters lack in what she calls the sad meaning of missing a chance and of failing in one's civic or maternal duty. Generally she misses him, but he does not miss her. After having described how she was lying on the hard, cold balcony, she adds: "I soon felt my lowness (that of all these last days with you — oh, no offense! — I was a coward, and you were you). I know that I am not that way, it is only because I am trying to live" (9: 43). And there follows her definition of what living is: "To live is to cut in pieces and inevitably miss and then put the pieces back together" (9: 43). One can say that she writes the letters so that she can sew herself together again. There follows a whole semantic scale on patching. Her definition of living also defines her relation between living and writing. When she writes, she cuts and patches. Her dashes first cut, then she sews together again: " — and nothing holds (and nothing is yours, and one does not hold on to anything any more — forgive me this sad and serious word play)" (9: 43).

She describes herself as a pitiful little seamstress who tries to patch things together: "a miserable seamstress who will never do beautiful things, who only knows how to spoil and hurt herself and who, putting everything down: scissors, pieces of cloth, spool, begins to sing" (9: 43).

Who could have picked up her scissors? She had distant partners and one cannot see any other possibility for her. She sings, as she says, at a window where it rains forever. Such a flow opens onto an eternity that Tsvetayeva puts in relation with those instants, these days that are always missing and that never take place. And each time, she cuts. But life forces her to scream. For Tsvetayeva, it is not only the separation between men and women, not only impossible love, but also a primal drama, something originary that takes place between life, of which one did not ask anything, and the one who put us in the world, that is to say, the real author or the mother. Tsvetayeva keeps insisting that she is being forced, and that she is capable of great violence in order to go from force to farce.

Her work on the signifier is not gratuitous. The most insistent is "I was born carried away [Je suis née emmenée]." People like Clarice Lispector or Marina Tsvetayeva were born from a tomb. Their relation to their mothers, to birth, are failed, so they are painful. For both, the question of the maternal is raised in a strong sense, since they were both daughters of sick mothers. The questions remain: "What is it to be born? For what am I born? Of what? Why? And who looked over my cradle?" (8: 23)

The same scream is at the basis of all of Tsvetayeva's letters: Take me away, once, carry me once. But the situation is constantly reversed, since she is the mother and the man is the child. At the same time, everything is fictitious, since nothing happens. Everything is about a desire that neither dies nor tells itself what it is: "You must know that you do not take me away from anywhere, that I am already taken away from every place in the world and from myself toward a single one, where I never arrive. (What cowardice to tell you this!)" (8: 39). Tsvetayeva constantly reproaches herself for her cowardice, which can be heard, the way she formulates it, as: I am a coward (je suis lâche), in its overdetermination of *lâche* and *lâch(é)e,* "coward" and "having been dropped, abandoned," but also "she who abandons." To be taken away or carried away is stronger than to be exiled. But Tsvetayeva is carried away into language. She lives in, and covers herself with, language. In "carried away," "taken away," "*em-me-née,*" we can hear that she cannot bring about her own birth. She absolves the man by stating that she is nowhere, carried off in a movement of infinite skidding. The drama is played out over an originary absence that precedes everything. Hence her love through writing, through the letter that only speaks of absence. Hence also the fact that words are but "palms," simulacra of hands. She says things that are terrible and true: "There are words of tenderness in your letter that caress my heart: palm-words *[mots-paumes].* It is good to sleep with such a letter. Thank you" (8: 38–39) This is the most that can happen to her. And she continues:

"And words of precision in mine: which must redress your heart: palm-words *[mots-palmes].* It is good to wake with such a letter. Do thank." (8: 39).

Her logic of spending is very real:

"Because, you see, it is only when one is at the end (of tenderness or of any other force) that one recognizes its inexhaustibleness. The more we give, the more we have left; as soon as we give prodigiously — it flows forth! Let us bleed ourselves — and here we are, a source of life!" (8: 40).

She has the palm-words, he has the apple. The nourishment that is supposed to come back to the woman goes to the man:

"Of course you do not write me any more — since you have them, my poems. You are like a baby who is taught to walk with an apple — always offered, never given, since as soon as he has it, he will stop. You have it, the apple" (8: 40).

From the beginning the text separates at the level of the letter-signifiers that represent masculinity or femininity. For example, Tsvetayeva declares *f* to be her virile letter. There is a lot of work on *f*'s. Words carry masculine and feminine sonorous effects, always in the mode of a claim, of a need, or of an impossible demand.

Etty Hillesum: How to Plant Flowers under the Nazi Occupation

I would like to assume, without assuming, something that is not very far from a central preoccupation in me and that is less a form of worry than a kind of stubbornness that moves toward a form of pleasure and joy. This worry or pre-occupation is that the texts I am currently reading are without pity. They are linked to a certain period that was probably more familiar with darkness than with light. Texts like those by Etty Hillesum take up the survival of art in a world that corresponds to the Shakespearean description of "sound and fury." Etty Hillesum's texts are but sound and fury and an immense struggle for meaning. They can nevertheless be read as a Bible of *savoir vivre,* of how to live and how to experience pleasure. My own recipe stays always the same. It consists in urging readers to plant flowers, both metaphorically and concretely. This is a little what happens in Etty Hillesum, who answers the onslaught of Nazism and its destruction not only through death but with all living means: She urges people to go and buy melons while there are some left and when there will be no more, to write a poem about them.

In her *Diary,* she says:

"Wednesday morning, 8 am. O Lord, on this early morning, give me fewer thoughts, less cold water and gymnastics. How can you lock life into a few formulas? But that is what preoccupies you constantly and makes your thoughts run. You try to reduce life to formulas, but it is impossible, it is nuanced infinitely, it can neither be enclosed nor simplified. But you could be simpler. . . .

"In a moment I will undoubtedly write: how beautiful life is and how happy I am. But right now, I cannot figure the state of mind this presupposes."

The beauty of life is given to her and then taken away again in an inexplicable, mysterious manner. We can hide behind Etty and perhaps we will succeed in making melons or roses grow. We can try in any event.

The reader of Tsvetayeva's *Nine Letters* is struck by the insistence on sexual difference in grammar. From the beginning, she organizes a play between masculine and feminine around a semantic proximity: "I do not exaggerate to you, all this stays within the limits of darkness . . . — of furs and thickets *[de fourrures et de fourrés]*" (1: 7). *Fourré* (thicket) is called up by *fourrure* (fur). The distribution between masculine and feminine, the play of the masculine with the feminine, is always in the same mode. Tsvetayeva insists on a kind of relative obscurity. At the same time, since she gives them to us, we can take the *f*'s in *fourrés* and *fourrures.* There are hundreds of them in the text. I call this letter *f* the first letter, the letter that burns *(fait feu). Feu,* with all the effects of meaning, carries in French "fire" and "deceased." Tsvetayeva plays with the letter *f,* a masculine letter for her, on every page. Sparks fly and fall everywhere. The text burns *(fait feu de)* everything and ends up in ashes. The text loses the thread and, often, it loses us. At the same time, from this masculine *f, féminine* and *femme,* "feminine" and "woman" are going to emerge. For Tsvetayeva, divisions and oppositions do not exist:

"My tender one (he who makes me . . .), with all my indivisibly double being, doubly and indissolubly one, with my whole being of a double-edged sword (gifted with this reassuring virtue of being able to hurt only myself) I want in you, *in-you,* as in night" (2: 11).

Tsvetayeva tells the reader: Be careful, this is double, do not bring it back to woman. "You liberate in me my feminine being, my most obscure and most hidden being" (2: 11). Though there is an association between feminine and obscure, there is strictly speaking "no pure feminine." It is right away accompanied by the masculine *r.*

Yet this kind of nondivision divides itself. The double has to be cut into syllables to find something soft that circulates everywhere. Tsvetayeva consciously plays on *le* and *la:* "The skin *[la peau]* as such does not exist. . . . The skin *[le pel]* is not only beast but plant" (2: 11). *Peau* and *pel* are the same word, "skin," but we slip from one end to the other of the grammar of gender, while saying more or less the same thing. In the play on *peau/pel,* the message is not to pay attention to the skin. One can see only fire: "You make me soft (humanize, feminize, animalize) like fur." We have already seen how in Clarice Lispector's text "Tanta mansidão" (Such mansuetude), woman was the equivalent of nobody.[8] For Tsvetayeva, there is something else:

"Descent into night itself. That is why I am so comfortable with you without light. ('A village of forty fires . . .' With you I am a village with not one fire, perhaps a big city, perhaps nothing — 'erstwhile there was . . .' Nothing will prove me since I extinguish myself entirely.) . . . Without light, lying in wait of our voices" (1: 8).

A whole scale of meaning comes out of fire. "Without light" is similar, though not identical, to "obscure." It has to be brought back to Rimbaud, toward a night that cannot be without light, but full of light. Perhaps it is a day without light and here we could touch on the value of day, or perhaps the sensation of a world without light, which someone might feel who has not been given or who thinks he has not been given the day. This is also one of Rimbaud's themes. Perhaps the liberation of her "most feminine hidden being that does not succeed in seeing the day" is also that.

The letter is marked by the insistence of fire, *feu.* But *feu* can also be read in French as "deceased, the departed" from *fatum,* "destiny." *Feu* is he who has accomplished his destiny.

"But is fur less? Hair *[le poil]* is night — the lair — the stars — the voice that screams *[pel-appel],* both as hair and calling and even the spaces . . ." (1: 10–11).

The passage can be put side by side with a multiplicity of other texts. In a specific cultural context, in a French space, Tsvetayeva might have read Mallarmé's poems. The *antre/entre* is everywhere in her writings and she exploits it extensively.

"I do not even know: *are* you in my life? In the space of my soul — no. But here, near my soul, in a certain in between *[entre]:* sky and earth, soul and body, dog and wolf . . ." (1: 9).

Tsvetayeva works on punctuation like a seamstress. She cuts and patches. She cuts in such a way that the negation comes at the end and that the sentence is also affirmation: "In the space of my soul — no." But the reader had time to believe that it *is* "in the space of my soul." Tsvetayeva advances and withdraws constantly in a space in between *(entre)*. Dashes symbolize the *entre* visually. Tsvetayeva links animal to *anima/âme* (soul). The value of *anima* is in "a certain in between: sky and earth." *Entre* (in between) is emphasized and interrupted by the colon. Sky and earth are joined. Soul and body, dog and wolf are married in a similar fashion. "Dog and wolf" *(chien et loup),* in French an expression referring to a moment in between day and night, are literally hostility personified, erased here in a dream where "I am no longer I, and my dog is no longer mine" (1: 9). Attributes of the proper are also dissolved.

We can think here of Jacques Derrida's study of the *antre,* the cave, in his text entitled "La double séance,"[9] a reading of Plato and Mallarmé that deals with the phonic confusion of *entre/antre* (between/cave) and the imperative of the verb: *entre!* (enter!) The question is: Does the *antre* (cave) have a bottom *(fond)*? Plato says yes and Mallarmé says no, because the *antre* (cave) is but an *entre* (between) and an *entre!* (enter). In this undecidable space *entre-deux,* between the two, genders circulate. In a contemporary vocabulary, this is called the structure — or the logic — of the hymen. The word itself is undecidable, since it is at the same time hymen, the membrane of virginity, and, as in the classical theater, marriage. As Mallarmé says, and Derrida takes up, a *hymen* is something paradoxical since marriage is going to undo the hymen. Hymen is something that gathers and separates. It is both closure and that which undoes it. We have a structure of relays. Mallarmé's economy is interrupted and undecidable. But Tsvetayeva's is more cruel: her *entre* (between) is both separation and being separated.

The work on genres, on the empty space, is assigned to man: "Without your emptiness" (2: 13) implies that you are hollow and I am full. It is a frank opposition, but in Tsvetayeva, the woman is full of emptiness, of empty sky, and vice versa.

"I know everything, Man, I know you are superficial, light, concave but your deep animality touches me more profoundly than other souls. You know so well how to be cold, warm, hungry, thirsty, sleepy" (2: 12–13).

We read between the lines: "and I do not know." The man's lack becomes positive and her positivity becomes lack. In man, it is a need that has to be satisfied.

"I do not know if you are overloved (overnourished with love) in your life. Probably yes. But what I know (and if you had to hear it for the thousandth time) is that no one *[nul (nulle!)]* ever has you thus . . ." (2: 13).

The verb is missing. It may be "to love" or "to hate," the place of affect is too strongly marked. The reader is struck by *nul (nulle!)*. The feminine word in parentheses, *nulle,* is like the secret of the masculine *nul.* The text plays simultaneously in different directions. In Mallarmé, the subject skids incessantly but the subject of the poem is about the figuration of the hymen. In Tsvetayeva, the poem is about *all* of life. It is at the same time troubling and cruel. As a reader, I do not know whether to defend, admire, or console her, but I will insist on this particularly beautiful page:

"Faithfulness: impossibility of another (to be other). The rest is Lucifer (pride) and Luther (duty). As you can see, my head takes advantage of my heart.

"And take me away, some evening — for a whole evening. So that I forget you a little by finding you. So that we will be two to carry you" (2: 17).

"Fidelity" is something out of Kafka, on the order of: I cannot be otherwise. It is not easy. The title of this fidelity is marked by a fatal "That's the way it is." If I hurt you, forgive me for being the way I am. Her pride becomes apparent in the impossibility of her being other, as Kafka would say.

"One thing I have just understood: with the other one, there was *r,* my favorite letter, the most myself of the entire alphabet, my essentially virile letter:

> froid, roc, heros, Sparte (renard!) —
> tout ce que j'ai de droit, de dur, de fort.
> Avec vous: chuchotements, chaleur, lâcheté, relâchement,
>   et surtout: chéri!

> [freezing, rock, hero, Spartan (fox!) —
> all I have that is straight, hard, strong.
> With you: whispering, warmth, cowardice, softening, and
>   especially: darling!]

"My darling, I know that this is disorder: from the morning, to love rather than to write. But it happens to me so rarely, if *ever!* I always fear that I am dreaming that I am about to wake up and again: rock, hero . . ." (5: 24–25).

R is the menace. But why did she choose not to include "to write" *(écrire),* curiously omitted? *R* is virile, *ch* is softening. One could find in it a separation between virile and feminine, but it does not hold because *r* is altered by what follows. In "rock," it is clear but in *chéri* (darling), an *r* is also written. Is this her ploy, or a mark of her blindness and her deafness? After having played the mother of this "child," she lets through an *r* altered in the presence of a feminine *ch.* Elsewhere, we read:

"My dear child, I take your dear head with both hands — what a strange sensation, [to feel] the eternity of the skull through the temporality of the hair, the eternity of the rock through the temporality of the grass . . ." (6: 27).

R and *ch* reappear but escape us. *R* is masculine but is also present in the feminine since *l'herbe* (grass) is feminine. Head and body are in constant metamorphosis.

Clarice Lispector, "Pertenecer": "I was born cut off from the source"

Marina Tsvetayeva's insistence on having been born "carried away" can be read next to Clarice Lispector's birth story, which begins with a somewhat banal remark: "A friend of mine, a doctor . . ."[10]

We are in a chronicle. We leave from the remark of a friend and arrive in the desert. The whole text turns around the problem of the unspoken word "crime." Clarice is the author of an originary crime that she did not commit.

The text is double. Clarice wrote it as a kind of criminal who assumes responsibility for the crime. Yet underneath it, another text cries out silently, I am not a criminal, I am paying for a crime I did not commit. But nobody knows this. "Pertenecer" ("To belong") is a wonderful example of a double-bind in writing. In *Near to the Wild Heart,* she is the daughter of a dead mother. But the worst is said in this text in relation to the way she was conceived:

"And yet I was prepared to be given birth in such a pretty way. My mother was already ill, and due to a very widespread superstition, it was believed that having a child cured a woman of disease. So I was deliberately created: with love and hope."

The text above says that Lispector forgives her parents, but that *she* cannot be forgiven. The text below is but one inaudible scream. Clarice goes beyond the parental pardon, since she does not talk about it. She takes on the discourse of the parents, the way she heard it as a child, and that is criminal. It was not *she* who was conceived but her mother. Whence Clarice's writing of despair and solitude: to say, my father and my mother killed me, is prohibited. If she did, she would kill her parents. So she does not say it, and accepts being the most solitary human being from the cradle onward. "I am sure that in the cradle, my first desire was to belong." Clarice has a false memory of this founding scene, which, in any case, is a reconstructed scene.

"I am almost able to visualize myself in the cradle, I am almost able to reproduce in myself a vague and yet pressing sensation of needing to belong. For reasons that neither my mother nor my father could control, I was born and remained only: born."

Had she been conceived to be simply their child, she would have become the child or the daughter. But she was pure "being born." How could she write this chronicle that decries the crime perpetrated against her? Perhaps Clarice wrote this story to her parents or perhaps to the readers of the *Jornal do Brasil,* the national newspaper in which it appeared — that is, to her dead parents.

Certainly, she sees herself in the cradle. She assumes the position of the parents and of those who looked at her in the cradle. She must have a memory of herself as a child abandoned in the cradle. Afterward, she was loved and brought up. But the way of looking at herself in the cradle with pity and tenderness as someone more conscious than her parents is a way of giving herself to herself: "Who knows if I began to write so early in life because, writing, at least I belonged a little to myself." And she wrote how she saw herself in the cradle.

There is an unbearable tragedy in this text. Where Tsvetayeva says: I was born carried away, Clarice says: I was born: born. I was born nobody. I lost the way of becoming somebody.

Clarice makes up for this by belonging to Brazilian literature. In appearance, she has nevertheless become somebody. It is a minimum of belonging. "I belong, for example, to my country and like millions of other people, I am belonged by it to the point of being Brazilian." Here is a definition, expressed in her strange syntax. She is not a child, but is she a woman? She does not know. We have benefited from her ability to say: Perhaps I am animal, I would have liked to be a tiger, or, I will regret forever not to have been a cockroach. She is deprived of a self and succeeds in qualifying herself as Brazilian. It can be understood by the Brazilian reader as a patriotic ferocity, but in reality it is something completely different.

Clarice knows well what giving and receiving mean. Like Tsvetayeva who says: the more one gives, the more one has, Clarice knows all the secrets, including that not to give is not to give to oneself. There must be circulation. The gift exists only as a possibility of bringing forth the source. Clarice was born cut off from the source. She was only born, and this troubles her. The question is: How can she be a source for others when she does not have her own source? Or, when I have pleasure, how do I transmit it?

"It is like standing with a present all wrapped up in adorned wrapping paper in one's hands—and having no one to say: Here, it is yours, open it!" One cannot imagine greater poverty. Clarice is deprived of the gift. How can one represent oneself with the present one has in one's hands? "Not wanting to see myself in pathetic situations and . . . avoiding the tone of tragedy, I therefore rarely wrap my feelings with wrapping paper."

Paper is everywhere: When I write, I write as if I were naked, and I do not make a present. As in an infernal machine, what was missing at the beginning cannot be made up.

Later Clarice goes further. "With time, above all the last few years, I lost the way of being a person. I don't know how to be anymore. And a totally new kind of 'solitude of not belonging' began to invade me like ivy on a wall." Solitude covers her and clings to her. From not having an other, the void is filled by the ivy that climbs on her, and carries in itself the motto: I die or I tie myself to something. Fidelity and infidelity at once climb all over her. In a lengthy meditation, she tells us that to know how to belong is one of the secrets. One belongs only inasmuch as the other gives himself or herself to you. In Clarice, everything is cut off from the beginning, since no one gave himself to her. She was abandoned, though the event did not *really* take place. She feels that from the cradle on, she does not belong to anything or anybody. Obviously, when she writes this chronicle, her parents are already dead.

Having been born cut off from the source is going to shape her trajectory, situated between the need of a baby, human hunger, and the way ivy clings at the moment of maturity. Hunger is going to accompany her throughout her life. It transforms itself into thirst, the key to all of her texts. Yet her thirst, of a terrible beauty, is the kind one feels in the desert.

Clarice works on the signifier: "And yet, I was prepared to be given birth in such a pretty way." The work of the signifier on body and soul can be followed. The fact of having been deserted leads her to the desert: "It is really in the desert that I walk." The crime she did not commit is translated into desertion: "I was made for a determined mission and I failed. As if they counted on me in the trenches during the war and I had deserted." And later, she says: "As a deserter, I knew the secret of the flight that, out of shame, could not be made known." She deserted as a deserter. She changed her sex and fled from a frightening scene, that is, from the war her parents waged against her. She fled reality, life, unhappiness. Her desertion produced a desert, the equivalent of an absence of world.

"I know my parents forgave me for having been born in vain and having betrayed them in great hope. But I, I don't forgive myself. I would simply have liked a miracle: to be born and to cure my mother." That would have been a miracle. "Then yes: I would have belonged to my father and my mother." Clarice would have had to be mother in order to be admitted in her family as a child.

The door to the second, unwritten text, hidden under the first one, reads: "I could not confide in anybody this kind of 'solitude of not belonging.'" When saying this, she confides in thousands of readers of a Brazilian newspaper, *Jornal do Brasil*. Can all these readers be called "nobody," simply because she herself is nobody? For Clarice, the desertion is infinite. At the same time, she confides: I will not tell you that I fled. But perhaps she is saying something else. Perhaps the very secret of her flight is that she herself had been "fled."

An accusation against her parents is unthinkable and would have turned her into a criminal. To accuse, to denounce is criminal in any case. That is Clarice's double-bind. Her being ashamed to tell this secret put her apart in the world, with few moments of exception: "Life made me from time to time belong." It is not a person, but life. She is the adopted child of life. Because she has a mind of quasi-philosophical power, she asks: How do I know what I have lost if I never had it? She knows because at times life has made her brief favors. But Clarice always loses: "I experienced it with the thirst of someone who is in the desert and who avidly drinks the last sips of water from a canteen." Though she has an interminable thirst, she knows what it is not to be thirsty. She stands in the desert, in front of us, and her gesture reveals the measure of the abandonment that constitutes her. She screams without screaming, before hundreds of thousands of people: I am abandoned.

There follows an explanation: Write to give yourself a little water, a little paper to eat. We know her passion for rain. In many passages of *Agua viva,* she divides herself into two—and a little girl dies. Clarice continues to relive the abandonment in her mother's belly. She was the victim of a false cradle. This may have been her own fabrication, but the history of the conception to cure the mother is true.

Being supremely intelligent, Clarice does not take the wrong road and put her parents on trial. The parents committed a crime, but they are completely innocent. In a similar situation, Tsvetayeva would arrive with her battle ax. Her world of vengeance and retaliation, in the style of the Russian revolution, is completely different. Yet Clarice also says: There are moments when one must not forgive. She lives in a universe of inequalities, social violence, and pain, but not in that of a Russian monstrosity where, to survive, one had to become cruel. Clarice has not been abandoned. In her biography we read that she was loved, courted, adored, surrounded by friends. This did not in any way diminish her solitude, since her abandonment was infinite. Tsvetayeva has known the betrayal of all of her close friends. In her world to love someone was even too dangerous.

Tsvetayeva's text is spiked with an armor like that of an Amazon, while Clarice chose the most absolute bareness *(dépouillement)* and remained faithful to her poverty. Tsvetayeva, at the bottom of her misery, died of hunger, so to speak. But to the outside world, she constantly showed her wealth. With fury, she tells the world: I am rich, with me, you are going to lose a great poet. We can understand her distress. But Clarice, with an extraordinary audacity, says: I, Clarice Lispector, famous and celebrated, I am very poor. The two women are at opposite ends. They share being without a mother, without something maternal. But both have been mothers. Betrayed by their mothers, they make an effort to *be* mothers.

Desert Writing

In the correspondence that took place in the summer of 1926 between Pasternak, Tsvetayeva, and Rilke, published as *Letters, Summer 1926* in their writing, the three poets were at a kind of summit with no more room for another step before the fall. One more step and Rilke died. One more step and Tsvetayeva entered the hell that led her to what I do not want to call suicide but rather her assassination by history. One more step and Pasternak took a fatal step backward and fell. Ten years later — and I say this without judgment, because I think of the implacability of history, which is the real author of these autobiographies — Pasternak did not die of despair, but he paid (and everybody always pays). He paid his customs duties in order to remain in a minimal security. And the second Pasternak is but a souvenir of the great Pasternak of his youth. I do not know who is the one that comes afterward. Such things are hard to say. They have to be said without judgment because we do not know if, in the place of Pasternak or Tsvetayeva, we would have chosen one suicide over another, one death over another. And no one ever knows.

Pasternak's *Essays in Autobiography* date from the fifties. They write of the same passionate period that concerns us. Reading across the French, they could be read as the essay of essays or of *décès,* that is, of death. We can find the same period, told otherwise, in texts like Mandelstam's admirable *Noise of Time,* where we see the word "revolution," almost erased in the text, somewhat like the devil in person. These texts date from the beginning, the rise, and the accomplishment of disaster. I take this word literally, to the letter, in the manner of Blanchot, that is as a *dés-astre,* or a falling of the stars, as the extinction of the stars in a sky that is now black. Can one be a witness of disaster strictly speaking? Is it possible to see the stars being extinguished? And, at such a limit, what does one see and do?

I want to situate these comments between a writing in the desert and a writing of disaster. They are not the same but at some point they touch and could be confused. When I speak of a desert writing, I allude to a formidable gift, a poisoned gift, as we know from the overdetermination of the German *Gift* — a terrible gift bestowed on some people in the cradle, a kind of malediction that is also a benediction and that condemns, "elevates and educates" them to poetry. The works of human beings like Clarice Lispector and Arthur Rimbaud come from the desert. This kind of primal scene is the awakening of the baby to the absence of everything, to the absence of milk, of light, be it imaginary or real. The originary effect, when its repercussions are played out, produces a kind of music. Everything happens as if the non-milk, the absence of milk, gave way to a milk of the ear, or to music, hence a death and a kind of birth in the desert. This leads us to the Bible, where there are also deserts, as in most great poetic works. In the Bible, the deserts are crossed mainly in conjunction with scenes of encounter with the absolute. It is the abandon, or as Tsvetayeva would say, in her usual play on the signifier, "le banc *d'a-ban-don,*" the bench of abandon. Tsvetayeva worked on the value of the word "abandon" at the level of the signifier. In French, the word exudes "gift" *(don)* and its opposite, *abandon*.

In the desert one lives a solitude and its contrary. The bottom of solitude may be the encounter with the absolute, but this encounter also opens onto solitude. The absolute can be the entrance to the desert. We can see it in Kierkegaard where Abraham is in communication with God. He loses the world in order to speak to God. But he will never be able to tell humans of his divine conversation. The desert can give us a little bit of God, or God can give us a little desert.

Paul Celan, "Und mit dem Buch aus Tarussa": A Written Desert

The desert always shows ambivalence. That is where we can put Celan's poem "Und mit dem Buch aus Tarussa," written after Tsvetayeva and Mandelstam, but in the same tradition. The German *aus,* "from," indicates an origin, a departure. The text resonates with *vom, von,* a "from," similar to *aus* but closer to the presence of a source. The text sings of a special desert, of Tarussa, a place also named in Tsvetayeva's writings. Celan speaks of a city on the Oka river where Tsvetayeva and Pasternak, among others, spent their summers. His poem surges from this lost childhood.

I place Celan's poem among all the writings of the desert. We hear the poem as a written desert, but we also hear that it takes the desert as subject. At the same time, it is a writing of disaster, a writing that speaks of and through disaster such that disaster and desert become the author or the spring. Can the desert be spring? Rimbaud tells us how, paradoxically, the desert *can* be spring. Some deserts do produce blossoms, water or milk. The desert can be an originary or an imaginary experience, something that surges from the unconscious. The desert points to an originary lack of engendering and to a family history. Disaster is something else. Historically, it can be inscribed at the other end of time. It means the falling of the stars, the *déchéance* (crumbling) of the sky. At a certain moment, Mandelstam says somewhere that the earth costs as much as ten skies. That is what it means to be a witness of the night, that is, of a denatured earth. The writings of Etty Hillesum, Paul Celan, Anna Akhmatova, and Marina Tsvetayeva are on the side of the desert *and* of disaster. Pasternak's are on the side of disaster. He did not have an originary desert. The desert makes one cry, but disaster dries up language. The devil may induce us into temptation but God keeps us from passing judgment on the people at the scene of disaster. We can never know what position would have been ours in the hour of disaster.

Why did Etty Hillesum stay? is a question which in other times I could not hear. After 1945, when people began to understand what had happened to the Jews, everyone began to ask the question: Why did they stay? For a long time, I did not have an ear for this question. For me, everything could be explained very simply. I did not understand the question nor the greatest masterpieces written from it, such as those of Hannah Arendt, who was able to reach the United States, and who wrote very beautiful sociological texts in which the passivity of the Jews is put in question. Now, I am able to accept the question because it teaches me something incomprehensible and how — like salt, sand, sugar — the incomprehensible is widespread. People do *not* understand each other. The incomprehensible part of each of us makes up the entire basis of life. Perhaps by reading these texts, we can work toward an effort of meditation on the incomprehensible. I do not say that we are going to understand the incomprehensible, but we have to accept it. Perhaps we have to look for what is human beneath it all. Why did Etty Hillesum stay? What does it mean? Why did Pasternak, a great poet, lose his greatness by staying? Why do we choose certain paths? Should we not forget that we are blind and move along our paths in blindness? We tell ourselves a legend while we move, but we move blindly. Some people do see. What does seeing give us? To Tsvetayeva, it gave what she saw. Before, she wandered around in the desert, itself already a kind of dreadful agony. But seeing even took the desert away from her. She started to see when she was at the end of the world, when she no longer had even an earth to put her feet on or a human being to speak to.

We can also let ourselves be haunted by the Sakharov couple. In my view, they ask the same ultimate and necessary question. Next to the fact that they are venerable, they must have in themselves that treasure of treasures, the inextinguishable spark of faith. They must have faith to remain alone, a trinket of voice against eight hundred million deaf ears. These are people who decided to stay where there are no ears. Their faith is that some day, somewhere, there will be open ears. It is not necessarily for tomorrow, but perhaps in two hundred years.

What produces springs in the desert? For the poet Sakharov, it may be God or a synonym. It may be childhood. Some people had a childhood, but a great many never did. Their childhood blew away like dead leaves and nothing remained. Those who keep their childhood already have a world behind them. Sometimes, there may be another childhood, something that comes in its place, old age for example, with an immense memory. It can be the heritage of those who wander, like the Jews, or of those who have behind them the Book of History and a very long story that made them cross time. Those who have five thousand years behind them say to themselves that perhaps, in another five thousand, there will be something else. That is why it is not surprising to read in a text by Tsvetayeva the words we have seen addressed to Mandelstam, "All poets are Jews." And then there are those who were given poetry in their cradle, and who know that if there is nothing left, there still is the world of language. I take the risk of saying that these people answer nothingness, from the desert to disaster, poetically. They are people who at the very moment of struggle, of encounter with historical disasters, work on language, transform it, work it, garden it, graft it. They are masters of the signifier. Language is their universe and with it they build a little house that is a palace. They grow forests, gardens, build mountains. They need and transform language. It is of no surprise that one finds that work on the signifier is formed among people who staked their tents in language: Rimbaud, Lispector, Tsvetayeva, Celan, and others.

Marina Tsvetayeva, "The Devil" and "Mother and Music": The Verbal Parent

In her short stories Tsvetayeva tells us her sumptuous childhood memories. Tsvetayeva can be related to George Sand, with whom she has in common an imaginary that is feminine. George Sand and Marina Tsvetayeva are probably not the only ones to have seen the devil, their devil, their god-devil. An essential and secret story circulates between the maternal and the child, but what will it be? For Tsvetayeva something undecidable remains. We constantly see here and in her other texts — especially in her *Nine Letters* — a very strong accent on virility. From her early childhood, a sexual struggle is waged with the maternal. The real mother exists, but somewhat like Virginia Woolf in her biography, Tsvetayeva benefited from a variety of maternal elements. First of all, there is another mother, since Tsvetayeva's father had a first wife. Tsvetayeva is determined by a family history that she retells at great length. The first wife was a singer, and the second, Tsvetayeva's mother, plays the piano. The whole house is swept away in a torrent of music. But, like the work of the devil, everything can be divided. There is another mother who dies and there is the mother, Meyn, who is Polish and speaks German. Tsvetayeva speaks of her in relation to the German signifier, *mein,* "mine," that is also related to *mind,* "thought." She always hears these signifiers.

The mother tongue is double, it is fractured. From early childhood on, everything is sung and played in German, preserved in the text, especially through nursery rhymes. Hence the maternal prevails in Tsvetayeva's writing. The father's first wife, the singer, was Russian. Valeria, her daughter, is Tsvetayeva's half-sister. We can sense in the pages of these stories conflict and concord in a family with two mothers, both of whom had the same fate. They both died very young, probably of tuberculosis. The mother's illness becomes a recurring theme that can be put side by side with Clarice Lispector's texts. Everything is troubled, divided through doubling and loss.

At the beginning of "The Devil" Tsvetayeva imagines that she enters his house, which has a woman as doorkeeper. She enumerates a series of women, all nurses, but never "my mother." It does not matter because the space of the "mother" is quite vast: The first and the second mother; the one who gives permission and the one who prohibits. Valeria herself is also a form of mother. Everything is under the sign of the mother, for or against her, with or without her, but the accent is on the mother.

One discovers also — since everything is divided and mirrored — that hell is paradise. In the room of the house, fruit is given. The room is a paradise garden, a prohibited paradise, the way the Devil is God and Tsvetayeva commits the supreme sin by calling him God-Devil.

"Mother and Music" can be put side by side with "The Devil." Tsvetayeva could have said "My Devil and Music," or "My God and Music." While reading these two texts, I chose as a title for meditation: "The Verbal Parent." I found this expression in the first text, where the entire world was engendered by the piano and its "other world." Tsvetayeva's sources — and she is very conscious of it — are the world and the names of the world; in other words, everything that deals with naming. She goes from one world to the other literally by "swimming" in a verbal flow. In "Mother and Music," for example, the piano is decomposed into each of its real elements. Tsvetayeva tries to become conscious of all the mysteries of the world that are produced by a cosmic, even maritime piano. The piano tells us how it is earth and sea and how it contains all the words. Each word opens and divides indefinitely. The piano makes her cross over into another world, that of language. She struggles with each element of the world of music and is at war with the metronome.

The story of the pedal ensues. The mother constantly enters the text. She is repression personified and at the same time a genius. She is a magnificent and terrible being but in all the texts the reader can feel that the mother made her children pay for her oncoming death.

"She can't even reach the ground, but she already wants the pedal! What do you want to be: a musician or (swallowing the 'Liora') a lady who, except for the pedal and her rolling eyes . . . No. You must learn with your *hand* to give the pedal! I did it, with the foot, only in the absence of my mother, but at such length that I no longer knew if it was I who was pressing or if it was still the pedal (that I imagined in fact as a golden shoe, *Plattfuss*, of Cinderella!). The pedal, this *Plattfuss* or flatfoot, also had a verbal parent *Pedell,* the inspector of student meetings who, at one of these reunions, had taken away Arkadi Alexandrovitch (Arkaexanytch) whom Assia and I were crazy about, the Arkadi Alexandrovitch of André's repertory. This pedel brought about the second poem in my life:

> Everybody runs to the meeting.
> Where is the meeting, the meeting is where?
> The meeting is outside.[11]

The little poems are similar to those we read at the beginning of Joyce's or Clarice Lispector's work. Pedell is a man, but also the pedal.

"Mother and Music" opens on all the books Tsvetayeva was reading when she was little, especially on Hector Malot's children's classic *Sans famille,* published in 1878. In *Sans famille,* there is a little boy whose name is Remi. He is named implicitly in Tsvetayeva's text, the beginning of which reads: do, re, mi, do, re, mi. Tsvetayeva discovered when she was little that there was another side of the mirror and that there were verbal parents. On the one side, the family was complicated, divided, doubling itself, playing at life and death like musical instruments, and killing, because the two mothers, the first and the second, killed their children with music. On the other side, another, immense family was linked by contamination: a metonymic family that goes through language. In the verbal family, *Pudel,* the poodle, *Pedell,* meetings, revolution, repression, the *pedal* of the piano all engendered one another. And they all constitute a universe that makes music and produces meaning. If Tsvetayeva had studied English, she could have used Alice's mirror, but given her cultural context, she takes her treasures from German and French.

In George Sand's world the child has an originary access to language that is mostly going to be quickly prohibited and repressed through hierarchization, classification, both at home and at school. In Tsvetayeva, probably because her mother was dedicated to music, but also because elements of foreign languages were scattered everywhere, language floats unfettered. The mother is a foreigner, several languages are spoken at home and one can go from one drawer to the other. To give homage to such a rich text we would have to take up each little anecdote, because each is like a little door that opens. Following the mirror and study of the mirror we can tell the whole story.

I come back to "The Devil," a text of apprenticeship. The unfolding remains completely poetic because the text is absolutely faithful to childhood experiences and to an economy that is going to exceed the family and include fatality, death, and prohibition. All the characters are admirably encamped in an oblique way. The father, a university professor, is always absent, always distracted. The mother loves only music. There are the half-brother and half-sister, and the two worlds simultaneously representing life and death. Above all, the question of survival reigns. The constant reinscription of the first, respected, dead mother is always there and incarnated in the children of the first marriage, of the first "bed." In a certain way the first bed is important. The devil is in the first bed. This whole world defends itself against its end, against its limits and its disappearance. It has found its infinite quality in this mirror that — as in Lewis Carroll — does not simply refer to the side of the same, but opens onto the infinite registers of the other.

The devil is a composite character, between lion and Great Dane. He is naked, without fur. The devil's nakedness is quite insistent. At the beginning of the story, we are told that the little girl is bareheaded and the "back of her head is shorn of hair."[12] Tsvetayeva, ahead of her times, insists repeatedly on being a woman with short hair.

The devil has mixed features. He is at the same time a peasant woman from Ryazan and a pharaoh from the Louvre. He embodies the most archaic elements of Russian soil, and the most ancient cultural memory. The Great Dane is one of Tsvetayeva's favorite characters. He can be found in *Nine Letters* as a cross between dog and wolf. In some passages of her correspondence with Rilke and Pasternak, he reappears in the form of a beloved dog with which she exchanges kisses. She makes mention of it in one of her first letters, dated May 12, 1926, written from Saint-Gilles-sur-Vie, and this is not by chance.

On Ascension Day, 1926, she writes:

"Your penciled notation (is this right? no, annotation, I suppose!) — those dear, airy three words: to a dog [a quote from Rilke's *Sonnets to Orpheus*]. Dear one, this takes me right back to the middle of my childhood, age eleven; that is to say, into the Black Forest (into the very middle of it!). And the headmistress (Fräulein Brinck was her name, and she was gruesome) is saying, 'This little Satan's brat, Marina, makes one forgive anything; all she has to do is say "a dog"!'

"(A dog — yowling with ecstasy and emotion and wanting — a *Hund* with three *u-u-u*'s. They weren't pedigree dogs, just street mongrels!)

"Rainer, the purest happiness, a gift of happiness, pressing your forehead on the dog's forehead, eye to eye, and the dog, astonished, taken aback, and flattered (this doesn't happen every day!), growls. And then one holds his muzzle shut with both hands (since he might bite from sheer emotion) and kisses, just smothers him."[13]

Marina is diabolical. She plays on dogs and words, with this privilege constantly given to the protective dog who is at the same time part man. In "The Devil," Tsvetayeva herself plays the devil as part lion and mastiff. S/he is sitting in Valeria's room:

"There was no movement. He sat, I stood. And — I loved him" (296).

Love is linked to contemplation and the absolute. Why is she in Valeria's room? Analyzing it, she notes that it is a room with books, that is, a library. This library has a mirror:

"I move with my eyes . . . from the screen to the book cabinet, such a strange cabinet where instead of books you see yourself, and even to the little cabinet with its — as Nurse says — "good-for-nothings" (299).

The room cannot be exhausted since there are not only books in which one sees the other but a mirror in which one can see oneself, and so on.

This place has been called "the tree of knowledge" (300). Here the war with her mother begins since the latter prohibits the reading of the books, which, of course, makes them passionately interesting. Gogol's *Dead Souls,* forbidden by the mother, is the first title to come up. In a slippage, Tsvetayeva writes that the dead souls are prohibited by the mother:

"I would press against [the stove] with the back of my head, shorn of hair, burning hot from summer, while I read aloud to Lera what was forbidden by mother and therefore permitted — put into my hands — by Lera: *Dead Souls,* which — the dead bodies and the souls — I never did find, never read up to, because at the last second when they were supposed to, were just ready to appear — the dead bodies and the souls too — as if on purpose mother's step would be heard (incidentally, she never did come in but only, every single time, at the right moment — as if run on a mechanism — went walking by) and, feeling weak from quite another fear, a real live one, I would stuff the huge book under the bed (that very one!)" (296).

All the secrets are here in the library. In addition there are forbidden fruits:

"Love *was there* in [Valeria's] room, love lived there, and not only her love and love for her, for the seventeen-year-old girl; all those albums, notes, patchouly, spiritualistic seances, sympathetic inks, tutors, tutoring, dress-ups as marquise, oiling of eyelashes — but stop there! Out of the deep well of the dresser, up and out of the rustle of velvets, corals, combed-out hair, paper flowers . . . they were focused on me — eyes looking my way! — the silver pellets" (300–1).

Again, we find the eyes of the devil, these metal eyes that looked on in a mysterious manner:

"Candies, but terrible, pills, but silver, edible silver beads that she for some reason devoured just as secretly (blocking the view with her back and with her forehead on the dresser) as I devour (with my forehead on the book cabinet) the 'Pearls of Russian Poetry'" (301).

Everything is here: the dangerous pieces of candy, the silver pills that also become poisonous metal eyes and resemble the poetic pearls that become edible. Valeria swallows it all in a scene revealing the world of femininity.

"Subsequently (so as to put the reader at ease) it turned out that the pills were the most innocent kind, *'contre les troubles'* etc., the most usual, young ladylike pills" (301).

The reader guesses that they are some kind of aspirin, taken most likely at the time of menstruation, something that cannot be named. Tsvetayeva associates femininity with the pearls of Russian poetry.

In the episode of the drowning she is saved by the devil. Tsvetayeva narrates a form of birth. The card games matter to her. Among them is the story of the green character with a red carbuncle. Everything takes place in German. The green character quoted by the mother is once again the devil. A long meditation on cards ensues and if Lewis Carroll fixed once and for all the play with the mirror, Tsvetayeva can be said to have done the same for card games. She meditates at length on the mystery of cards, on this strange tribe of beings with two heads, upside down and refusing to have legs, these homeless characters reigning over numerous subjects, three or four of the same color. Tsvetayeva fashions a God-Devil from the world of cards. The cards constantly reverse themselves, since the other side is the same. God is the Devil and at the same time secrets abound. A whole people, a system of mysterious power is a key for history when Black Peter *(Der Schwarze Peter)* emerges. The latter has to be gotten rid of at all costs. The secret of this game is that it is the key to Tsvetayeva's economy of passions. It shows how dangerous it is to play cards when one is not even fifteen years old.

"The point of the game was to foist off on another person the Jack of Spades, the *Schwarze Peter,* the way in old times you passed on a fever to a neighbor and even now you pass on a cold: you pass it on and by bestowing it, you get rid of it. At first, when there were lots of cards and players, there wasn't any game at all, properly speaking" (305).

She describes the game. The mystery begins with the *Black Peter* who is Tsvetayeva's devil:

"Never, perhaps, did he feel me so much his own as when I so cunningly and dazzlingly gave him away, got rid of him, once again concealed my secret and his, and perhaps the main thing, once again was able to get along — even without him" (306).

This may remind the reader of how much, elsewhere, she does without those she loves, in particular throughout her correspondence.

"So as to say it all: the game of *Schwarze Peter* was the same as a meeting with someone secretly and burningly beloved — in a crowd: the colder — the hotter, the farther off — the nearer, the more a stranger — the more mine, the more unbearable — the more blissful" (306).

That is where God and the Devil are interchangeable. We can read it in her *Letters* of 1926 and also in her *Nine Letters.* Is Tsvetayeva a monster? No, she is a poet. She is God, Devil, and the Black Peter. She moves in an inverted economy where she can find only through loss. And she has an infinite capacity for loss.

The text bursting forth from this burning source has a most rigorous construction. At the end Tsvetayeva received the devil from her mother. As she is very sick, she has the right to ask for a gift. She dares to ask her mother for the devil. It is the first time that the mother gives her the devil. The mother brings her the devil in a small bottle. There follows a funny scene in which the mother tells her to be careful, because if she heats the bottle it will explode. As in the story of Solomon, Tsvetayeva smashes the devil during the night. In the epilogue, we can see the difference in economies between mother and daughter:

" 'There now, you see,' said mother, sitting over my quiet tears, 'you must never become attached to a thing that can break. And they — they all break! Remember the commandment: "Do not make thyself a false idol"?'

" 'Mama,' I said, shaking myself away from the tears like a dog from water, 'and what makes a rhyme with "idol?" "Adele"?' " (317).

She never loses her tongue. In the struggle for the devil, the mother has given up for her daughter a little bit of devil that the latter loses right away. The mother's advice is not to get attached to objects — or subjects, men, or even mothers. Everything dies, disappears. But in the mirror there remains "Adele," the "idol." The infinite entry into the world of poetry remains. If she does not have a mother, at least she has a verbal parent.

Tsvetayeva's texts are both infinite and very harsh, but they are without hatred. When the daughter goes over to the infinite of language, she experiences a great love for the mother and for what she lets the mother do to her.

I come back to the *Letters* of 1926 to read these effects in Tsvetayeva's creations. In the introduction to the French translation *Correspondance à trois,* a quotation from Tsvetayeva's *Quelques lettres de Rainer Maria Rilke* (31–32), omitted in the English translation, shows how she insists on translation as *nachdichten.* The passage is a translation, a passage, a transference, a traversal of the mirror, or of what she called in a German neologism *nachdichten,* from *dichten,* "to compose poetry," and *nach,* "afterward."

"Today I want Rilke to speak through me. This is called translating in common language. (How much better it sounds in German: *nachdichten!*) Following the trace of another poet, to fray once more the road he already frayed. So much for *nach* (afterward), but there is *dichten,* something always new. (*Nachdichten* is to fray anew a path that grass invades instantly.) But translation also means something else. One does not simply make one language pass into the other (Russian, for example), one also passes a river. I make Rilke pass into Russian, the way he will one day make me pass into another world" (14).

The stakes of poetry consist in crossing over, through the river of language, to the other side, into another language and another world. Poets are passers or trespassers. We could also add in this context the English expression: *No trespassing.* These poets succeed in "trespassing" from one language to the other, and within language itself. They ascend, decompose, recompose incessantly with words, images, and genres. They manage to give their hands to one another without concretely doing so. They give a hand to each other through a symbolic marriage of poets, of poetry, of something that to this very day cannot be effaced.

Tsvetayeva's "Lettre à l'Amazone" takes up the problem of female homosexuality.[14]

Though its pronouncements on the topic are dated, the letter can hold our interest in relation to Tsvetayeva and writing. The text can be situated not far from what I just discussed, on a border both strange and familiar. The poet is looking for an interlocutor, a descendant, a child-echo of her own poetry, of her own music. I want to speak of this child-echo. One can find in Tsvetayeva — as in Clarice's texts traversed by desert and absence — a certain way of treating this "theme." In the antigarden represented by the desert, the question accompanying the poet like her shadow under the sun is: Who am I to be so alone? Who am I if I am not with another? The demand for another is always mute but piercing. All these texts ask for another and all the poets ask for another language, even for a foreign language perhaps, because the essence of poetry is to find strangeness in language. Every great poet translates another, out of love, but also because the calling of a foreign tongue is quite unlike one's own familiar language. All these poets are accompanied, doubled, divided by the other, in particular around sexual difference or something they do or do not take into account.

In "Lettre à l'Amazone" Tsvetayeva's work on language is of a poetic kind, but the content deals with female homosexuality. Tsvetayeva is in two places at once: in that of the homosexual who is alone, absolutely, because she has no descendants, and in her own place. The question is: Who in Tsvetayeva is the woman who writes this letter?

The repetition of "You will go away, you will go away," can be taken as refrain or exorcism. The myths that cross this letter all refer in a banal way to what one encounters in such situations, that is, the myth of the couple. What is the destiny of the couple? Tsvetayeva describes mythological couples who are with or without children. While noting a list of famous couples, she says something perfectly true: Lovers have no children. In her letter many remarks are made that a woman analyst could have written in the 1920s on both the homosexual and the heterosexual situation in relation to amorous passion. There is the list of absolute lovers, that is, of those who *cannot* have another, and then we have the old lovers like Philemon and Bausice.

"Ile. Cime. Seule" (44).
In a sliding effect we move from *Ile* (Island), to *cime* (summit) to *seule* (alone). Then we slide to a new paragraph with *saule* (willow):

"Saule pleureur! Saule éploré! Saule, corps et âme des femmes! Nuque éplorée du saule [Weeping willow! Tearful willow! Willow, body and soul of women! Tearful nape of the willow]" (45).

Tsvetayeva goes from the feminine *seule* (alone) to the neuter of *saule pleureur* (weeping willow) to finish in a kind of uncertainty of gender with *saule pleureur, saule éploré* (weeping willow, tearful willow). Then, very quickly, she catches up with the feminine in *nuque éplorée* (tearful nape).

The effect on the reader is most painful. In Clarice Lispector, we often hear a silent scream. Tsvetayeva too screams — and we have to bear it — though it may be hard—but in *both* instances of the enunciation. In her letter we can hear her own complaint as subtext. The text is truly sad. It is not Tsvetayeva's genius, but her poverty that comes across in this key sentence:

"L'enfant refoulé remonte à la surface de ses yeux comme un noyé. Il faut être aveugle pour ne pas l'y voir [The repressed child comes back to the surface with the eyes of a drowned person. One has to be blind not to see her]" (19–20).

Here she is not clear with her "friend" or her "enemy," to use her terms. She is confused and her pronouncements are unacceptable. The truth of the text is hidden, covered up. She narrates a brief but universal story where the characters are in the third person: "she," "the oldest," "the youngest," and from time to time "me" or "him." The question is: Who does Tsvetayeva think she is? But this is not even a question. She does not even know how to ask it. She is too confused. The very idea of writing this letter to Natalie Barney to say: Listen to me but you do not need to answer me, is unacceptable. Rather, she should say: Don't listen. Tsvetayeva is very violent but at the same time exudes love. We cannot doubt some moments of identification, tenderness, and a certain type of comprehension.

The text is dated and could be inserted in a history of homosexuality, or an account of what it means to be homosexual at a certain period. Tsvetayeva is not antihomosexual. She remains glued to a cliché of homosexuality rather than trying to listen to something more profound in herself. Tsvetayeva describes the abandonment of the older woman by the younger one, an episode taken from everyday banality. Her transmission of this kind of constituted discourse does not work. But something else is disengaged from the text, that is, the marvelous and inalterable figure of the older woman who remains alone, very dignified. What is at stake for the couple? The desire for a child. Tsvetayeva writes in fact a text *on* and *of* a child.

The text is rather strange since, as a heterosexual, Tsvetayeva gives advice to Natalie Barney, who must have dealt very well, in her life, with this kind of abandonment. She was a very powerful, phallic woman for whom everything always happened in a nonanalyzed way. Nothing could move, because nothing was really being symbolized. And when one begins to call oneself an "Amazon," as Natalie Barney does, one's destiny has already been decided.

To understand where this bizarre, illegitimate text comes from—it is as the younger of the two women that Tsvetayeva speaks to Natalie Barney—we have to go back to "Mother and Music."

As a bearer of the signifier for the "Lettre à l'Amazone" I will take the word "lacuna," which can carry both black and white. There is "lacuna"; in other words, there is nothing. It is the black hole whence the text emerges screaming or moaning, but that I would write as: *Il n'y a là qu'une,* a pun in French on "lacuna" and "here there is only one." Tsvetayeva does not know, she cannot know for whom she is taking herself. The one there *(là qu'une)* is also the missing one that she herself is. Tsvetayeva is someone—and this is both a malediction and a benediction—who is completely at the mercy of the signifier. In German, "Marina" has echoes of *See,* both as sea and lake and, containing it, of *Seele,* soul. The lake recurs in all of her texts, particularly in "Lettre à l'Amazone."

I will come back to the sentence, "The repressed child comes back up to the surface with the eyes of a drowned person." In Tsvetayeva a hidden yet insistent protest is made against drowning. Do not drown me, she seems to say. This reminds us of Freud's analysis in *The Interpretation of Dreams.* A father who is holding a wake over the body of his dead child dreams that the child tells him that he is burning. The father wakes up and sees that a candle has set fire to the room. Tsvetayeva seems to say continuously: Mother, don't you see that I am drowning? She has a very strong rapport with the sea. One can say that her name, Marina, is her destiny.

"Mother and Music" contains the keys to her oeuvre. Tsvetayeva constantly tries to get away from the infernal machine in which she is caught. Her mother drowned her and she will eternally remain the drowned child. Hence she pleads for the cause of a drowned child, as in "Lettre à l'Amazone," where she says that as a woman, she is on the side of women and that she is afraid of men. At the same time, she tells Natalie Barney that she is afraid of her too because she thinks that in a homosexual relationship the child who should be saved is being drowned. And *she* is the child! The whole text says: If you drown the child you drown me, I am drowning.

I recall the beginning of "Mother and Music"; it begins with a nonbirth:

"When, instead of the longed-for, predetermined, almost preordained son Alexander, all that was born was just me, mother, proudly choking back a sigh, said: 'At least she'll be a musician'" (271).

The musician-mother was expecting a son. She is not going to make a son of her daughter, but she gives her over to the Minotaurus and decides to orient her toward music. From the first page we will see how she is going to be surrounded by music and musical exercises. She will be submerged with music and her immense verbal universe will be "caused" by music. Music *talks* to her. That is where she saves herself. Like a drowning person who tries to hang on to something, she hangs on to words in order to escape music. The musical "do, re, mi" resurges in the name of the little Remi, of Hector Malot's *Sans Famille,* a popular children's novel of the time. Tsvetayeva is going to cross music like deadly waters. She is going to make up with the words in music, including the names of musical notations. She begins with the beginning, with little Remi, who has no family. There are three dogs in Malot's novel: Capi, Zerbian, and Dolce. Capi reappears in German as *Pudel,* "poodle," related by Tsvetayeva to the pedal of the piano. From the beginning she has a good rapport with Remi's dog. From the time she is four years old, she relates music to an absence of family.

There is also the other, later message she sends out:

"That *do-re* soon turned into a huge book, half as big as me — a 'koob' as I said it, for the time being only into its, the 'koob's,' cover, but it turned into a gold of such strength and fearfulness piercing forth from that violet that still to this day in a certain reserved, isolated Undinian place in my heart a fever of heat and fear persists, as if that murky gold, melted down, had settled at my heart's deepest depth and from there, at the slightest touch, would rise and suffuse my whole self right up to the edge of my eyes and burn out my tears" (271).

In this sumptuous passage, "Undine," who will recur a few more times, re-appears. She is one of these identificatory figures that come up as Tsvetayeva reads. Undine is from a German romantic story. Fouquet, an old emigré of the French Revolution, became a German romantic writer. His most famous text, *Undine,* tells the tale of a young woman who comes out of the water and feels an extraordinary passion for a knight. She is another form of, a kind of aquatic version of Psyche. The condition is always the same. The message is that one should not violate the secret of the origins. When the silence is broken, the secret is violated. Undine dies, and so does her knight. The story deals with a question of appurtenance to a very ambivalent and mortal water.

"Pater noster qui es in coelis [Our Father, who art in heaven]" (272) makes the father quasi-absent. He comes out of the library like a ghost. The watery element marks Tsvetayeva, and she might entertain with him the same relationship as water does with the skies, with something that is not mortal, that would be posthumous, in a restful place. The earth and the mother are not very restful. It is only as a dead person that one accedes to the skies. For Tsvetayeva, salvation goes toward heights. But salvation is always paradoxical, since it occurs in the midst of solitude. A recurring thought seems to be: I liked you at such heights that I am now buried in the sky. For her, an unhappy choice has to be made between acceding to the summit, the sky, and man on the one hand, and trying to "un-drown" herself from the mother on the other. As she says:

"I was also put in touch with the piano — *do-re-mi* on keys — right away. My hand proved to have an amazing reach. 'Five years old and it almost takes an octave, a li-i-itle bit more to reach,' mother would say stretching out the missing distance with her voice, and, so that I wouldn't get conceited: 'But then of course her feet are like that too!' " (272).

The mother fills everything. With the extension of her voice, she fills the missing space. While the little girl begins to climb musically, the mother already invades the entire space. The longer it lasts, the worse it becomes. The mother was in a hurry because she was going to die:

"Oh how my mother hurried with musical notes, with alphabet letters, with the Undines, the Jane Eyres, the Anton Goremykas, with contempt for the physical pain, with Saint Helena, with the one against all the many, with the one — without all the many, as if she knew that she didn't have time, no matter what she wouldn't have time for everything, no matter what she wouldn't have time for anything, so here — at least this and at least this too, and this too, and then this . . . so there'd be something to remember her with! So as to feed them full all at once — for a whole lifetime! From the first minute to the last, how she gave to us — and even pressed upon us!–not letting herself be calmed, be depressed (or us be set at rest), she poured down, she pounded down right to the brimful — impression upon impression and memory upon memory, as if into a trunk already crammed full (which, however, proved bottomless), inadvertently or on purpose? Pounding it down deep — what was most valuable — to protect it longer from eyes, as a stock against that extreme eventuality when 'everything is sold,' and beyond the extreme — the dive into the trunk where, it turns out, there is still — everything. So that the trunk bottom at the last moment would give us something. (Oh, the bottomlessness of mother's depth, the perpetualness of her giving!) Mother truly buried herself alive inside us — for life eternal" (275).

Tsvetayeva is taken up with excess, with what is overfull, too painful, or too forceful. She is a victim of her mother's excess. At one point, she says:

"[Mother] tested our strength of resistance: would our ribcages fall in?" (276). And further:

"Mother deluged us with music. (We never again floated free from that music turned into Lyricism — out into the light of the day!) Mother flooded us like an inundation. Her children, like those poor people's shacks on the banks of all great rivers, were doomed from their inception. Mother deluged us with all the bitterness of her own unrealized vocation, her own unrealized life, she deluged us with music as if with blood, the blood of a second birth. I can say that I was born not *ins Leben,* but *in die Musik hinein*" (283).

Hinein really implies going into an interior, as if music were a place into which one could penetrate.

"From the beginning I heard the best of everything that could be heard (including the *future*). How could I, after the unbearable magic of those streams every evening (those very Undinian, forest-kingly, 'pearly streams') even hear my own honest, dreary 'playing' that crawled out from under my skin to my own counting and the metronome's clicking?" (283).

She is clearly swallowed up by the mother-music who impregnates her almost through the skin with lyricism and who threatens her to death. This produces an extraordinary dislike for the sea. When Tsvetayeva lives in France, she has a most ambivalent relation with the sea and with everything maritime, hence maternal; she will invest herself in the mountains. She has an extraordinary and abstract passion for mountains, as we can read in this letter of May 23, 1926, to Pasternak:

> But there's one thing, Boris: I don't like the sea. Can't bear it. A vast expanse and nothing to walk on — that's another. Why Boris, it's the same thing all over again, i.e., it's my notorious, involuntary immobility. My inertness. My beastly intolerance, whether I want to be tolerant or not. And the sea at night?–Cold, terrifying, invisible, unloving, filled with itself — like Rilke (itself or divinity, no matter). I pity the earth: it feels cold. The sea never *feels* cold, it *is* cold — it is all its horrible features.

They are its essence. An enormous refrigerator (at night). An enormous boiler (in the daytime). And perfectly round. A monstrous *saucer. Flat,* Boris. An enormous flat-bottomed cradle tossing out a baby (a ship) every minute. It cannot be caressed (too wet). It cannot be worshipped (too terrible). As I would have hated Jehovah, for instance, as I hate any great power. The sea is a dictatorship, Boris. A mountain is a divinity. A mountain has many sides to it. A mountain stoops to the level of Mur [Tsvetayeva's son] (touched by him!) and rises to Goethe's brow; then, not to embarrass him, rises even higher. A mountain has streams, nests, game. A mountain is first and foremost *what I stand on,* Boris. My exact worth. A mountain is a great dash on the printed page, Boris, to be filled in with a deep sigh (119).

The parentheses require analysis. As *apartés,* they go far. Perhaps they are places of childhood. Of course, it can be said that she takes herself for a mountain or for a divinity. In order not to bother Goethe, she overtakes him. Indeed, she has a double image of herself that is immense and completely desperate. But while she dislikes the mother, the mountain functions as divinity.

I come back to ''Mother and Music,'' to a passage that Lacan would have liked. It could be called the piano stage. Tsvetayeva analyzes the different pianos she knew in her childhood:

''The third and maybe the longest piano — is the one you sit under: the piano from below, the whole underwater, underpiano world. Underwater not only because of the music poured on your head: behind our piano, between it and the windows, which were blocked by its black earthen mass, set off and reflected by the piano, as if by a black lake, stood plants, palms and philodendrons that turned the subpiano parquet floor into a real watery bottom, with green light on faces and fingers and with real roots you could touch with your hands, and where, like great wonders, mother's feet and the pedals soundlessly moved.

''A sober question: why did the plants stand behind the piano? So it would be less convenient to water them? (It could happen, with mother in charge and her disposition!) But from that combination: of piano water and watering water, mother's hands that played and mother's hands that watered, hands that poured out in turn first water, then music, the piano was forever identified in my mind with water, water and green: leafy and watery sounds.

''That's — mother's hands; and now — mother's feet. Mother's feet were separate living beings completely unconnected with the edge of her long black skirt'' (288).

After this lengthy evocation of a visit into the maternal subworld, she arrives at the piano stage:

''The fourth piano — the one you stand above: you look and looking you enter it, and the one which, in years' gradations, the opposite of going into a river and of every law of depth, is first over your head, then up to your neck (and seeming to cut your head clean off with its black edge colder than a knife!), then up to your chest and then up to your waist" (289).

An inversion of movement occurs. The piano changes in size. This kind of mirror movement involves a transference of activity onto the other:

"You look and in looking, you look at yourself, gradually bringing first the end of your nose, then your mouth, then your forehead in contact with its black and hard coldness (Why is it so deep and so hard? Such water and such ice? Such yes and such no?). But besides trying to get into the piano with your face, there was also simple childish playfulness: blowing the way you blow on a windowpane, and on the opaque, already receding oval breath, hurrying to get your nose and mouth printed; the nose comes out like a round five-kopeck piece, and your mouth — all puffed out as if a bee had bit it all around! in deep lateral bands like a flower, and twice as short as in real life, and twice as broad, and it disappears right away, merging with the piano's blackness as if the piano had taken my mouth — and swallowed it" (289–90).

The piano *becomes* the mother. It shakes everything up and carries off Marina's mouth:

"And sometimes, short on time, with a check on all the music room doors: into the front entrance — one, into the dining room — two, into the living room — three, into the mezzanine — four; from which, from all of them at once, mother might come out, I simply kissed the piano for the coldness on my lips. No, you *can* go twice into the same river. And there, from the darkest depths, a round, five-year-old, inquiring face comes toward me, with no smile, rosy even through blackness — like a Negro plunged into dawn, or a rose in an inky pond. The piano was my first mirror and my first awareness of my own face was through blackness, through its translation into blackness, as into a language dark but comprehensible. That is how it was my whole life: to understand the simplest thing I had to plunge it into poetry, to see it *from there*" (290).

The piano is in the place of the mother. To look at oneself in the piano is also to look into the mother-sea-mirror, and at that point it is to see in this mutation of colors an indication of *how* one can read the *lacuna,* both black and white. What remains is white but at the same time there is this black hole and these roses plunged into the ink-lake, this return of an image in black that carries all the connotations of black, since it is said to be a black person. There is an associative whole, so to speak, of black and ink, of yes and no, as it were. And then, in true blackness, or as she says, "into a language dark but comprehensible," the other side of the black mirror is going to be there. The other world, the black sea, is in relation with the "rose in an inky pond," whence surge these lines. It is necessary to pass through the bad mother in order to find the good source. Writing surges from the mirage, from the mirroring of the self in the black mirror of the piano. Writing is the hollow of the mother, her inverse. As soon as the mother-music dies, as soon as she withdraws, Marina stops playing.

"I didn't stop, but I gradually reduced it to nothing" (293).
She effectuates the mother's death by reducing her to zero.

"The teachers of my numerous schools, who at first had oh'd and ah'd, soon stopped ohing and ahing and then oh'd and ah'd in a very different tone of voice. I taciturnly and stubbornly reduced my music to nothing. Thus, the sea, receding, leaves pits behind, at first deep, then getting shallower, then barely damp. Those musical pits — the traces of mother's seas — stayed in me for good" (293).

With less mother and with more earth and mountain Tsvetayeva advances into writing, but all the while keeping some archaic humidity.

This dilemma will reappear in "Lettre à l'Amazone," which is full of sea:

"And she who began by not wanting a child from him, will end up wanting a child from her. And, because it cannot be, she will leave some day, loving but persecuted by the lucid and powerful jealousy of the other — and still that some day she will fall, a wreck, into the arms of the first passerby" (18).

After her mother's death Tsvetayeva becomes sometimes daughter, sometimes mother. The island is both sea and earth: "The island — earth that is not earth." That is how, in "Lettre à l'Amazone," the relationship between mother and earth is played out in the older woman. An earth from which one cannot leave; an earth one has to love since everyone is condemned to it. A place whence everything is seen. The relationship between sea and mother has to be heard in it. "Only in the convent we have God to help us, here, in the island, the sea to drown ourselves." The love of the older woman in a homosexual relationship pushes the child toward the mother:

"Looks can kill. There are none, since the dark-haired woman is leaving, alive and well, on the arm of the older one — the loved one. Enveloping her in the blue folds of her long dress that physically put between the one who stays behind and the one who leaves the irremediable limit of the seas" (37).

Elsewhere, she marks a strong opposition between sea and mountain (43). Nothing meaningful can be taken from the sea. The image of the willow with which she identifies resurges: "Tearful nape of the willow. Grey hair brushed forward into the face in order not to see anything anymore. Gray hair sweeping the face of the earth" (45). That is what remains of the mother. "Water, air, mountains, trees have been given us in order to understand the deeply hidden soul of humans" (47). Water is acceptable only on condition that it be tears, regulated and not immense like the "saucer" of the sea.

This is one of the stakes of the text. The other can be found at the level of Tsvetayeva's extraordinary technique. We have to hear what emerges from Tsvetayeva's own pain, that is, where she, like the older abandoned woman, is the victim. She insists on pain to the point where we could speak in her text less of the eternally feminine than of pain as woman. We can take this statement in parentheses:

"(Why did she come? To hurt herself. At times, that is all we have left.)" (35).

All these murmurs are Tsvetayeva's own pain that she shares through identification.

"The child begins in us well before his beginning" (20) is what she indicates as a feminine destiny. It can be contested by those who do not consider themselves defined by the child. But the fact remains that the child is expected, sometimes as in a trap. It is the *coup* of Alexander. The mother expects Alexander but Marina comes out. In my reading, I want to plead Tsvetayeva's cause a little bit. Her text is unacceptable, but the reader has to see from where it is written.

Poetry and the Jewish Question

The poet is, like the Jew, without property but distinguished nevertheless by a mark. For the Jew the mark will be a cut, a cut he carries ritualistically on his body — that is to say, circumcision. The cut distinguishes, separates, and puts in place symbolic exclusion. It is the very cut experienced by the poet who is expelled from the city. For the Jew, the mark becomes literal and legible. We need to deliteralize and resymbolize circumcision. I associate its circumference with what poets, such as Celan, have called "the meridian." I choose to read the meridian as a strange circle that traces the separation of the universe into two sides. For the Jews, this circle would divide the world into those who are on the side of alliance and those who are not. In its origins, circumcision is an Egyptian practice that the Jews adopted very late, long after Abraham's sacrifice, considered by us to be the origin of circumcision.

The English word is different from the Hebrew, in which circumcision opens a semantic field of benediction, sanctification — much more than a simple cut.

Yet the cut, the separation, marks poetic texts such as those of Paul Celan, or here, for our purposes, that of Marina Tsvetayeva, who went so far as to feel herself "Jewish." It refers in her text to a feeling of strangeness, to an element that marks her positively and negatively, voluntarily and involuntarily. It is the fact that the poet is unappropriated or expropriated. The poetic condition is marked by this very condition of estrangement. This could be a restriction but, in fact, it functions as its opposite. It is often inscribed, as in Celan, as an opening. *I* opens and flows into *you*. The other Jew is also the same but especially other, even other than Jewish. We have the same in Clarice Lispector where a wound opens onto the other, but as a good wound. All those who inhabit language as poets — this is a quote from Hölderlin — are Jews, and vice versa. To say that is already a trope. Only a poet is capable of uttering it. I will add, in order to show the opening, the flowing of the term "Jewish" into the other, that anyone can be a Jew, anyone who is sensitive to the cut, to what, by marking a limit, produces otherness. The cut or the limit is also in language. And, finally, a flow of breath, a continuous ribbon, is interrupted by a movement of the lips that cuts words and syllables. Clarice Lispector says in *The Passion according to G. H.* that we should no longer talk about creating such units, such pieces of flesh.[15] This means that she knows flesh does not consist of blocks of meaning, but of sonorous units and stellar fragments.

Tsvetayeva was obsessed with the pain of not being loved. Celan talks of pain for the unloved "Jewish" other. The theme of being unloved recurs in Tsvetayeva, for example in "Poem of the Mountain" and in "Poem of the End." "Poem of the Mountain," a poem about nonseparation, writes a kind of meridian:

> You are a full, unbroken circle, a
> whirlwind or   wholly turned to stone.
> I cannot think of you apart from
> love. There is an   equals sign.[16]

Such an effort at gathering will also occur in Celan's texts where, after a gap, a violent separation and a departure, a reunion takes place near the earth.

"Poem of the Mountain," written on the mountain of a city, that is, on Prague Mountain, and "Poem of the End" are related to each other. What is the relationship between the mountain and the end? We know from Tsvetayeva's correspondence how she is obsessed with mountains. She loves mountains — while hating the sea — and attributes an entire system of psychological traits to the mountains. She puns on something between "mountain" and "suffering." All the beings are dedicated to mountains. She *is* Prometheus. She tells us that she is on top of one mountain and underneath another. Persephone is going to be subterranean. Tsvetayeva is both on the ground and underground. "Poem of the Mountain" alludes to the whole mythology of the Titans hidden in the mountains. The Titans, having been defeated by the gods and buried by the mountains, have seizures underground — which cause earthquakes. Freud constantly reminds us of it in the metaphor stating that drives are like the Titans who agitate and shake the entire globe. It could be a simple metaphor, but it goes much further, declaring that we are human giants whom the gods and the superego try to reduce, repress and kill.

> Mountain   many worlds   the
> gods take revenge on their own likeness! (44)

Tsvetayeva refers to the story of the Titans who pretended to imitate the gods. Apropos of Tsvetayeva's style, Rilke says that her *I* is thrown like a pair of dice. We can even say that she throws herself from the height of her mountain toward the other-as-chance. This describes her relation to the other, especially, as in these two poems, to a man. In her writing, texts are produced that are unleashed, liberated from syntax, composed of a handful of words that strike the page.

The exclamation point strikes like an arrow that is shot *(décoché)*. Only few poets dare to strike and whip their texts with exclamation points that are like "dashes standing up." Translations usually cannot deal with Tsvetayeva's punctuation (like Lispector's) and modify it. The exclamation point is a vertical dash, the exclamation of the dash or the dash exclaiming, rising up like a monument, like an index. This goes very far. Tsvetayeva's text in Russian is written horizontally and vertically, in a movement that at the same time she continues to describe and that functions like a kind of morse, a kind of appeal in ciphers. She is someone who lets musical signs pass through a poetic text.

As a result, reading the poems in translation is disastrous. A word cannot be displaced without destroying something. This happens with all texts of poetic value, such as Clarice Lispector's. It is a function of poetry that confers responsibility on the reader. As Celan's themes tell us, poetry addresses and moves toward the other. Eventually, it becomes a calling to the other. It is the hope of the other, the other in us, in despair. What will happen if we don't know the language in which the poem moves? We have to go to its encounter. Such is poetic process, a move that becomes a political activity in an ethical mode. If we have a sense of the delicacy of the world, this is exactly what we have to do. One can do something else, somewhat as I have just done. We have several languages, but some are missing. We have to put our ears to the ground and listen in order to make the poem advance.

"Poem of the Mountain" and "Poem of the End" are linked by Tsvetayeva herself like two sides of a mountain, but the metaphor is more specific. In "Poem of the Mountain" she climbs a mountain, at least before she herself rises like a mountain. In "Poem of the End" she says that she is lying under a mountain. The poem writes the story of a separation, or rather of a rupture, the end of a love that moves along a path that goes from the city to its outskirts. This city — and it is a moving one — is Prague, which has been at the center of one of Tsvetayeva's passions. The movement of walking through this city, with its extraordinary presence in this poem, something of a passion, of a power to tear apart, and something of its furor and force of destruction is inscribed on the outskirts of the city and on the adjacent hills:

> Rain rips at us madly.
>   We stand and break with each other.
> In three months, these must be
>   The first moments of sharing.
>
> Is it true, God, that you even
>   tried to borrow from Job?
> Well, it didn't come off.
>   Still. We are. Outside town.
>
> Beyond it! Understand? Outside!
>   That means   we've passed the walls.
> Life is a place where it's forbidden
>   to live. Like the Hebrew quarter.

And isn't it more worthy to
    become an eternal Jew?
Anyone not   a reptile
    suffers the same pogrom.

Life is for converts only
    Judases of all faiths.
Let's go to leprous islands
    or hell   anywhere   only not

life   which puts up with traitors, with
    those who are sheep   to butchers!
This paper which gives me the
    right to live — I stamp. With my feet.

Stamp! for the shield of David.
    Vengeance! for heaps of bodies
and they say after all (delicious) the
    Jews didn't want to live!

Ghetto of the chosen. Beyond this
    ditch. No mercy
In this   most Christian of worlds
    all poets   are Jews![17]

Tsvetayeva's chaos, her ruptures — inconsistently reproduced in English — are quite regular. Destruction and disarticulation, another rhythm, pervade. Tsvetayeva seems to be drawing a kind of harmony from her chaos. The poem is of an unheard violence, again that cannot be sufficiently rendered in translation. Her association of poet and Jew — she actually uses the term "Yid" — will serve as epigraph to Celan's poem *Niemandsrose (Nobody's Rose),* even though Celan's rhythm differs greatly from Tsvetayeva's.

For Tsvetayeva, all indications are that something of a Jew is in every poet or that every poet is Jewish. The point has nothing to do with religion but with what it means poetically to "be Jewish." She suggests that we are better off as wandering Jews, belonging where we cannot belong: "Life is a place where it's forbidden to live." And her insistent cry is: "Outside! Outside town!" Maybe the equivalent of "outside town" is the mountain. Maybe the place the most outside town *is* the mountain.

There are several registers to the mountain in Tsvetayeva's poetry, just as later on in Celan's. The mountain is the antitown. It is uninhabitable and forces one to wander. One cannot live in the mountain, which, as in Nietzsche's *Thus Spake Zarathustra,* is nevertheless also a place of magnificent isolation. It is the summit from where one looks on to infinity, toward the horizon and beyond.

Writing after and taking his cue from Tsvetayeva, in his "Conversation in the Mountains," a kind of staged dialogue, Paul Celan will go beyond "Poem of the

End." He will even insist on the geological side of the mountain, on its constitution from the first waters to the last waters. For him, the mountain folds and unfolds, so that it can be seen into to its very depths, or to the very heart of the globe.[18] And what will the Jews see in Celan's poem? They will see that they belong *neither* to the earth, to the mountain, nor the town.

And that is how poets will be able to discover their status again.

1985–86

Notes

1. Anna Akhmatova, *Poems of Akhmatova,* ed. and trans. Stanley Kunitz with Max Hayward (Boston and Toronto: Little, Brown and Company, 1973), 72–73.

2. Martin Heidegger, "What Are Poets For?" in *Poetry, Language, Thought,* trans. Albert Hofstadter (New York: Harper and Row, 1971), 91–142.

3. Etty Hillesum, *An Interrupted Life: The Diaries of Etty Hillesum, 1941–1943* (New York: Pantheon, 1984). *Letters from Westerbrook,* trans. Arnold J. Pomerans (New York: Pantheon, 1986).

4. Marina Tsvetayeva, "Lettre à l'Amazone," published as *Mon frère féminin* (Paris: Mercure de France, 1979), 12. Translations mine.

5. Clarice Lispector, *The Passion according to G. H.,* trans. Ronald Sousa (Minneapolis: University of Minnesota Press, 1988), 10.

6. Paul Celan, "Und mit dem Buch aus Tarussa," in *Die Niemandsrose, Gedichte I* (Frankfurt: Suhrkampf, 1978), 287.

7. Marina Tsvetayeva, *Neuf lettres avec une dixième retenue et une onzième reçue* (Paris: Clémence Hiver, n.d.). Translations mine.

8. Clarice Lispector, "Tanta mansidão." See *Reading with Clarice Lispector,* ed. and trans. Verena Andermatt Conley (Minneapolis: University of Minnesota Press, 1990).

9. Jacques Derrida, "La double séance," in *La dissémination* (Paris: Seuil, 1973). Trans. Barbara Johnson, *Dissemination* (Chicago: University of Chicago Press, 1981).

10. Marina Tsvetayeva, "Mother and Music," in *A Captive Spirit: Selected Prose,* ed. and trans. J. Marin King (Ann Arbor: Ardis, 1980), 271–94. See also "Ma mère et la musique," in *Le diable et autres récits,* trans. Véronique Lossky (Lausanne: L'Age d'homme, 1979), 45–78, especially 62–67, missing in the English translation. For a slightly modified Russian version of this missing passage, see Marina Tsvetaeva, *Prosa* (New York: Izdatelstvo Imeni Czecova, 1953), 85.

11. Marina Tsvetayeva, "The Devil," in *A Captive Spirit,* 295–317.

12. Boris Pasternak, Marina Tsvetayeva, and Rainer Maria Rilke, *Letters, Summer 1926,* trans. Margaret Wettlin and Walter Arndt (New York, London, and San Diego: Harcourt Brace Jovanovich, 1983), 92.

13. Boris Pasternak, Marina Tsvetayeva, and Rainer Maria Rilke, *Correspondance à trois,* trans. Lily Denis (Paris: Gallimard, 1983), 14. Translations mine.

14. Marina Tsvetayeva, *Mon frère féminin* (Paris: Mercure de France, 1979), 44. Translations mine.

15. Clarice Lispector, "Pertenecer," in *A Descoberto do mundo* (Rio de Janiero: Nova Frontera, 1984), 151–53. Selections in this chapter were translated by Claudia Guimarães.

16. Marina Tsvetayeva, "Poem of the Mountain," in *Selected Poems,* trans. Elaine Feinstein (New York: E. P. Dutton, 1987), 40–47.

17. Marina Tsvetayeva, "Poem of the End," in *Selected Poems,* 48–72.

18. Paul Celan, "Conversation in the Mountains," in *Last Poems,* trans. Katharine Washburn and Margaret Guillemin (San Francisco: North Point Press, 1986), 206–12.

Index

Compiled by Hassan Melehy

Theory and History of Literature

Hélène Cixous, born in Algeria in 1937, is head of the Center of Research in Feminine Studies at the Université de Paris VIII (Saint Denis). Since the publication of *La jeune née* in France in 1975, Cixous has become one of the major writers and theoreticians to come out of the French feminist intellectual movement. She received the Prix Medicis in 1969 for her first novel, *Dedans*. Her latest text, *Jours de l'an* appeared in 1990. Many of her books have been translated into Dutch, Danish, Japanese, Portuguese, German, and English, including *The Newly Born Woman* (Minnesota, 1986), and *Reading with Clarice Lispector* (Minnesota, 1990). She has written many plays; her two latest — one about Cambodia, the other, *The Indiad* (on the partition of India) — were performed by the Théâtre du Soleil.

Verena Andermatt Conley is professor of French and women's studies at Miami University in Ohio. She attended the University of Geneva and received her Ph.D. in 1973 from the University of Wisconsin. Conley is also the author of *Hélène Cixous: Writing the Feminine*.